GW01366874

A Worms' Eye View

FRED S. WORMS

A Worms' Eye View

A Selection of Interviews, Letters, Essays and Reviews

Isaiah Berlin, Teddy Kollek, Natan Sharansky, David Hartman,
Amos Oz, Yeshayahu Leibowitz and others

Weill Publishers
Jerusalem

@ Fred S. Worms, Jerusalem, 2012

All rights reserved. No part of this publication may be reproduced, stored in a retrieval system or transmitted in any form whatsoever, without the prior permission in writing of the author.

Editor: Asher Weill

ISBN: 978-965-7405-02-4

Designed by Youval Tal, Jerusalem
Printed in Israel, 2012

For Della
The Love of my Life

Contents

Preface	9
Introduction	11
David Brinn: "A 50 Year Aliya Bears Fruit"	18
Review of "A Life in Three Cities"	23

Religion, Faith and Jewish Education

Abraham and Sarah	25
The *Akeda*	28
Mordecha's: Strategy for Jewish Survival	33
King David – the Unlucky Monarch	38
An Interview with David Hartman	40
The Religious Credo of Yeshayahu Leibowitz	54
New Anti-Semitism and the Catholic Church	60
Education Above All	63

Zionism, the Diaspora, the Jewish People

So How Many Are We?	67
Post-Zionism Combat Fatigue	71
What are our Priorities?	74
Israel and the Diaspora: is there a Dialogue?	77
A Letter to Professor George Steiner	84
Rabbi Menachem Hacohen	87
"A Taste of Freedom", Interview with Natan Sharansky	89

Jerusalem

Interviews with Teddy Kollek	98
Rabbis of Rejection	104
The Teddy Kollek Award	107

The Mount Scopus Campus	108
The Hebrew University Dormitory Village	111
"Yerushalayim shel Zahav"	113

Isaiah Berlin

Zionism and Sir Isaiah Berlin	118
Book Reviews	125
Ephraim Halevy letters	134
The Berlin and Worms Correspondence	136

Sport and the Jewish Question

"Muscular Judaism"	174
Address to the Maccabi World Union	183

Book Reviews   186

Reviews of books by Thelma Ruby and Peter Frye, Amos Oz, Michael Bar-Zohar, Martin Gilbert, Wim Van Leer, David Sorkin, Moshe Kaveh, Philip Klutznik, Hillel Halkin, Harold Fisch, Alan Dershowitz, Arthur Miller, Conrad Black

Miscellaneous

Frederic Raphael: Correspondence	229
Thinking Aloud	233
Hot Under the Collar	236
Modern Art	238
The Vwlls Lngg	243

Index of names   245

Preface

My autobiography "A Life in Three Cities, Frankfurt, London and Jerusalem" was published in 1996 to unexpected acclaim. "Well, what happened since?" I am often asked by friends and even total strangers. The present book, then, is in response to what seems to be a genuine interest. So much has happened in the intervening years that it is difficult to choose what to include and what to omit. During that period we finally immigrated to Israel (or made aliya in the felicitous Hebrew phrase; literally meaning "going up"), thus joining our children, grandchildren and great-grandchildren. This book is an anthology of articles, interviews, letters and book reviews I have written over the years.

I should note that these pieces should be read in the context of the time in which they were written. Since then, inevitable changes – political, economic, demographic – have occurred both within Israel and the Jewish world at large. This then is a mirror of the events I describe at the time I described them.

Nothing that I may have achieved could have been realized without the active assistance and encouragement of Della. My greatest stroke of luck was to have had her for a life companion. At 91, having reached "Middle Age," it is wonderful to be able to rely always and absolutely on one person. I also owe an enormous dept of thanks to the two medical practitioners who look after my health with constant devotion, Dr J. Maresky at the Wolfson Medical Centre, Jerusalem and Dr Stephen Frank of the Department of Oncology at Hadassah Hospital, Ein Karem.

I would like to thank Asher Weill, one of Israel's leading editors and publishers, without whose expertise, editorial skills and perseverance, this book might well not have seen the light of day.

Fred Worms

Jerusalem
Sivan 5772, June 2012

Introduction

The following will serve to bridge the gap between my previous book and the present day.

On 31 December, 1997, Her Majesty the Queen was gracious enough to bestow upon me an OBE (Officer of the British Empire) in recognition of my forming and chairing the B'nai B'rith Housing Society, providing secure apartments for the elderly.

I have served on the Board of Governors of the Hebrew University of Jerusalem for more than 30 years. I heard one consistent complaint year after year: "We are losing some of our best students because we cannot give them suitable accommodation." In 1998 I was awarded the Rothberg Prize for Jewish Education and in 2008 the university gave me an Honorary Ph.D. In the intervening years I concentrated on solving the accommodation problem and eventually lit upon a proposal that achieved the desired result. The Israel Lands Authority informed us that the stretch of land between the then Hyatt Regency Hotel (it is now the Dan Jerusalem) and the buildings of the university on Mount Scopus was available for public purposes. We appointed an architect, Arthur Spector, to draw up detailed plans down to the last doorknob, reflecting our requirements. We invited developers to quote for putting up the buildings, for which they would have to provide a 90 percent mortgage, repayable over 25 years. Today we have possibly the finest student village in the Middle East, eleven tower blocks providing 1,800 rooms forming part of five-room apartments with shared lounge and kitchens. The place is full up with a long waiting list (see page 111).

In May 2010, I retired as honorary president (having been president for many years before that) of the Maccabi World Union, one of the most consistent affiliations of my life. I have since been elected as honorary president of the Maccabiah Village, which I helped to found, having recently donated the elegant Business Centre, with the latest technology, available also for non-Maccabi members (see page 183). In August 1999, I had the honour of being enrolled in the International Sports Hall of Fame at the Wingate Institute of Physical Education, Netanya.

In 1995 Della retired as a Justice of the Peace in the London Borough of Haringey after having served on the bench for more than 25 years. Marking the occasion, the chairman of the Magistrates' Probation Liaison Committee wrote "…we all felt that we should write, saying how much we all regret your premature retirement and with it the loss of your contributions and wise counsel in the work of the committee…you must be by far the most senior member of the PLC in terms of unbroken service…Thank you for all you have done and all best wishes for the future." Della remains deeply involved with the work of Emunah and the Jerusalem Botanical Gardens and recently we sponsored the "Living Water" section of the wonderful gardens which will be the first station in a new Children's Discovery Park with a 95 metre treetop walk and nine interactive stations. We laid a time capsule to be opened by future archaeologists and Della told the audience that it gave us great pleasure "because it represents renewal and hope for the future, in personal relationships as in nature."

As honorary fellows of the Israel Museum, Della and I remain in close touch with its brilliant Director James Snyder and his colleagues. In addition to the Cochin Synagogue which we brought over in its entirety from Kerala in South India, we endowed a gallery for European Art.

One of the most respected rabbis in the world is Rabbi Adin Steinsaltz, who has translated both the Jerusalem and the Babylonian Talmud into modern Hebrew and English, with French to follow. It is a privilege to sit with him as we do and listen to his explanations of any problem you pose to him. His weekly session in English is akin to a superior university course. In February, 2012, he received the newly inaugurated President's Prize.

Rabbi David Hartman, founder of the Shalom Hartman Teaching Institute has handed over the reins to his son, Rabbi Donniel Hartman. The institute continues to train rabbis, educators, teachers, army officers and lay leaders in Jewish studies. It also has two high schools, for boys and girls (see the interview with David Hartman, page 40).

In 2011, The Jerusalem Foundation honoured me with the Teddy Kollek Award, in the presence of the Knesset Speaker, Reuven Rivlin, the Mayor of Jerusalem, Nir Barkat, and the long-time chairperson of the Foundation, Ruth Cheshin (see page 107).

Sir Isaiah Berlin OM, is considered by many to be among the most brilliant Jews of the 20th century. He was president of the British Academy in 1974-1978, Fellow of New College and All Souls at Oxford University. He was also the first president of Wolfson College, Oxford, which he co-founded. For ten years from 1957-1967, he was Professor of Social and Political Theory at Oxford. In 1979, he was awarded the Jerusalem Prize for "The Freedom of the Individual in Society." We were friends for many years and exchanged letters on stimulating subjects, a selection of which are reproduced here (see pages 136-173). Among his comments in this correspondence is his rejoinder to a question on religion, "As far as God is concerned, I am tone deaf." Nevertheless, on his deathbed he asked that the act of tahara be performed (religious cleansing and purification of the body before burial). His memorial service at the Hampstead Synagogue was one of the most moving I have ever attended – and there have been many! His close friend, the pianist Alfred Brendel, played, as did the violinist Isaac Stern. Lord Annan gave a brilliant oration and many members of the House of Lords were present together with leading personalities from all walks of life.

We are members of both the Beit Israel Synagogue in Yemin Moshe near our home, as well as the Great Synagogue in the centre of Jerusalem which is not only a house of prayer, with world renowned cantors and a superb choir, but also a famed cultural centre under the inspired leadership of its president, Asher Schapiro. It sponsors lectures and debates, concerts and the remarkable "Lone Soldiers Friday Night Dinners" for IDF volunteers from abroad and Israeli soldiers without family in Israel.

One of my main interests in Britain was Jewish education. I wrote numerous articles on the subject and after the publication of the "Worms Report," in 1992, the Joint Israel Appeal was persuaded to become the United Joint Israel Appeal, to subsidise Jewish schools and the Hillel Foundation in the UK. I wrote extensively on this subject in my first book. After coming to Israel it was natural, therefore, that I join the board of the Pardes Institute of Jewish Studies in Jerusalem. Pardes brings together men and women of all backgrounds to study classic Jewish texts and current Jewish issues in an open, warm and challenging learning environment. It offers a number of programmes for educators in Israel and North America throughout the year. The Pardes experience goes beyond the Beit Midrash (study hall), and students are given the opportunity to explore Israel, celebrate Shabbat and festivals as part of a dynamic community and participate in various social action projects. Pardes is a non-denominational institution, and diversity is an important part of its learning mission; we attend many lectures there. Its chairman and primary activist is John Corre who was preceded in those twin roles by Libby Werthan and then Moshe Werthan. Pardes has a world-class faculty and an outstanding ulpan (Hebrew classes).

A Family Update

We are very content in our wonderful penthouse on King David Street overlooking the walls of the Old City. The English-speaking circle of which we are a part (our offspring make fun of our Hebrew accents) is alive and kicking in Jerusalem, and our children, sons-in-law, grandchildren and great-grandchildren are in and out of our home on a daily basis. The Almighty has been kind to us.

Nadia, our eldest daughter, is a clinical psychologist specialising in working with people who have experienced psychological trauma. Alan Hoffmann, her husband, is the director-general of the Jewish Agency for Israel and travels the world. Their sons, Noam and Matan continue their M.A. studies at Tel Aviv University, combined with work, while Noam's wife Zohar pursues her career as an actress. Tal is enjoying her service in the Israel Defence Forces. Ayelet is busy with her thesis for a Ph.D. in Talmud, while her husband Adi completes a Ph.D. in law. They manage to do this while caring for three delightful children – our great-grandchildren, Kaveh, Eden and Hallel, who give us enormous pleasure.

Hilary, our second daughter, is a counsellor for women with emotional problems, and runs a fascinating course on mid-life issues. Her husband, Shimon Ilani, continues his geological research around the country. Hilary's children: Maor, studies at the Hebrew University and also works as an assistant lecturer; Kinneret is continuing with her nursing studies and sees lots of babies being born; she and computer expert husband, Amir Friedman, have their lively three-year-old Noam and a huge dog; Ma'ayan is on her way to being a social worker and is an energetic activist for social causes. Shimon also has two children from his first marriage, Inbal and Nadav. Della's only brother, Arthur Harverd has represented us in London most efficiently since our departure and nephew Dan Harverd, is a leading financial analyst. Fred's only sister, Vera, widow of Ken Gradon, a great Maccabi and B'nai B'rith leader, still lives in her house in Hampstead Garden Suburb, London.

Our youngest daughter, Caroline and her husband Nitzan Gaibel, live in Sharon, near Boston, Massachusetts. He is involved in mediation and marketing – especially of Israeli products, while Caroline is an active advisor of women's groups on health, infertility problems and adoption. Their eldest daughter, Sigal, served in the Israel Defence Forces as a tank and firearms instructor in the Armoured Corps. Twin sons Roi and Barak are spending a year in Israel on a pre-army leadership course. Shira, the youngest, is a champion swimmer, a chorister and a budding dog trainer.

My late mother's sister, Claire, married a Hungarian Jew, Sandor Kevahazi, and moved to Budapest. They suffered under the Nazis and the Communists and had some narrow escapes. They sent their only child, Michael, to London in 1948 and he lived like a brother to me in our home. His parents managed to come to London in 1956. In 1952, he married Gene Preger. He had extraordinary capabilities and I introduced him to my accountants, Blick, Rothenberg, where he became a senior partner. At the peak of his career in an act of supreme courage, he decided to move his wife, his four children and his parents to Israel. Here he joined the leading accountancy firm of Kesselman and Kesselman and again became a senior partner. He took over the running of the Maccabiah Village and turned a losing concern into the prosperous and thriving country club and hotel that it has become today. He died in 2007, and Gene, who had worked closely with him, died in the Maccabiah Village in 2012.

Fare-Thee-Wells

February 2001 marked our 200th anniversary based on a simple computation – Fred was 80, Della was 70 and together we were celebrating our golden wedding – 50 years of married life. Parties duly took place: one at the Israel Museum in Jerusalem and another in the Lynbury Theatre in Covent Garden, London. The children and grandchildren delighted us with some brilliant songs about the family. A trio of musicians played and a film edited and narrated by Della was shown – a highlight being a shot of a Nijinsky-like Fred pirouetting on the sands of Herzlia egged on by the children, back in the 1970s. Della rounded off the proceedings with a speech about coping with Fred for 50 years. We ourselves could hardly believe that we had enjoyed so many exciting moments through this time.

The Anglo-Jewish community gave us an aliya farewell party at Hillel House. The speeches, especially that of the Chief Rabbi, Sir Jonathan Sacks (now Lord Sacks) were most moving even if Della and I thought we were having the rare privilege of listening to our own obituaries. Rabbi Liss of the Highgate Synagogue, which we joined after 50 years at the Norrice Lea Synagogue in Hampstead Garden Suburb, organized a communal farewell from our local friends.

Ten years later, the clock had moved forward to our 230th anniversary (Fred 90, Della, 80, and a diamond wedding of 60 years). Once again, we celebrated at the Israel Museum. The evening was divided into three parts: following a buffet dinner, the 200 or so family and friends were split into groups for guided tours of the refurbished and extended galleries, including the new lane of synagogues (among them the Kadavumbagam Synagogue which we brought over from Cochin), and gathered together in the Springer Auditorium for speeches and entertainment.

Once again, the show was stolen by a family ensemble –a skit about immigrants struggling with the convoluted grammar of a new-old language. This time it was the turn of our 11 grandchildren to make fun of our Hebrew. Attired in caps, hats and shawls borrowed from our extensive collection, they acted out Fred (the boys) and Della (the girls) in very funny Hebrew. Della followed with a hilarious speech on the trials of wading through the thicket of Israeli bureaucracy and the health services with her very British accent. Then Fred turned the tables in a fluent and totally impromptu Hebrew rejoinder.

A 50-Year Aliya Process Bears Fruit

David Brinn

90-year-old British businessman and philanthropist Fred Worms has played a huge role in the development of many of Israel's hallowed institutions like the Hebrew University and the Israel Museum. Now he and his wife Della are finally living here for good. For some people the decision to move to Israel is a snap judgment, and for others it takes a lifetime. Fred Worms' aliya story is a little bit of both.

"We've been making aliya for 50 years, but two years ago we completed the process and did it properly. Now we're here permanently and very happy, having joined our children, grandchildren and four great-grandchildren," the 90-year-old Jerusalem resident and renowned British businessman and philanthropist said last month. He was sitting in the spacious living room of the two-floor luxury apartment overlooking the Old City that he shares with his elegant wife of 60 years, Della.

While Worms may physically be in Israel full-time now, his presence in the country has been felt in remarkable ways almost since the founding of the state. Over decades of philanthropic endeavours, Worms has been involved in building some of the country's hallowed institutions. His contributions include founding Kfar Hamaccabiah, which hosts the Maccabiah Games; building wings and funding exhibits at the Israel Museum; helping to raise funds for the Scopus Student Village at Jerusalem's Hebrew University; and playing important roles in maintaining the capital's Botanical Gardens, the Pardes Institute of Jewish Studies and the Hartman Institute, among others.

On the way to Jerusalem and on a first-name basis with various prime ministers and mayors, Worms has had many honours bestowed upon him: the presidency of the Maccabi World Union (MWU) from 1982 to 1986 and honorary presidency from 1994; the chairmanship of B'nai B'rith Hillel; an honorary doctorate in 2008 from the Hebrew University, where he has served on the board of governors for 35 years; and in 1998, an OBE (Officer of the Order of the British Empire) from Queen Elizabeth II for exceptional efforts as chairman of the B'nai B'rith Housing Association of Great Britain, which secured housing for the elderly.

"I had a remarkably lucky business career, and I knew I had to pay something back to *Medinat Israel* [the State of Israel] and to *Hashem* [God], so I've been busy for many years doing just that," said Worms, who became independently wealthy as an entrepreneur in the engineering, automobile accessory and real-estate sectors in post-Second World War Britain.

Born in Frankfurt, Germany, in 1920, Worms developed a strong combination of Jewish traditionalism and Zionism as a youth, as well as an affinity for sport. "On the one hand, I was learning in an ultra-Orthodox school during the day, and on the other hand, I became a counsellor in the Habonim movement. I also played football for Bar Kochba," said Worms.

His parents divorced, and in 1937 Worms, his mother and sister fled Nazi Germany for England. He was interned briefly as an "enemy alien" but eventually settled into his new country, becoming an accountant. One day in the post-war period, when supplies of everything were short, Worms was at his local garage and heard the manager complain about the shortage of rear-view mirrors.

"I employed an engineer and five workers and started making a new type of mirror. I built it into a group of companies with factories in England and Australia employing 700 people," said Worms. The entrepreneur also went into first gear on windshield-wiper washers and sun roofs, becoming one of England's biggest suppliers of both.

His livelihood thriving, Worms committed his time to raising his three daughters with Della, whom he married in 1951, and promoting Jewish education and sports at every turn. In addition to developing a lifelong passion for tennis, he continued the allegiance to Maccabi that he had forged in Germany, joining Maccabi Compayne Gardens and eventually climbing the ranks of the organization until he became head of the Maccabi World Union. He was present at the first Maccabiah Games after the establishment of the state in 1950 (two games took place in pre-state Palestine in 1932 and 1935).

"We slept in tents where the Tel Aviv Hilton is today. It was called Mahaneh Yehuda," he recalled. After the 1955 games, Worms co-founded and helped build Kfar Hamaccabiah to permanently house the Jewish athletes who arrived from around the world for the subsequent games. He proudly stated that he has attended every Maccabiah since then.

As avid a sportsman as he was, Worms was just as committed to Jewish education and its connection to Israel. He was chairman of B'nai B'rith Hillel for 25 years, and enrolled his daughters in Bnei Akiva. They became *madrichot* (counsellors), and upon reaching age 18, each moved to Israel.

"Israel was always an integral part of our lives. We would ski in Switzerland in the winters and spend each summer and the festivals in Israel," said Worms. "We've had a home here since 1965, when we bought a place in Herzlia Pituah." He expanded his holdings in Israel after becoming friendly with then-mayor of Jerusalem Teddy Kollek, when the venerable city leader came to London to speak at a Worms-sponsored Hillel event.

"Fred, I want a promise from you – next time you come to Jerusalem, I want you to call me," Worms remembered Kollek telling him. "Look Teddy, if it is money you want, I can't spare any. Whatever I have goes into my movements and organizations," I told him. But he didn't care, he just said to call him."

That connection resulted in Worms buying a plot of land in Yemin Moshe from the Jerusalem Foundation that housed an old shack and building a second home in Israel. The house became the residence of one of his daughters and her family and more recently Worms and his wife bought and renovated their current home, near the King David Hotel. Worms' connection with Kollek continued, and one day he wanted to thank the mayor for helping him find the Yemin Moshe property.

"I asked Teddy what he wanted for his 75th birthday, and he said, 'I want to pray in a synagogue in Cochin," said Worms. "Teddy, I didn't know you were religious, but okay, I'll pay for your fare to Cochin," I told him.

"'No I want the Cochin synagogue to come to Israel,' Teddy said, so that's how we ended up bringing the Kadavumbagam synagogue to the Israel Museum," recalled Worms, referring to the 1991 purchase, shipment, renovation and reconstruction of the synagogue interior that is now featured in the museum's "Synagogue Row." He also endowed the Della and Fred Worms Gallery in the European art wing of the museum.

Since making aliya two years ago, the Worms' have become active in local Jerusalem activities, attending lectures with Rabbi Adin Steinsaltz, weekly classes at Pardes, events and services at the Great Synagogue, and – for Fred, until recently – tearing up the tennis court at age 90 in weekly doubles matches with opponents half his age.

"I have no regrets. I went to shul yesterday morning, and a fellow gave me his book that included a number of essays by prominent people dealing with the subject of happiness. It turns out that most people don't know it when they have it," he said.

"I said to Della last night that I was sitting here thinking what a lucky man I've been. All my life has been more *mazal* [luck] than *sechel* [brains]. All I know is that I have a personal God who looks after me," he said. "Here I am sitting in this beautiful home with one of the most famous views in the world; out on the patio is an assemblage of flower pots with flowers that are Della's pride and joy and surrounded by lovely sculptures by Menashe Kadishman."

Finally living full-time in the country that his passion, determination and money helped build, he reflected without rose-tinted glasses on the accomplishments of the country after 62 years – and what still needs to be done. "I'm not sure if the term *ness minhashamayim* ["miracle from heaven"] is quite true. I think the real ness is the aliya after aliya from different countries that have brought fresh thinking and new concepts to Israel. I'd say we've had pretty rapid integration, all things considered, and that what the Russian aliya has done to this country has been just terrific," said Worms.

"However, I think that education in Israel, its universities and schools reached their peak about three or four years ago, and at the moment I fear, because of budget cuts, there's been a bit of decline that must be stopped. This is a great danger," he went on.

"But living in Eretz Israel is such a pleasure. Israel is a lifesaver. My life didn't need saving, but I could feel the pressure in London. If you walk around [there] with a kipa in the open, there's a good chance that you'd be attacked. Look out the window here," he said, pointing to the vista outside, "and you can see people walking around with their *tzitzit* hanging out. We really are in our own country and can feel at home."

Worms singled out his own family experience – his grandson served in the Golani Brigade and his granddaughter is in an IDF intelligence unit – and connected it to Independence Day. "Yom Ha'atzmaut is a great thing – it's our independence, the fact that we can stand up for ourselves. I take pride in contributing to the fact that Israel is a strong country," he said.

Indeed, without Fred Worms, the landscape and complexion of Israel at 63 might have looked very different.

The above article appeared in the Independence Day issue of The Jerusalem Post *on 9 May, 2011, and is reproduced here by permission.*

"A Life in Three Cities: Frankfurt, London and Jerusalem"

Fred Worms' autobiography, (Peter Halban Publishers, London) was published in 1996. The following is a review that appeared following the book's publication.

Shirley Kleiman in *HaGan*, London, 1997

It gives me particular pleasure to review this book by Fred Worms as he is not only a friend of more years than I care to recall, but he has been a regular contributor of literate articles to our magazine.

Everyone's life has a certain interest – how they arrived at where they are – and in Fred's case it is a fascinating story, although he says that he has "no delusions of grandeur that my life has been extraordinary." Yet this is an extraordinary story from a man we know as a modest member of our community – no red carpet or fanfares when he regularly arrives for services, usually via the side door.

The book is not only divided into three cities but also into the different spheres of his life – a life that has spanned the period from 1920 to approaching the millennium, which has certainly been a remarkable period of history. We hear first about the early years in Frankfurt where he was born and attended the ultra-orthodox Samson Raphael Hirsch School. In Habonim, a basically secular youth movement, he was labelled a religious fanatic. This has led to him embracing tolerant orthodoxy ever since.

1937 saw the sudden transition to England and to the totally different environment of St. Paul's School in Hammersmith, which in those days had a regime which seems to belong to a different century from the relaxed school atmosphere of today. The personal reminiscences include the war years, his marriage to Della, subsequently their three daughters, and concludes with thoughts about taking his grandchildren back to Frankfurt for a visit.

There is a definite pioneering spirit in all these endeavours which are chronicled in the second part of the book. In his business life he became an entrepreneur in the engineering and motor industry, which ultimately led to the location of a factory in South Wales, injecting new life into the development of the area. In communal life he has never been involved in the "big" committees, concentrating all his efforts on neglected areas of Jewish communal life – those which enhance essential facets of our Anglo-Jewish community. There has been great emphasis on education, especially on student life, which resulted in the creation of Hillel Houses and recently in the founding of Immanuel College. His passion for sport forged a lifelong association with Maccabi. More recently he became involved in housing and caring for the aged. He has the ability to interest other people in these enterprises and, as he points out, it is invariably the same people who are the "movers and shakers" in most endeavours. He likes to emphasize that he is not the only person involved in all these projects, which results in the book containing a rather numerous lists of names.

Israel, and especially Jerusalem, where they have a home and where their three daughters live, plays an enormous part in his and Della's life, and again he is involved in education – with B'nai B'rith – and with the Israel Museum where he can indulge his love of art. Fred is really something of a philosopher and makes perceptive comments on whatever topic is discussing. This book is a celebration of a life lived and continuing to be lived to the full.

The last section of the book is a series of pen portraits of people who have played a part in his life. Perhaps inevitably, the first extremely moving account is of his mother who was obviously an outstanding personality and a great influence on Fred and all the family. He dedicated the book "To my grandchildren who wanted to know." This is the best reasons for writing an account of one's life and guarantees a kind of immortality.

Religion, Faith and Jewish Education

Abraham and Sarah

Every word in the Torah has been weighted and measured by our exegetes. Every philological nuance has been scrutinised. The conduct of our forefathers has been discussed, analysed and cited as role models in countless words, written during the last 2,000 years. It is a mystery, therefore, why Abraham's cavalier conduct in exposing Sarah to the tender mercies of Pharaoh's and Abimelech's sexual acquisition instincts has provoked so little attention from the commentators.

> ### Genesis 12: 10-20
> And there was a famine in the land; and Abram went down into Egypt to sojourn there; for the famine was grievous in the land. And it came to pass, when he was come near to enter into Egypt, that he said unto Sarai his wife: "Behold now, I know that thou art a fair woman to look upon: therefore it shall come to pass, when the Egyptians shall see thee that they shall say: This is his wife; and they will kill me, but they will save thee alive.
>
> Say, I pray thee, thou art my sister; that it may be well with me for thy sake, and my soul shall live because of thee." And it came to pass that, when Abram was come into Egypt, the Egyptians beheld the woman that she was very fair.
>
> And the princes of Pharaoh saw her, and commended her before Pharaoh; and the woman was taken into Pharaoh's house. And he dealt well with Abram for her sake; and he had sheep, and oxen, and he-asses, and men-servants, and maid-servants, and she-asses and camels. And the Lord plagued Pharaoh and his house with great plagues because of Sarai Abram's wife.

> And Pharaoh called Abram and said "What is this that thou hast done unto me? Why didst thou not tell me that she was thy wife? Why said'st thou: 'She is my sister?' So that I might have taken her to be my wife; now therefore behold thy wife, take her, and go thy way." And Pharaoh commanded his men concerning him; and they sent him away, and his wife, and all that he had.

Abraham's action deserves nothing less than outrage. Our marriage ceremony makes the wife the husband's sacred property, restricting, at least in those days, her public appearance *(Kiddushin 26)*.

Famous for his quality of *hesed* (compassion), Abraham takes the incredible risk, not just of allowing Sarah to emerge from her sheltered background, but of creating a crisis situation which in accordance with his own forecast, could only result in Sarah being sacrificed for his own survival and enrichment.

It cannot be claimed that he found himself in an impossible dilemma. There was a famine but was it necessary to take his wife to Egypt, when he knew of the attendant dangers? Would it have not been possible to send his trusted servant, Eliezer, to buy food? Did not Jacob send his sons whilst he stayed at home? It is clear from the text that he set out deliberately on a course of action which, without the miraculous intervention of the Almighty, would have led to utter disaster, aborting the future of the Jewish people.

Imri na achoti at – "say you are my sister" – A dangerous half-truth. Thousands of words have been written, mostly justifying the use of "sister" because of their close kinship (Sarah was the daughter of Haran, Abraham's elder brother), and also because of the special meaning which this description had at the time. Rabbi Adin Steinsaltz, in his book "Biblical Images," refers to the Song of Songs – "My sister, my spouse" (5.1) and "My sister, my love (5.2)." One wonders why so much energy has been expended on the sister issue, which is relatively unimportant. The fact remains that above everything else, Sarah was Abraham's wife.

Of the leading commentators, only Nachmanides (Ramban) states categorically that Abraham had sinned. Those who express this view take the attitude that the uniqueness and beauty of the Bible is that it does not varnish the truth and that our revered forefathers had human shortcomings like everybody else.

I find this hard to accept. To sleep with a "prostitute" (who turned out to be his daughter-in-law in disguise) as Judah did or to steal another man's wife as did King David, can be excused as human frailties, but for a man of Abraham's calibre the surrender of Sarah is hard to fathom. Having got away with it, Abraham tried it for a second time:

Genesis 20: 1 -14

And Abraham journeyed from thence towards the south country and dwelt between Kadesh and Shur; and sojourned in Gerar. And Abraham said of Sarah his wife: "She is my sister."

And Abimelech king of Gerar sent, and took Sarah. But God came to Abimelech in a dream by night, and said to him: "Behold, thou art but a dead man, for the woman whom thou hast taken; for she is a man's wife." But Abimelech had not come near her; and he said: "Lord, wilt Thou slay also a righteous nation?"

And again Abraham was showered with gifts. "And Abimelech took sheep and oxen, and men servants and woman servants and gave them unto Abraham and restored to him Sarah his wife."

Genesis 20 – 14-17

This also does not make sense unless the phrase *somchin al haness* – "to rely on miracles" was suspended for Abraham's benefit. Having set such an extraordinary example, can one be surprised that his son, Isaac, followed in his father's footsteps?

Genesis 26: 1 et seq

And there was a famine in the land ….and Isaac dwelt in Gerar. And the men of the place asked him of his wife and he said: "She is my sister" for he feared to say "she is my wife" lest, said he, the men of the place should kill me for Rebekah because she was fair to look upon. And it came to pass when he had been there a long time, that Abimelech, King of the Philistines looked out of a window and behold Isaac was sporting with Rebekah his wife.

The Hebrew word translated here into English as "sporting" is *mitsachek*, which literally means "having fun," a euphemism for sexual intercourse. Here we have a situation where an important man stays temporarily in another country, claims that his principal lady companion is his sister and then makes love to her, not in secret but in front of an open window.

What are we to make of this? Short of ascribing suicidal tendencies to Isaac, we can only presume that he, the gentlest and most innocuous of our forefathers, had such complete trust in God that, like his father Abraham, he would be able to rely on him unconditionally.

The *Akeda* ("Binding")

We now come to the greatest mystery of all, the *akeda* which has been the subject of more analysis, commentary and artistic interpretation than any other event recorded in the Hebrew Bible. God promised four times to make Abraham the progenitor of a great nation through Isaac. Abraham therefore "walked with the Lord" in the secure knowledge that the Promised Land would be inhabited by Isaac's descendants.

Genesis 22: 1-19

And it came to pass after these things, that God did test Abraham, and said unto him: "Abraham." and he said "Here am I."

And He said, "Take now thy son, thine only son Isaac whom thou lovest, and get thee into the land of Moriah, and offer him there for a burnt-offering upon one of the mountains which I will tell thee of."

And Abraham rose early in the morning, and saddled his ass, and took two of his young men with him, and Isaac his son; and he cleaved the wood for the burnt-offering, and rose up, and went unto the place of which God had told him.

Then on the third day Abraham lifted up his eyes, and saw the place afar off. And Abraham said unto his young men: "Abide ye here with the ass, and I and the lad will go yonder; and worship, and come again to you."

And Abraham took the wood of the burnt-offering, and laid it upon Isaac his son; and he took the fire in his hand and a knife; and they went both of them together. And Isaac spoke unto Abraham his father, and said: "My father." And Abraham said: "Here am I, my son." And Isaac said: "Behold the fire and the wood; but where is the lamb for a burnt-offering?"

And Abraham said "God will provide Himself the lamb for a burnt-offering." So they went both of them together. And they came to the place which God had told him of; and Abraham built an altar there, and laid the wood in order, and bound [*akeda*] Isaac his son, and laid him on the altar, upon the wood.

And Abraham stretched forth his hand, and took the knife to slay his son.

And the angel of the Lord called unto him out of heaven and said: "Abraham, Abraham." And he said "Here am I." And he said: "Lay not thy hand upon the lad, neither do thou anything unto him; for now I know that thou fearest God, seeing thou has not withheld thy son, thine only son, from me."

And Abraham lifted up his eyes, and looked, and behold behind him a ram caught in the thicket by his horns. And Abraham went and took the ram, and offered him up for a burnt-offering instead of his son.

We know from the biblical text that Abraham had a cast-iron, unqualified promise from God that through Isaac his seed would be multiplied. Either God was reneging on his word, which is inconceivable, or he was a moody, unpredictable and unreliable God, in which case the supreme sacrifice made no sense.

Descartes put it well. "If God is perfect, he cannot deceive." Abraham knew that he was going through the motions of a symbolic test, as evidenced in the sentence, "And we will worship and will come back again to you." Abraham had tested God twice. Twice he received confirmation of the Almighty's plan to create a great nation through Isaac. It was inconceivable that the same God would turn capricious and undo a special relationship built over a period of a hundred years.

In his book "Fear and Trembling," Kierkegaard wrote, "Faith begins precisely where thinking leaves off…" Abraham did not doubt that he would get Isaac back. Had Abraham no faith he would have thrust his knife into his own breast. All along he had faith that God would not demand Isaac of him.

His faith was built upon complete trust. Perhaps the unique relationship which God had established with Abraham was based on an unprecedented I and Thou continuum not granted to lesser mortals.

To the Chief Rabbi, Lord Jakobovits
28 November 1994

My dear Immanuel,

I am truly most grateful to you for having taken the enormous trouble to photocopy extracts from the commentary of some of our luminaries on Abraham's conduct vis-à-vis Sarah. Knowing of the enormous pressure of your time, this is truly appreciated.

It is all the more disappointing, therefore, that none of them throw any light on this miasmic subject. Hirsch does not answer the problem why Abraham should have taken [Sarah] to Egypt at all and why, having got away with it once through a miracle, he tried God for a second time. Hirsch says that in pretending she was his sister, he was trying to "gain time." Gain time for what? Is the rape of your wife two months later more pleasant than two months earlier?

Hirsch also says we should not judge with hindsight. However, since Abraham himself forecast precisely what would happen, where does the hindsight come in? I am afraid therefore, that whilst his illuminating commentary on Isaac's deception is absolutely brilliant, I find him not helpful on this occasion.

Similarly, Elie Munk and B. Jacob do not deal with the dilemma. They wander off into side issues. Munk quotes, "if there is a famine, move to another place, even if it is dangerous," whilst Jacob says that Abraham's whole wealth arises from this subterfuge which does not exactly alleviate my problem.

Finally, Hertz seems to share my puzzlement. He says [Abraham's] conduct was quite unworthy of his majestic soul? Bearing in mind that it was the royal custom in those days to kill the husband of beautiful women, and then take them to the king, I fear that the conclusion must be that not only were our forefathers men of exceptional qualities, but also of quite exceptional shortcomings and it is just as well that we do not have icons in our religion.

Fred

To Prof. Jerome I. Gellman, Hartman Institute, Jerusalem
11 August 2003

Dear Jerome,

When you were kind enough to give me your latest book "Abraham! Abraham!" I responded immediately that this was a subject close to my heart, that I have wrestled with it and that I would respond to you. I do so with a certain amount of diffidence as a mere layman venturing into the overcrowded camp of the professionals.

It is not just a question of the two good Abrahams, the *zadik* [righteous man] who stuck his neck out when pleading for Sodom, and the zadik who was apparently prepared to cut his favourite son's neck. These majestic incidents were preceded by most unacceptable conduct in relation to his two wives. He sent Hagar and Ishmael into the wilderness with one pipe of water. Their chances of survival were remote. Here is this rich sheik, with hundreds of fighting men at his disposal – could he not have sent an escort of three or four warriors to see them safely through the desert, all the way to Egypt?

His conduct vis-à-vis Sarah defies description. I enclose an essay which I wrote in 1993 and then sent copies to various *gedolim*, asking for their comments. By gedolim I mean right-wing Orthodox rabbis plus one or two leading thinkers.

The majority avoided the issue by sending me photocopies of the leading commentators – with which I was familiar. The commentators all defended Abraham, often with spurious Mishnaic arguments – all except Nachmanides. He was courageous enough to say that Abraham's conduct was unbecoming to a Jewish icon. Incidentally, the wife-sister motif was dealt with at length by E.A. Speiser of the University of Pennsylvania.

Let us return to the Akeda now with the knowledge that Abraham's character was flawed. Fair enough – nobody is perfect and that is the strength of the Torah. Of course, one agrees with David Hartman that the courageous Abraham, reminding God of his eternal values, which were incompatible with the total destruction of all of Sodom if there were ten righteous men, is a true role model.

On the other hand, I also agree with Kierkegaard that Abraham knew all the time that the murder of Isaac would not take place but that it was a show ritual against sacrifice. You state that individuals and communities should be flexible enough for a total change in perspective. You just try and place such a dilemma before a haredi community! The slightest hint of our friend Rabbi [Adin] Steinsaltz (to whom I am sending a copy of this letter) that Avraham Our Father was not perfect brought an avalanche of condemnation from the stone-throwing camp.

I am afraid that your example of the pacifist who volunteered for the army so as to fight the Nazis is no analogy to a God who will say evil is good, go and kill your son and heir. Leibowitz as usual has his own barren views. Abraham learns that his faith is not defined by any human moral definitions. God is the centre. Morality mixes with religion only to the extent that religion becomes idolatrous, placing human beings in the centre instead of God.

I am afraid that this is meaningless. We are human beings – full stop. God-like assumptions do not become us. We must know the difference between good and evil in terms which we can understand. Kierkegaard slightly contradicts himself: "The Knight of Faith believes that he will be losing Isaac forever and he believes with no less fervour that he will get Isaac back."

Teiku – a draw.

I have a question: Who was there at the Akeda? Abraham and Isaac. Did either of them give a blow-by-blow description for posterity? Or are we relying on God dictating the whole Torah to Moses? When the ultimate editors refined old folk tales with their nuances changed in the miasma of the centuries, did they ever envision the dilemmas that the inclusion of the Akeda would produce?

It is a pity that they did not allow for the possibility that Abraham knew about the goat, conveniently caught in the thicket, before the ascent to the mountain!

Fred

Mordechai's Strategy for Jewish Survival

One of the principal reasons our sages included the Book of Esther in the Bible was to pay tribute to human ingenuity and self-help. Although the principle *ein somchin al haness* ("do not rely on miracles") was enshrined in our tradition only in the later Talmudic period, freedom of choice and the obligation to survive have formed part of our way of life since the Giving of the Law at Sinai.

Life in Babylon was not easy for the remnants of a once-proud Jewish state with the glorious Temple as its focal point, but Mordechai, a descendant of the family of King Saul was a privileged courtier who had built up his own network in royal circles. He was alarmed by the seismic shift in the political constellation under a weak king and feared the worst, when Haman, from the tribe of the Amalekites, the traditional deadly enemies of the Jews became the virtual dictator of the vast Persian empire *(Deuteronomy 25:17-19):* "Remember what Amalek did unto you as you came out of Egypt... when you were faint and weary... blot out the remembrance of Amalek, do not forget."

Mordechai decided to embark on a high-risk strategy, presumably because he saw no alternative to prevent what could have been the ultimate annihilation of Persian Jewry. The outcome was a personal triumph and indeed, in Hasmonean times, Purim was known as "The Day of Mordechai" *(II Maccabbees: 15:36).* It is inconceivable that a man of his integrity would have allowed his orphaned cousin, who was also his ward, to join the debauched king's harem unless there was an emergency involving *pikuah nefesh* (the saving of lives). Having made the fateful decision, he left little to chance:

> So it came to pass, when the king's commandment and decree were published, and when many maidens were gathered together unto Shushan the palace, to the custody of Hegai, that Esther was taken into the king's house, to the custody of Hegai, keeper of the women. And the maiden pleased him and she obtained kindness of him.

Here is the first example of Mordechai's largesse distributed in the right quarters at the right time. The second example occurs not long after:

> ... in those days, while Mordechai sat in the king's gate, two of the king's chamberlains, Bigthan and Teresh, of those that kept the door, were wroth and sought to lay hand on King Ahasuerus. And this became known to Mordechai, who told it unto Esther the queen; and Esther told the king thereof in Mordechai's name.

Contrary to common misunderstanding that Mordechai had personally overheard the conspirator, it was his private network that brought this vital information to him before it reached the king's security officers.

When the king promoted Haman to become his prime minister, there was no reason for Mordechai to react in a provocative manner unless he was determined to force a showdown before Haman could consolidate his position before the king. Haman declared:

> There is a certain people scattered and dispersed amongst the population in all the province of your Kingdom. Their laws are

> different from ours and they do not observe the King's laws...
> we should not tolerate them – let it be written that they should be
> destroyed, young and old, children and women, all in one day.

This was the prototype of anti-Semitic manifestos through the ages from the Crusaders to the Inquisition to the Holocaust. Mordechai must have known that his refusal to bow down before Haman would have dire consequences. That Haman wanted to destroy an entire people for the "sins" of one man proved the accuracy of Mordechai's prognosis. Following the decree of genocide against the Jews, Mordechai's conduct became even more eccentric – unless, of course, he was following a master plan (which he was). Again he acted provocatively:

> Now, when Mordechai knew all that was done, he rent his clothes
> and put on sackcloth and ashes, and went out into the midst of the
> city, and cried with a loud and bitter cry: and he came even before
> the king's gate; for none might enter within the king's gate clothed
> in sackcloth.

The time had come for Mordechai to call on Esther's help inside the palace, the very place into which he had so skillfully manoeuvred her. When Esther appeared, unbidden, before the king in her most alluring apparel, he was delighted; he had not seen her for 30 days. In typical mid-Eastern tradition, he overreacted:

> Then said the king unto her: "What wilt thou, Queen Esther? For
> whatever thy request, even to the half of the kingdom, it shall be
> given thee." And Esther said: "if it seem good unto the king, let
> the king and Haman come this day unto the banquet that I have
> prepared.

Ahasuerus' pleasure on being invited to Esther's chambers was marred when he heard that Haman would be there as well. Was there something going on of which he was unaware? He began to be worried; Haman had become a rival. That night the king could not sleep. No wonder; he may have been naïve but, like most despots, he had a nose for self-interest.

> He commanded that the Book of Records be read to him. And it was found written that Mordechai had revealed that... two of the king's chamberlains... had sought to lay hands on Ahasuerus. And it was revealed that nothing had been done for Mordechai.

Once again we see the hand of Mordechai. Was it mere coincidence, when the royal chronicles were read to the insomniac king, that they were opened at the very page which had such a crucial bearing on subsequent events? When, during the same night, Haman, came to seek permission to hang Mordechai on specially-prepared gallows, he was asked by the king what should be done to the man whom the king wished to honour? Haman in his self-glorious vanity proposed that such a man should ride the king's horse and should wear royal garments and the crown; an impudent proposal which the wary Ahasuerus interpreted as a challenge from a potential rival.

The next evening, a second dinner party took place in Esther's chambers. Again Haman was invited. By now Ahasuerus had formed a deep dislike of him; only then did Esther, with immaculate timing, tell the king of her Jewish origins and of the danger facing her people. After Ahasuerus had rushed out in fierce anger, Haman tried to save himself with one last desperate act, encouraged, perhaps by Esther, He did what no sane man would have dared to do: he fell on the queen's bed. She listened to the pleading long enough for the king to re-enter to witness the extraordinary scene.

After the hanging of Haman and his sons, Mordechai felt that his carefully planned campaign had only partially succeeded. There was still the matter of the impending destruction of the Jews. Once again, Mordechai showed his consummate negotiating skills. He suggested to the gullible king that decrees bearing the royal imprimatur could not be annulled. A mere revocation of the edict would have been insufficient, since it would have left Haman's private army intact. Mordechai wanted nothing less than the total destruction of those who sought to wipe out his people.

> Then were the king's scribes called at that time ... and it was written according to all that Mordechai commanded concerning the Jews. And they wrote in the name of King Ahasuerus and sealed it with the

> king's ring and sent letters by posts on horseback.... that the king had granted the Jews that were in every city to gather themselves together, and to stand for their life, to destroy and to slay and to cause to perish all the forces of the people and province that would assault them, their little ones and women, and to take the spoil of them for a prey.

The impact was immediate:

> And all the princes of the provinces, and the satraps and the governors, and they that did the king's business, helped the Jews because the fear of Mordechai was fallen upon them.... and the Jews smote all their enemies with the stroke of the sword ...

A master plan, carried out with great courage and with total disregard for personal safety, had succeeded. The Jews of Babylon had been saved. When we celebrate Purim, it is well to remember its principal architect – Mordechai

Purim, 2002

Part of the above article was published in The Jewish Chronicle, *London on 17 March, 1989*

King David - the Unlucky Monarch

The general impression of King David's reign is that he was one of the highlights of Jewish history. Here was a man with extraordinary charm, lyrical qualities, courage and fighting abilities, all of which camouflaged a deeply trouble family life, beset by one disaster after another. His name first appears in *I Samuel 16,* when he met the Prophet Samuel, "David was glowing with beautiful eyes and good looks, and the Lord commanded him to anoint him."

When King Saul had his first nervous breakdown David was summoned to play the harp and "Saul found relief and the evil spirit departed from him" *(I Samuel 16:23)*. A Philistine warrior, Goliath, taunted Israel on the battlefield; no one dared challenge the giant. David volunteered to confront him. "And David put his hand in his bag and took a stone and a sling. He smashed the Philistine forehead, who fell upon his face *(I Samuel 17:49-50)*.

Saul employed David as his army commander to fight his many enemies. He did this with great success, and Saul gave him his daughter Michal as his wife. As David's popularity grew, Saul became intensely jealous and tried to kill him. "And Saul cast his spear to nail David against the wall" *(I Samuel 18:11)*.

From here onwards David led a life of a fugitive to escape from Saul's wrath. Jonathan, Saul's son and ironically David's best friend, warned David from time to time. "Samuel died and all Israel gathered to lament him." *(I Samuel 25:1)*. Surprisingly, the Bible goes on for another six chapters, dealing almost entirely with David's affaires. I use the word "affaire" deliberately. Amongst the various women in his life was Bathsheba whose husband he sent to his death.

The whole of II Samuel has nothing to do with the dead prophet, but is a recitative of King David's reign. It is even more surprising that yet another book deals with David's last years *(Kings I:1-2)*. It is generally thought that these arbitrary divisions were made by non-Jewish redactors. In a war against the Amalekites, King Saul and his son Jonathan were killed. David's genius as a lyricist is shown by the epic lament deploring the death of Saul and his son. "How have the mighty fallen" *(II Samuel 1:18-27)*.

David took more wives, who gave him ten sons, including Solomon. David brought the Ark of the Covenant to Jerusalem and danced enthusiastically half-clad in front of the Ark. When his wife Michal looked out of the window, she was appalled and told David that his affair with Bathsheba whose husband Uriah he had sent to his death, was disapproved of by Nathan the Prophet, who said: "Because of this great sin the sword shall never depart from thy house."

Quite apart from the continuous warfare, David had little joy from his children. His son Amnon raped his half-sister Tamar, whose brother Absalom killed Amnon. Absalom then rebelled and claimed the King's crown for himself. He surrounded himself with a group of bullies and David tragically exclaimed: "Let us flee or else none of us will escape from Absalom." Absalom entered his father's harem to sleep with his concubines – a symbolic act of claiming the kingship *(II Samuel. 16: 22)*. Later, in hot pursuit of his father, Absalom's horse galloped under the boughs of a terebinth tree and Absalom's magnificent tresses were caught in the branches and he died. David wept bitterly, "Absalom, my son, my son, I wished I had died for thee" *(II Samuel 19:1-2)*. II Samuel concludes with a long hymn which David addressed to the Almighty for having saved him so many times. But this was premature: "For the Lord sent pestilence upon Israel and twenty-seven thousand men died from Dan to Beersheba.

We now switch to *Kings I:1*. Having lived a long and troubled life with a dysfunctional family, it was not given to David to die in peace. While he was on his deathbed his son Adonijah proclaimed himself king. Due to the last minute intervention of Bathsheba, Zadok the Priest and Nathan the Prophet, King David rallied and made it clear that Solomon would be his successor.

And David slept with his fathers and was buried in the City of David.

An Interview with David Hartman

Rabbi David Hartman is the Director of the Shalom Hartman Institute in Jerusalem which teaches Jewish studies to a wide range of educators and laymen, and also administers two high schools, one for boys and one for girls. This interview was conducted in April, 1987. Professor David Hartman's book, "A Living Covenant: The Innovative Spirit in Traditional Judaism," received the 1986 National Jewish Book Award given by the Jewish Book Council for the best book of the year on Jewish thought.

FW: Could you tell me something about your background?

DH: I was born into a very religious home. My father and his parents were born in Jerusalem; my mother and hers in Safed, the ancient Jewish hilltop town in Galilee. Our family not merely lived a Torah life, it was deeply in love with the Torah. The central value in our life was to become a *talmid hakham* – a Talmudic scholar. Our parents never asked their children to ignore their Torah study in order to earn money. Their greatest joy was that all their four sons went to yeshivot and eventually received rabbinic ordination. My father's joyful spirit had a permanent effect on my own appreciation of Judaism. He was a Hasidic Jew, as also was my mother. His Hasidism was expressed not in his garb or by having a beard, but in a joyful appreciation and natural trust of feelings in religious life.

Although it was a deeply religious home, it was not a rule-dominated one in which the *Shulhan Arukh* (a codification of Jewish law and practice) would be quoted daily. Our life was led with a very natural piety which ensured total commitment without rigidity. For we were not newcomers to this way of life, but it had been ingrained in our ancestors for centuries. How should I describe a life in which piety was part of the character structure rather than some sort of rule-book to be followed slavishly? Well, when my mother baked a cake, she never consulted a recipe book to get the right proportions of ingredients or the order of steps, but rather she knew it all intuitively. In the same way, Judaism was an intuitive part of how we lived.

It was thus a classical Jerusalemite home in which I grew up. Love for Torah and willingness to sacrifice everything for the sake of observance of the *mitzvot* – the divine commandments – pervaded every action. We would live in poverty, if only we were able to buy Talmudic literature and other Judaic sources. We had to have those books, even if there were no chairs to sit on.

FW: Was your primary language Hebrew?

DH: No, it was Yiddish. My father spoke Hebrew at home as well, but the main language was Yiddish, because that had predominated in the Old City of Jerusalem where my father was born.

FW: Could you elaborate on the aims of the Shalom Hartman Institute in Jerusalem, which you direct?

DH: The Institute is named for my father of blessed memory. He was conscious of being a Jerusalemite; it was always his pride to be referred to as "Shalom Hartman the Jerusalemite." When he died as a poor man, but a man of unshaken religious faith, I longed to perpetuate his memory in Jerusalem.

After the Six-Day War, I underwent a major spiritual transformation, with the emphasis shifting from existentialism to political thinking. The most important question was no longer the struggle of the "lonely man of faith," but how Judaism could guide our people in its renaissance in its own state. I saw no choice but to go on aliya to Israel, although many people tried to convince me that I was needed more in North America.

It was too obvious that something very important was happening in Jewish history. The question was not only what kind of Jewish individual we were producing, but how we should form a nation together when we had the responsibility of political sovereignty? Was Judaism capable of offering something beyond ways of perpetuating Jewish identity in an alien world? In the Diaspora and also for many Jews in Israel, the Sabbath and kashrut and all the other mitzvot give a sense of sacredness to a Jew in opposition to his or her environment. *Kedusha* – holiness often means to be separate, supported by Jewish ritual and *halakha* in which the passion of Jewish identity is focused. Building a sense of self, independent of our environment, for me became the controlling idea of what it meant to be a Jew. Orthodox Jews, committed halakhic Jews, were not involved in the social transformation of society at large, in concern about poverty, alienation or injustice in society; these were not the things into which Orthodox Jews really poured their passion. Since human beings have limited energies, religious Jews put their energies into building schools and observing kashrut and Shabbat. For them, *tikkun olam* – "transforming the world" – was a messianic idea. You prayed for it, you talked about it, but it was not what Jews saw as primarily characterizing their identity.

I was brought up in that spirit and deeply loved it. I danced with passion on the festival of Simhat Torah. All this lives deeply in my soul. However, this does not do justice to the totality of Judaism. Judaism, in its classical sources, is not only a way of life in opposition to the world, but a way of being in the world, even a way of transforming the world. Zionism and the creation of Israel was the decision of the Jewish people to remember that broader vision and leave the ghetto behind them.

A ghetto is not just a spatial idea. Israel is for me the attempt of the Jews to leave the ghetto – spiritually and intellectually. Now, what happens when you leave the ghetto? Does that mean you leave Judaism as well? Is Judaism fundamentally a ghetto concept? This was what many early Zionists thought. They believed that they had to reject Judaism in order to enter the world as a nation. They thought it was an either/or situation. If you choose statehood, national existence, building a serious economy, political reality and living in the world and taking seriously what the world says, you cannot go on living according to your ghetto heritage. I believe Judaism is not meant exclusively for a ghetto, but rather a way which connects you to the world. As understood by many, however, Judaism did not connect the Jew to the world; it protected him or her from the world. This was the whole structure of ghetto Judaism. It kept Jews as a distinct entity. Now suddenly comes along Zionism which wants to bring them into the world.

The problem is that a Zionism which repudiates our classical religious heritage weakens our nation's spiritual identity. Is Israel a place where you can assimilate without guilt, where your Jewishness is defined only by speaking Hebrew? Some Israeli thinkers promote the "Canaanite" ideal that Jewishness equals living in Israel. They say: Judaism is what Jews do. In my own view, Judaism is what Jews ought to aspire to do. Whatever Jews do is not necessarily Judaism. Judaism should act as a normative critique, a standard, but the question is – what standard does Judaism offer in Israel? What I saw going on in this country when I came here was not encouraging. I saw the polarization between religious and secular. I saw that people gave religion the same exilic definitions: Shabbat, kashrut, synagogue and marriage laws. Fundamentally, Judaism did not infuse the moral discussions of politics. That is why I volunteered to be an adviser to Zevulun Hammer, then minister of education, because I wanted to show that a person with a kipa on his head can be a bridge-builder between Jews and not only represent the sectarian interests of the religious.

The Shalom Hartman Institute was founded because I knew that not only must Jews leave the ghetto but Judaism as well must leave the ghetto. Our concern at the Institute is to build a new Jewish social and political philosophy.

FW: You underline the importance of halakha, yet I discern some sort of uneasiness with the Orthodox establishment. Where do you differ? If you were a practising rabbi today, under which particular flag would you preach?

DH: I would preach under the flag of a Jew deeply committed to Torah. I call myself an Orthodox rabbi, not for the sake of deceiving anybody. No, I start off deeply rooted in our tradition to which I am totally committed.

FW: Are you a fundamentalist?

DH: The covenantal moment of Sinai is the central pivot of my thinking. But the way it is understood is important. I would say that I understand the giving of the Torah on Mount Sinai in the spirit of Maimonides' appreciation of prophecy as a natural phenomenon

FW: Are you a follower of the Mishneh Torah or are you a follower of the "Guide to the Perplexed," because these are two very different faces of Maimonides?

DH: Yes, I realize that. I have written works to show that there are not two different Maimonides. While it is a mistake not to recognize the tensions between the Guide and the Mishneh Torah, it is equally a mistake to think that there were two people.

Fundamentally, at the centre of the Maimonidean understanding of Judaism is the relationship between philosophy and halakha. For Maimonides, the pole of philosophy, in which the study of nature mediates the spiritual consciousness, must be balanced against the pole of community, which requires a revealed law. Torah and halakha have significance because community is important. Community building always requires spiritual compromises; halakha is a great spiritual compromise in the best sense.

I am now working on a new book that deals with the implications of Maimonides' understanding of Torah as the great compromise. Chapter 32 in the third part of the "Guide to the Perplexed" boldly describes how God works with the limited abilities of human beings. The difference between the philosopher and the prophet is that the philosopher addresses the singular student, the prophet speaks to the nation. For Maimonides, Moses is different from Aristotle because Moses is primarily concerned to build a nation, but you cannot build community unless you have halakha. Abraham, who does not found a nation, did not have halakha. For Maimonides, halakha begins with Moses.

FW: Did he not say that the creation story in Genesis is mythology?

DH: It depends how you understand creation. I also believe in creation in the way Maimonides did. I see the world we live in as a creation, as a gift from God. But if you read the creation story in the way it is described in Genesis literally, and believe in the Torah literally, Maimonides says you are an idolator. Therefore, non-literalism has always been a very traditional mode of understanding Judaism. Jews always took seriously the Torah as the word of God, but felt it had many possibilities of interpretation. Therefore, dogmatically, I am Orthodox; I believe in the foundational principles of classical Judaism. I believe in the giving of the Torah on Mount Sinai, in creation, but how I make sense of those categories is mediated to me through the Talmud and the Maimonidean tradition. In other words, I begin at Sinai with God speaking; I end up with human beings mastering the text.

The commentator is the master of how the word of God is understood, so I do not blame God for the failure of halakha today. I think the lack of moral courage, the lack of boldness, have nothing to do with the authority of Torah, but rather with the inability of our interpreters to move the Torah in new directions. It is Jews who are responsible for what the Torah is becoming today. Therefore, I don't blame God for the way we dealt with the Ethiopian Jews, for the way we deal with women in Judaism, for the fact that so many Jews are alienated from Judaism. I blame the lack of nerve of our teachers. I am fortunate to have studied with a bold teacher such as Rabbi Joseph Soloveitchik. Maimonides and Soloveitchik enable me not to be intimidated by establishment figures or by chief rabbis. I worry only what the Master of the Universe thinks. It is He to whom I have to answer. He gave me a Torah and said: "You are now responsible to interpret it. I will not interfere in the process. My love for you is eternal. The word I have given you should always follow you. How you interpret that word, how you make sense of that, how you apply that word, is what you yourself must decide." This is how the Talmud understands the Torah's saying about itself – "It is not in heaven that thou should say 'who shall go up for us to heaven and bring it up to us that we may hear it and do it?'" *(Deut. 30:12).*

The Shalom Hartman Institute is an attempt to create an intellectual leadership deeply filled with passionate love for Torah, who will take the Torah into the 20th and 21st century, who will allow Israelis to look at Torah as a living option. The way the Torah is being taught here today is saying to Israelis: "Give up the state spiritually, go back into the ghetto." Now, if Judaism takes us back to the ghetto, it means that Judaism and the state are incompatible, because the main aim of Zionism and the state is to bring Jews out of the ghetto and into the world. The purpose of the Shalom Hartman Institute is to create an intellectual leadership that will demonstrate that Judaism and the Jewish national renaissance are not incompatible.

Even individuals educated in that spirit can bring about a great change in the situation. It was the individual, Maimonides, who changed a generation. Judaism was never a mass movement. There are always elites that make the difference, elites that are committed, that can lead the community, that do not hide in academia.

FW: As a pupil of the Samson Raphael Hirsch School in Frankfurt for nine years, I was imbued with the Hirschian principle of Torah *im derekh eretz* ("Torah and Respect"). To read today that certain yeshivot refuse to accept students who have been to university seems to me to be a contradiction in terms. Can you elaborate on your interpretation of the phrase, which I gather is not exactly the same as that of Samson Raphael Hirsch?

DH: Hirsch was a broad influence on my earlier youth. I read everything of his. He was the one who symbolised to me at least a desire to articulate a Judaism which takes seriously into account Western culture and Western ideas. For example, Hirsch never interpreted *ahavta et hager* ("You shall love the stranger") to mean a convert to Judaism, but that it meant a Gentile. There was a very deep desire in Hirsch that Judaism should evoke and embrace the universal dignity of humankind. Hirsch really tried to leave the ghetto, but I think in the end the Hirschian method failed. He thought it was easier than it was. What his great-grandchildren are now saying – "We have to go back to Eastern Europe" – would make Hirsch turn in his grave.

Early German Jewish Orthodoxy was the best Orthodoxy of its time. It was an Orthodoxy that wanted to be cultured, to be part of the world, to respect human culture. But it did not realize sufficiently that there were enormous intellectual problems in Judaism that had to be worked through. Therefore, there is a need to overcome the fear of thinking new thoughts and breaking into new conceptions. You cannot enter into the world and still build a concept of *kedusha* ("holiness") which protects you from the world. You need a concept of kedusha that leads you into the world. We have to deal with pluralism, with other faiths and communities – there are many new issues which surface as a result of the world we live in. We must create in the spirit of Hirsch, but not necessarily in accordance with his teaching.

FW: From your book, I gather that you are not satisfied with the type of petitional prayers with which we have all been brought up. Yet, petitional prayer is surely central to Judaism. For example, the whole of the Yom Kippur service seems to be one long series of petitional prayers asking for God's personal intervention. It seems to me that you have a different concept of prayer, that your basic belief lies more in the inner strength of human beings to rely upon themselves to shape their fate rather than rely on God. Is that not a little un-Jewish?

DH: No. I do not think that my approach – which is not exactly as you described it – is un-Jewish. It is not relying on oneself alone, but on God's love and faith in our ability to become responsible. In other words, I really believe it to be the very meaning of the covenant that God invites Jews to responsibility. But the fundamental difference between Judaism and Christianity is that we never gave up on God's faith in human beings. The Christian notion of the crucifixion is that God gave up on the human ability for repentance and therefore had to save humankind through His own sacrifice.

FW: So How do you pray yourself, every day? After all, a great deal of the daily prayers is petitional prayer.

DH: I say the same petitional prayers as any other Orthodox Jew. It is a question of how you make sense of petition. If you read Maimonides, he says the highest form of prayer is not petitional by silent contemplation. He categorized prayer as rungs on a spiritual ladder. You begin with petitional prayer; you end with silent meditative love. What meaning petitional prayer has is a very serious question for the modern Jew; I tried to face that issue in my book. I am not a Spinozaist or pantheist. I do not claim that God does not act in history. What I am saying is that I do not need that concept in order to build a fulfilled religious life. In other works, I bracket the truth question: I do not decide either way.

What I am trying to do is to build a spiritual life in which God's miraculous intervention in history is not a necessary requirement in order to live by Torah. Does He or does He not answer my petitions? That is up to God. I am not going to decide if He should answer prayer, if He acts, or how He should act in history. That is God's decision. What I have to become responsible for is: how do I educate Jews? Do I have to tell them that unless you believe in miracles you cannot put on *tefillin* (phylacteries) in the morning? Like Maimonides, I say that you do not have to believe in miracles in order to put on tefillin. For, even apart from miracles, God works through the given order of the world. God works through mitzvot, and God does not change human nature. Therefore, petitional prayer need not mean: "Please help me while I sit back and relax." Petitional prayer can also be to share with God my needy situation and to know that God never asks of me to be some sort of heroic person who dare not expose his vulnerability. I bring my needs to God. I do not necessarily expect God to solve them for me.

FW: I am not altogether clear about your answer. I am aware of the principle *ein somekhim al haness* ("We should not rely on miracles"). The Jew who sits back and lets God worry is not one I approve of. I am not talking about this but about a man who is in a deep state of crisis, a man who needs help desperately because of a family illness, if not a Holocaust. Is it not natural, therefore, for that man to go to his maker and say: "Look, I can't do it by myself; I need your help?"

DH: The question is, how do we feel in our crisis? Do we feel that God is going to do something miraculous, or do we believe that God has created the resources with which we can heal ourselves?

Now I believe that God has created the resources both within humankind and within the world to be able to meet our crisis situations. But the question is: where do we see God's gracious response? It is like when a person turns to another human being. If you turn to your father when you are five years old, it is one thing; when you turn to your wife in adult life, it is another. When a man turns to his wife, or a wife to her husband – say she is in urgent need or in pain – does she want her husband to solve it for her, or does he want her to solve it for him? Not necessarily. First and foremost, you want to share that need. The response of love, the acceptance, the caring suddenly provides resources for you to be able to deal with that issue. Similarly, I need to turn to God in petitional prayer, but the question is how I think He responds to me. I believe that within the world, within human beings, God has provided ways which, if we could only see and sensitize ourselves, would enable us to cope with those crisis situations.

FW: Are you saying that God makes the adrenalin flow?

DH: God creates the conditions for human beings to be able to live with dignity. That is the point. You say God healed the poor or sent food to the hungry. But must our only image of God be a care-package sender? An image of God which encourages us to use our resources, given by Him, will help us to discover ways of feeding the world. In other words, can we see the world as following a normal natural pattern and yet see God in that? My whole work is an attempt, in the spirit of Maimonides, to see God in the natural structures of the world. It is not denial of God's activity in the world. So therefore I am all for petitional prayer.

But who knows what God is saying? Who has a computer that determines whether God says yes, God says no? Did God decree that one million children should die in Auschwitz? Beware of those who know God's motives. They look for faulty mezuzot to see why people die; or they claim children died in a bus crash because a cinema was open on Shabbat. As if they were the accountants of the Almighty's actions. It is time to stop profaning God's name like that. I am trying to offer a humbler way of dealing with the world.

FW: You use the word "humble." In your book, you also say that observing mitzvot encourages humility. Is that really so? When we look at the ultra-Orthodox today, the one thing many of them seem to lack is humility. So why do you say mitzvot promote humility?

DH: This is a very serious question. To me, the biggest problem is the conduct of the religious Jews. What drives people away from Torah is the lack of compelling moral qualities in the life of some of the Orthodox. They are by no means all of the Orthodox, but their numbers are sufficient to make their attitudes very obvious.

The Gemara says: "You shall love the Lord your God – be like Abraham, in whom the name of God becomes beloved through his actions." In other words, God and His mitzvot become beloved in the way you conduct yourself, in never allowing yourself to respond arrogantly to people, conducting your business affairs modestly, letting your word be your bond, remaining always gentle, never trying to be nasty even though others are nasty to you. That is the Talmud's description of the way the pious Jew acts toward fellow human beings, as opposed to obsession with details of ritual as the only expression of religion. You show faith not just by correct ritual or by filling in a pledge card. You show faith, I believe, by your humility, by your attentiveness to other human beings. Faith must find expression in the total character structure of a human being. Mitzvot should guide you to that, but Judaism does not work as a mechanical pill. The attitude you bring to mitzvot will define the effect of the mitzvot on you. A wrong attitude will prevent mitzvot from having the effect they can. That, in a nutshell, is my whole philosophy. We have to bring our generation to an appreciation of what mitzvot were meant to create: what type of person, what type of family, what type of nation. Mitzvot are not automatic passports to the world to come.

FW: You lay enormous stress on human conduct in this world, on the human potential for self-reliance. I also gather from your book that the corollary is a somewhat unorthodox view on the world to come. Would you care to elaborate on this?

DH: I mentioned how the Talmud understands "It is not in heaven." To me, it means that I have to be responsible for what I do with my life. I am not claiming that belief in the resurrection of the dead is false. How would I know? Speaking as a religious philosopher, I have no metaphysical proof either way. It does not interest me to speculate about it. What does interest me is the question: "Is belief in resurrection a necessary presupposition in order to live by Torah?" Do I have to feel that God will put it all together in the end in order for me to live now? Can you be a committed halakhic Jew and yet live with tragedy as a permanent fact of life? Can you live by Torah without the guarantee of resolution?

Many Jews do need that guarantee. If they were told that their child had died because the nurse was negligent, it would destroy them; but if they can believe that God wanted the child back in heaven, it gives them comfort. I understand their way of reacting to tragedy and I do not think it is immature. But it is not my way. I had to face the tragedy of my son-in-law's death. He was killed in the Lebanese war as a beloved son of mine. My book "A Living Covenant," was written in his memory, when I had to face what my feelings were towards God. What I wrote, therefore, is a personal faith confession, not a metaphysical theory about the truth of the universe. I do not reject resurrection or the World to Come. I only ask: are they a necessary presupposition for me to live my Jewishness?

Can I live with the human potential for destruction? Can I live by the Torah knowing that an atomic holocaust might come? Can I live not knowing whether God guarantees that the world is going to turn out well in the end? Do I need God as the guarantor, or is it enough for me that God has given me the Torah? I have tried to show that it is possible to say "That is enough" and to remain in the Orthodox Jewish tradition.

FW: When we recite the grace after meals, we quote the verse: "I have never seen a *zadik* [righteous man"] abandoned…." Yet we see it all the time, and the only way that the zadik who has been abandoned can justify his existence is by looking for his reward in the World to Come. Now, are you saying that is not so, and that he should lift himself up by his bootstraps in this world and change it, because if he does not help himself, there will not be any help?

DH: I would say to him: let me offer you another way of dealing with it; then decide which way you prefer. Judaism does not dictate which of the two ways you must choose. My book is an attempt to offer another alternative, not a unique truth. Therefore, I called it "A Living Covenant" and not "The Living Covenant." I perfectly appreciate a fundamentalist position regarding messianism and resurrection and the World to Come. I do not reject those views outright, but only say that this is the only world I have to act in, and here is where I have to serve God. Can I find sufficient reason to serve Him in the way He wants in the world I live in? In other words, I keep the Sabbath and I am committed to Torah and to Israel, not because I want to get into the world to come, but because Torah is worth obeying *lishma* – for its own sake.

FW: We have had enormous difficulty with God over the Holocaust. For instance, I have heard people say that they could possibly forgive God for the Holocaust because it led to the creation of the State of Israel.

DH: I would never talk about "forgiving God for the Holocaust because He gave us our own state afterwards." It is too much like saying: "I don't mind other people dying as long as the rest of us benefit." That is obscene, when you think about it. Never bring God into such an obscene statement.

The Holocaust remains a total tragic moment in Jewish life, unredeemable by anything. The creation of the State of Israel was a response to the Holocaust, not a redemption of the Holocaust. It demonstrated awareness of Jewish vulnerability, of the horror of Jewish powerlessness, the horror of relying on mistaken moral humanism. It is the horror of knowing where Christian anti-Semitism can lead to, the horror of knowing what 2,000 years of dripping poison into human consciousness can do. The death of even a single Jew in the Holocaust is unredeemable.

So the State of Israel is a response of a people, a response which has absolutely no way of solving, healing or forgiving. Who are we to purport to forgive the Sovereign of the Universe? If anyone, the dead have to forgive him. When anyone hears them forgive him, let me know. People are too ready to talk in the name of the dead. Who made them the patron of those who died? We cry, we weep, but we cannot speak in their name. We can speak only in our own name. We must permanently mourn for the victims who are not here; it is a permanent pain, a permanent tragedy. *Lanetzah* – forever – that is my view.

As far as the State of Israel is concerned, I view it as the greatest event of the last 2,000 years of Jewish history, an event which challenges Judaism to the core. It is the greatest opportunity for Jews to become a holy people in the world and to reflect on the way they can build a society which is a sanctification of God's name. God in Judaism seeks to be in the market place of history. This is the mystery of Judaism: why is God interested in history and human beings? Aristotle's God is too aristocratic to bother with human beings. When Aristotle asked himself, "What does God think about, for it must be most perfect, and what is most perfect?" he felt obliged to answer: "He thinks about Himself." Aristotle's God has no interest in what happens to individuals, no interest in human history. To be a Jew is to believe that God indeed has a permanent interest in history.

My view is that God must live in the nation, in the total life of the community, in the quality of its social, economic, moral and political life. God seeks the fullness of life. That is what the Torah tells us. Look at *Leviticus* chapter 19. God is interested in an honest way of life and in meticulous forms of worship – both together in that chapter. He is interested in the way we deal with human beings in the totality of our interpersonal relationships. That is what kedusha is about, not just which meat is kosher.

For me, therefore, the State of Israel is a way of life. It gives me a whole society in which Jews are responsible. So I recite the Hallel prayer on Independence Day because I thank God for this great opportunity. I thank God for being privileged to participate in this struggle of making Torah a way of life, filled with passionate tolerance for those who are not observant, compassion for those who are not Jews, seeking to live in a spirit of humility with other people who disagree with me. Instead of talking about Judaism in a sermon, as I used to do as a rabbi, I am now challenged to implement Judaism in the living vibrancy of Jerusalem, a city filled with fanaticism and hate, yet filled with great potential for love. Our work in the Institute is a testimony to our belief that Torah can one day surface in the society in a way that will command the respect both of the Jews, but also of the peoples of the world, because it will show its power, not through its ability to do political deals in the Knesset, but through humility and justice, through the type of human society it will create. For me, therefore, the important challenge is not how much land we own, but what type of people we produce. We have to stimulate greater capacities of love.

FW: Is this not what Rabbi Kook said 50 years ago?

DH: Yes, that is what he dreamed about, that out of Israel should arise new powers of love, new capacities to appreciate the world. Israel should be a place which does not live in hatred and suspicion of the world, but Israel should help heal the Jewish soul from its exilic wounds, so that it may learn to love and cherish and respect all that is worthwhile in human culture and in the human experience of God. To live in Israel is not to live in a ghetto; it is to live in a new relationship to the world. It is not the land of assimilated Jews who try to be indistinguishable from everyone else, but of Jews who are deeply rooted in their own history and culture. They may be proud of what they can articulate from their own identity, but they should never claim chauvinistically that this is the only identity that is meaningful. That new spirit of saying "yes" to what we have, of affirming our own culture without delegitimizing others, is the great challenge which I and other people around me are prepared to face.

Am I certain we shall succeed? No. Am I certain that the destruction of our third Jewish commonwealth cannot come about? No. Nonetheless, in the midst of uncertainty, I am privileged to be a Jerusalem Jew.

The Religious Credo of Yeshayahu Leibowitz

Professor Yeshayahu Leibowitz has been the bête noire of the Israeli political, religious and military establishment for most of his 89 years. He was recently offered the Israel Prize, much to the consternation of the establishment. When Prime Minister Yitzhak Rabin declared that he would refuse to participate in the prize presentation, Professor Leibowitz declined the offer.

Born in Riga, Latvia, his family fled the Russian civil war in 1919 to settle in Berlin. He studied medicine, chemistry and philosophy at the universities of Berlin, Cologne, Heidelberg and Basel. Shortly after the Nazis came to power he settled in Palestine.

Anyone who has heard him lecture whilst in his eighties will have no difficulty in imagining the sensation he caused when he was in his thirties. Whilst ostensibly teaching chemistry at the Hebrew University, his unique methodology and polymath approach led his students over a vast field of seemingly unrelated disciplines.

Through the ensuing decades he taught, lectured, pronounced on television and launched regular attacks against the rabbis, general and politicians. He showed particular contempt for the rabbinical authorities who shrank away from pressing contemporary problems instead of agitating for a change in *halakha* (Jewish law). Their attitude of relying on non-observant members of the Jewish community to act as *Shabbes-goyim* made them parasites in his eyes.

His premise that halakha does not reflect the existence of the State of Israel since its laws were promulgated largely for Jewish communities under foreign rule, has upset the Orthodox establishment which is reluctant to disturb the status quo.

He reserves his special ire for religion in politics. The sanctification of territory is akin to *avoda zara* (idol worship). He states that, "The Land of Israel is the Holy Land and the Temple Mount is a holy place only by virtue of the *mitzvot* (good deeds) linked to these locations. The idea that a specific country or location has an intrinsic holiness is an indubitably idolatrous idea."

He is opposed to the political concept of Judea and Samaria and suggests that "the religious" arguments for the annexation of the occupied territories are only an expression, subconsciously or perhaps even overtly hypocritically, of the transformation of the Jewish religion into a camouflage for Israeli nationalism. Counterfeit religion identifies national interests with the service of God and imputes to the state – which is only an instrument serving human needs – a supreme religious value. "The halakhic reasons for remaining in control of the territories are ridiculous, since the State of Israel does not acknowledge the authority of the Torah and the majority of its Jewish inhabitants reject the imperative demands of its mitzvot. Our real problem is not the territory itself but rather the population of some million and a half Arabs who live in it and over whom we must rule. Inclusion of these Arabs (in addition to the half a million who are citizens of the state) in the area under our rule will bring about the liquidation of the State of Israel and result in a catastrophe for the Jewish people as a whole; it will undermine the social structure that we have created in the state and cause the corruption of individuals, both Jew and Arab."

So what is Leibowitz's credo? Halakha is the beginning and the end. It is sacrosanct, devoid of emotion, a barren paradise. He insists that, "the endurance and continuity of the Jewish religious collective result from the objective factor of halakhic practice rather than from some form of subjective consciousness that is likely to change as its individual bearers succeed one another. Halakha is founded on faith, yet at the same time constitutes this faith. In other words, Judaism as a living religion creates the faith upon which it is founded. This is a logical paradox but not a religious paradox. Halakha is not an external wrapper clothing Jewish religion and faith. It is the sole form in which they can be embodied: a collective manifestation of Judaism. Halakha as a religious institution cannot admit the category of the ethical. Needless to say, it cannot admit utilitarian justifications, whether it be for the good of individuals, of society, or of the nation."

This purely cerebral, circular approach appears to contradict his injunction to the rabbinate to update halakha so as to face the realities of a modern Jewish state.

We now come to his most controversial subject – that of prayer. By implication, he dismisses two thirds of our time-honoured rituals as set out in the Siddur. A person pouring out his or her heart before God is not seeking divine intervention, nor performing a mitzva. The Deity is not listening to him. According to Leibowitz, unscheduled prayer is a human-psychological phenomenon, the expression of an impulse from within, an action which springs from man himself, from an experience he has undergone, or from the circumstances in which he finds himself. It is an action performed for a man's own need, whether material, intellectual, or emotional. This is prayer for one's own benefit, a service to oneself. There is nothing worshipful about it. It does not represent acceptance of "the Yoke of Heaven." In other words, it is not essentially a religious act although, like many other psychologically determined events, it may occur in a religious context as a natural outcome of human manipulation of religious categories.

Spontaneous prayer is out. Fixed ritual is obligatory. Supplications for good health, wealth or wine for Kiddush are self-serving and not *lishma* (for their own purpose). What is lishma? The thrice daily fixed routine which he considers a religious imperative. Spontaneous prayer (when a person is overwhelmed and pours out a supplication before God) is, of course, halakhically permissible, but, like the performance of any act which has not been prescribed, its religious value is limited.

As a religious act it is faulty, since one who prays to satisfy a need sets himself up as an end, as though God were a means for promotion of personal welfare. As in the case of any mitzva, prayer – especially prayer – is religiously significant only if it is performed because it is a mitzva. Its religious value is minimal when it is performed out of free inclination.

According to Leibowitz, whoever worships a creator who has no body and cannot be corporeally conceived cannot imagine that he can truly praise God or that he need inform Him of his needs. He will certainly not seek to influence God, an idea which comes short of being blasphemous only because of its naiveté.

According to Leibowitz, we are also wasting our time praying for the welfare of the state or for soldiers in battle. God only helps those who help themselves. He says that "the various occasional prayers composed lend a religious halo to personal or collective interests – a prayer for the welfare of the state, a prayer for parachutists, a prayer for submarine crews, are ludicrous and insipid. All of these are either national-religious play-acting or expression of fears which have nothing to do with religious consciousness. By the nature of the training implanted in him and if the parachutist follows his instructions carefully and skillfully, he will land safely. If not, a special prayer will be of no avail."

This cavalier dismissal of the content of our prayers diminishes our liturgy which, admittedly, is man-made, albeit some of it deriving from the prophets. The difficulty we encounter focuses on prayers which are actually taken verbatim from the Torah, for example, "Hear O Israel" – *Shema Yisrael*.

The first paragraph of the shema prayer is perfect Leibowitz material a declaration of faith with no strings attached. The second paragraph, however, deals with conditional reward and punishment – something akin to petitioning on which he looks askance. When questioned, his answer was stunning in its simplicity.

"The first paragraph is lishma, the second is not. Central to this discussion is the sharp distinction between lishma and not lishma. Without this distinction the world of Jewish faith constituted by the Torah and mitzvot cannot be fully comprehended. God may be worshipped at two levels representing two different types of motivation. In the terminology of ethical theory, one might say that faith and Torah may be conceived deontically [ed. by free choice], and also along consequentialist lines. The Torah admits both levels. The first part of the reading of shema is an expression of faith for its own sake, which is called 'love.' This faith has no instrumental function and no ulterior purpose. It cannot be rationally explained. If it were capable of being justified for ulterior reasons, it would lose its character as a categorical imperative. What a person does for a specific reason is not, in itself, the direct outcome of his decision."

Does this not seem a rather barren way of communicating with the Almighty? Suddenly our daily prayers assume the mantle of selfish requests for favours that are not lishma.

From Moses' famous five-word prayer *El na refah na la* in which he pleaded with God to cure his sister (it worked) to the bulk of the grace after meals, we do ask for heavenly intervention in our health, well-being, worldly endowments and we also express fear of the Lord – as best summarized in the new moon monthly prayers.

In his explanation of the weekly biblical portion, quoted in *The Jerusalem Report* of 19 November 1992, Leibowitz wrote:

> I cannot resist telling of a certain person in our midst, a man of a high intellectual and moral calibre, who was also immersed in Judaism and who is reported to have said that after Auschwitz he lost his faith in God. My reaction to this is: You never believed in God, but in God's help. One who truly believes in God does not relate this to belief in God's help; nor does he believe that God ought to or will help him. He believes in God as Godhead, not in terms of functions that he attributes to Him concerning His dealings with man. And this is the significance of the *Akeda*, in which God appears to Abraham, not as He who protects him and not as He who rewards him, but as He who makes the most difficult and exacting of demands, a demand that Abraham can fulfil only by nullifying all human needs, interests and values, nullifying them in order to serve God.

One wonders how Chief Justice Haim Cohn, alluded to in this paragraph, liked to be told that he never believed in God.

Where Leibowitz's views are more popular is on the subject of state and religion. According to him they do not mix and religion involving itself in a political power struggle becomes fatally flawed. Leibowitz maintains that religion as an adjunct of a secular authority is the antithesis of true religion:

> It hinders religious education of the community at large and constricts the religious influence on its way of life. From a religious standpoint there is no greater abomination than an atheistic clerical regime. At present we have a state – secular in essence and most of its manifestations – which recognises religious institutions as state agencies, supports them with funding and administrative means, imposes, not religion, but certain religious provisions chosen arbitrarily by political negotiation. All the while, it emphasises its rejection of guidance by Torah (a state ruled by secular law, not by halakha). There is no greater degradation of religion than maintenance of its institutions by a secular state. Nothing restricts its influence or diminishes its persuasiveness more than investing secular functions with a religious aura; adopting certain religious obligations and proscriptions as glaring exceptions into a system of secular laws; imposing an arbitrary selection of religious regulations on the community while refusing to obligate itself and the community to recognize the authority of religion; in short, making it serve not God but political utility.

One may well wonder why Sir Isaiah Berlin endorsed the views of Professor Leibowitz with the following encomium:

> Yeshayahu Leibowitz, with total courage, independence, and above all, undeviating honesty and strength of character stood up; and when others were silent, he raised his voice for what he, and they too, knew to be right, when, for whatever reason, they, for the most part, failed to do so. Of him, I believe, it can be said more truly than of anyone else that he is the conscience of Israel: the clearest and most honourable champion of those principles which justify the creation of a movement and of a sovereign state achieved at so high a human

cost both to the Jewish nation and to all its neighbours. Yeshayahu Leibowitz is surely one of Israel's greatest moral assets.

When I tackled Sir Isaiah on this unqualified praise, he pointed out that he differed from Yeshayahu Leibowitz's religious pronouncements, and that the hallelujahs were reserved solely for his political courage.

Professor Leibowitz's book "Judaism, Human Values, and the Jewish State," *from which I have quoted extensively in this article, was published by Harvard University Press in 1992.*

New Anti-Semitism and the Catholic Church

Who would have thought in the late 1940s, in the wake of the Second World War, in which one third of the Jewish people were murdered and when Europe felt a sense of guilt after the horrors of Auschwitz, that anti-Semitism would again rear its ugly head and become rampant at the beginning of the 21st century?

The creation of the State of Israel, which should have been the solution, has become part of the problem. Anti-Jewish manifestations and anti-Zionism have become indistinguishable. The Chief Rabbi, Lord Sacks, interviewed by *Ha'aretz* earlier this year, stated that "anti-Semitism has moved from Europe to the Middle East, from Christian culture to Islamic, from the individual Jew to the Jews as a sovereign nation."

This is only partially correct. Whilst militant Islam is on the march with its fanatic fundamentalists threatening the very existence of the Western world, as we know it, it is ably assisted and abetted by the Catholic Church in general, and the Vatican in particular. This, at first glance, may seem an extraordinary assessment, bearing in mind the interfaith work so assiduously carried out from our side by the

Chief Rabbi and Sir Sigmund Sternberg, amongst others, but recent disclosures from the archives of the Vatican have caused a chilling resonance.

Three authors have recently grappled with this problem and their conclusions are not reassuring. John Cornwell, the Catholic author of "Breaking Faith – the Pope, the People and the Fate of Catholicism," (Viking Press), is deeply pessimistic on the state of his religion. As the influence of the Church rapidly declines in the Western world, the Vatican has moved to the right, eschewing pluralism and moving away from the benign declarations of the Second Vatican Council in the 1960s. Cornwell, in an earlier book, "Hitler's Pope," provided evidence of the close collaboration between the Nazis and the Vatican. The author now goes further and states: "John Paul II has described other faiths as 'deficient,' has eliminated freedom of speech within the church and has allowed the ultra-conservative Opus Dei to infiltrate the key departments of the Vatican."

This is in response to the worldwide diminution in numbers of practising Catholics and church attendance. In the United Kingdom, for example, only one million out of four go to church regularly; in France only seven percent of young Catholics set foot in a church and in Brazil, 600,000 are moving over to the Protestant faith every year. Inter-church ecumenism has been seriously damaged as seen in Argentine and Northern Ireland. In 2001 the Vatican issued a proclamation, *Dominus Jesus*, suggesting that Anglicans, Methodists and Episcopalians "are not proper Christians."

The move to the right to fundamentalism on the part of the Vatican and its relapse into mediaeval absolutism does not augur well for the Jews. According to Cornwell: "it threatens the future of civil society everywhere." Two Jewish historians go further. David Kertzer, a professor at Brown University in the USA, has written what Richard Morrison in *The Times* described as a savage book. In "Unholy War: The Vatican's Role in the Rise of Modern Anti-Semitism," published in the UK by MacMillan (in the USA the book is called "The Popes against the Jews – the Vatican's Role in the Rise of Modern Anti-Semitism," published by Knopf), Kertzer alleges that the Catholic church paved the way for the Holocaust, not only because of its appalling record in the Middle Ages and the Inquisition but right up to modern times.

In an interview with *The Times* (18 January, 2002), Kertzer stated, "anti-Semitism was nurtured by the church for centuries, making so many people susceptible to Nazi ideology." He was impelled to write his book of Catholic misdeeds by the spurious attempt of the Vatican to whitewash its record in "We Remember – a Reflection on the Holocaust" which he found to be a distortion of history.

Whilst acknowledging the progress in partly opening its archives, the Church has laid itself wide open to the examination of its chequered history. *The Times* described the material as "dynamite." Long after Napoleon introduced liberté and égalité to a war-shattered Europe, the Jews in the Papal States were subjected to the same discriminations that were thought to be inventions of the Nazis. Overcrowded ghettos, yellow badges, public humiliations, enforced 40-day indoctrination courses, were the visible symbols of the Catholic Church's deep-seated hatred of the Mosaic religion which refused to recognise the evolution to redemption by the son of God.

In 1880, the official journal *La Civiltà Cattolica* anticipated *Der Stürmer*: "The Jews are obstinate, dirty thieves, an enemy race." The blood libel was maintained by the Catholic press and in 1913, the infamous Mendel Beilis trial had all the appearances of a Dreyfus-like charade. When Beilis' innocence was established, the Church was not pleased.

Kertzer recognises that there were distinguished exceptions, such as Lord Bertrand Russell, Cardinal Vaughan, and the Duke of Norfolk, who protested against the blood libel accusations, but these were dismissed, hardly surprisingly, as coming from "Friends of the Rothschilds." Pius XI, before he became pope, wrote: "One of the most evil and strongest influences felt here [in Poland] is that of the Jews."

David Goldhagen, a Harvard professor and son of Holocaust survivors, who became famous through his controversial book, "Hitler's Willing Executioners," in which he holds the German population at large responsible for conniving in the Holocaust – has written another book, "A Moral Reckoning: the Catholic Church during the Holocaust and Today."

Goldhagen accuses Pope Pius XII, the very man whom the Vatican would like to canonise, as a willing collaborator with the Nazis who did not raise a finger when Italian Jews were deported to certain death. He maintains that, "there is no difference between the [Catholic] Church's anti-Judaism and its offshoot, European anti-Semitism." He condemns the Church's attempt to whitewash its record, which he equates with the Holocaust deniers.

David Cesarani, professor of Jewish history at Southampton University, believes that Goldhagen goes too far in his broad-brushed condemnation. "More Jews survived in Catholic Belgium than in Protestant Holland," he recalls. Goldhagen will not have this: "For every Catholic who helped the Jews, thousands more turned their back on their suffering."

In 2002, when Christians in Belfast murder each other in the name of their respective churches, can we Jews really expect preferential treatment from the Vatican embedded in its own inflexible dogma?

Education Above All

Recently, I had to attend an urgent meeting with the leadership of the Union of Jewish Students and the honorary officers of the Institute of Jewish Affairs who intend to organise a demographic survey of the Anglo-Jewish community. We need this very much. Whilst we know that our community has shrunk dramatically (down from 480,000 after the Second World War, to less than 300,000 at the present time), we do not have any reliable data on its composition. It is established that we are an upside-down pyramid where the shrinking younger age group is trying to support an ever-increasing over 60s sector.

Much has been written and said about the demographic decline of Jews in the Diaspora. Our numbers in the United Kingdom continue to diminish by 4,500 people each year. The chances are that in 20 years time we shall be down to 200,000. There is such a thing as a critical mass. Below a certain number we shall not be able to sustain our institutions.

Is this an inevitable state of affairs decreed from heaven, or is it, to some extent, a self-inflicted wound? For over 25 years I have made myself unpopular by preaching one monotonous theme, namely that we cannot afford to continue on our present path. Jewish education must become Priority Number One. Putting all our eggs into the Israeli basket has never been in the interest of Israel which relies on a virile and supportive Diaspora.

When, in the early 1980s, I appealed through letters and articles in *The Jewish Chronicle* that the JIA should become the Joint Israel Appeal and Jewish Education Fund, thus harnessing their tremendous fund-raising abilities for the benefit of Jewish education, the silence was deafening. On the whole my views were unpopular.

Today we reap the results. The community is shrinking because of lower birth rates, because of 40 percent out-marriage and because of lack of commitment. All three phenomena are self-inflicted and could have been prevented by education in its widest sense.

The Jewish Education Development Trust established a Committee of Enquiry into Jewish Education which I chaired and which conducted its research over a period of 18 months. In my chairman's summary I wrote:

> Education has been relegated to the bottom of the ladder, relying on haphazard competing fund-raising from a multitude of non-professional, well-meaning sponsoring organisations. Even what we have is maintained with difficulty. At any one time 40 percent of our children aged between five and 18 are deprived of formal Jewish education, 60 percent of our teenagers have opted out by not attending either Hebrew classes or Jewish schools after their Bar/Batmitzva and by the time they are aged 17, only ten percent will have stayed the course.

> Two predominant fund-raising bodies are active in the community – the JIA with its long history and sophisticated apparatus and Jewish

Fred was inducted into the Order of the British Empire (OBE) by the Queen in December 1977 (see page 11)

Fred and Della at Buckingham Palace

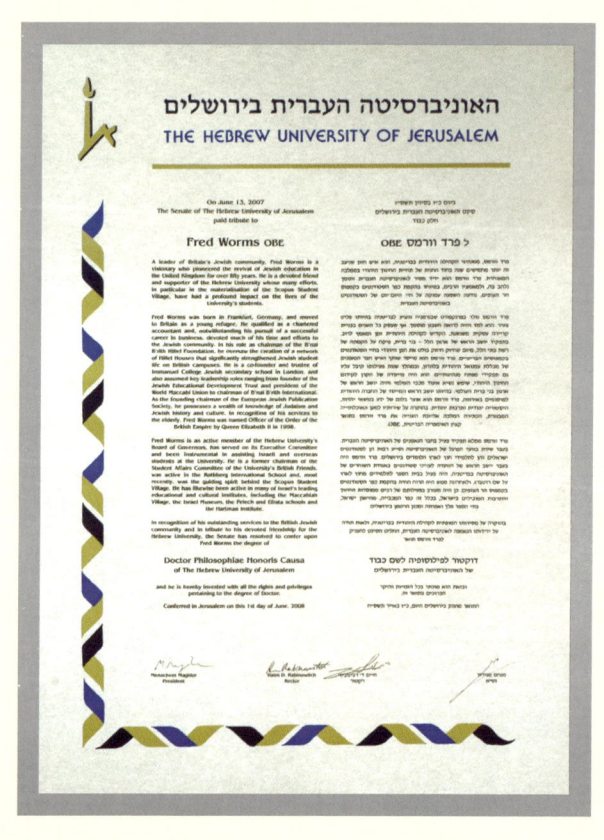

Fred is awarded an Honorary Doctorate by the Hebrew University, Jerusalem, 2007 by University President Menachem Magidor, right, and left: Chaim Rabinowitch

An Honorary Fellow of the Hebrew University

The Teddy Kollek Award, 2011
(see page 107)

Standing left to right: Amir (holding Noam), Adi, Ayelet, (holding Eden), Matan, Maor, Alan, Nadia, Noam, Zohar, Tal, Kinneret, Maayan, Barak, Roi, Sigal, Shira

Seated left to right: Shimon (holding Kaveh), Hilary, Della, Fred (holding Hallel), Nitzan, Caroline. (See "A Family Update" page 14).

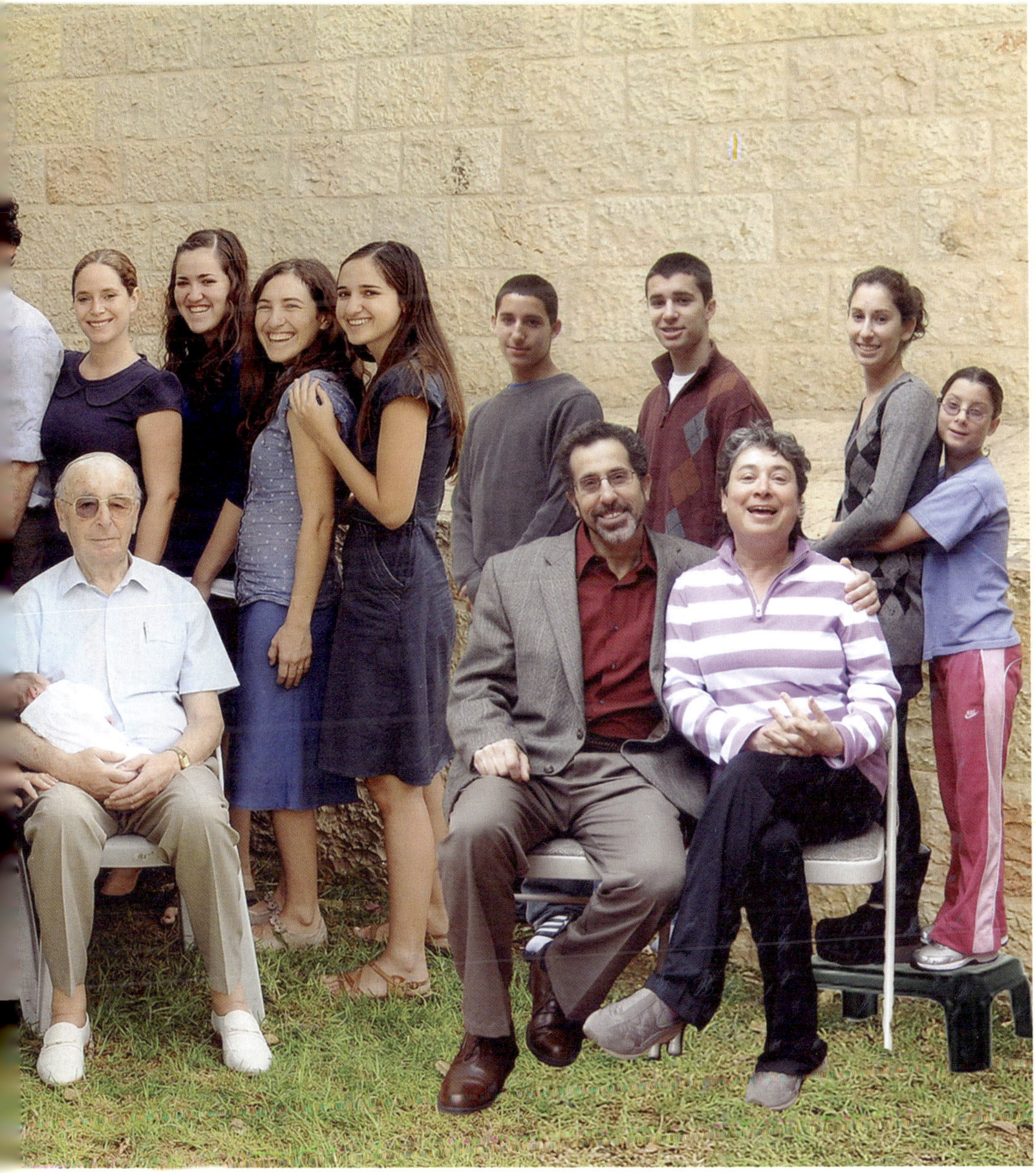

Prof. Hanoch Gutfreund of the Hebrew University with Fred and Della at the inauguration of earlier student accomodation on Mount Scopus

The Student Dormitory Village at the Mount Scopus Campus of the Hebrew University (see page 111)

Fred with King Hussein of the Hashemite Kingdom of Jordan during the king's visit to London in 1996. Centre: Lionel Gordon, Chairman of the Jewish Chronicle

Fred and Della with James Snyder, Director of the Israel Museum, Jerusalem

The Kadavumbagam Synagogue brought from Cochin in India by Della and Fred and reconstructed in the Israel Museum, Jerusalem

Mayor Teddy Kollek, Martin Weyl, Director of the Israel Museum, and Fred at the inauguration of the Kadavumbagam Synagogue

Care, which has attracted within its fold more charitable bodies engaged in the welfare of the elderly, the handicapped and the under-privileged. In theory we should create one central fund-raising organisation covering Israel, welfare and Jewish education. Whilst it would be far from ideal to have three major fund-raising bodies with permanent staff in our small community, it will take many years, as it has taken in the United States, to make a community chest function efficiently. We cannot afford to wait. The needs of the education sector are crying out.

The Chief Rabbi's plans for Jewish continuity in so far as Jewish education is concerned is based on the JEDT report. A separate strong third fund-raising body entirely devoted to Jewish education is in the course of formation. If the community begins to understand that it has to re-slice the shrinking cake and allocate a far greater portion to our self-preservation in this country, then there may be a chance for the future.

If we carry on at the present rate we are doomed. The most vulnerable stage in our youngsters' lives is when they go to university. Eighty percent do not study in their home towns. Severed for the first time from the family umbilical cord, left to their own devices in the heady air of freedom, the universities could have either a beneficial or a disastrous effect. The temptations of sex, drugs and the sacrifice of study to leisure activities could be ruinous. Political pressures from the extreme left where anti-Zionism is a disguise for anti-Semitism, coupled with the unholy alliance of a fascist right with Moslem fundamentalism, exert additional pressure on our youngsters.

Hillel, which is now active on 18 campuses together with the Association of Jewish Sixth Formers, where the students are prepared for the hazards of the campus, offers a haven in an area of uncertainty.

Now that the consensus of Jewish public opinion has at long last come round to appreciate the need to give priority attention to Jewish education, we must have a new vision. It is no use sending children to Jewish schools, particularly religious schools, if there is a dichotomy between the home atmosphere and the teaching at school. Parents will have to show commitment to fall into line with the aspirations of the school, and undoubtedly this will call for adult Jewish education without which the influence on the young will at best be ephemeral.

Are we able to live and survive without outside pressure? Are we able to look freedom in the face without being swallowed by it? This is the challenge facing us.

June 1993

Zionism, the Diaspora, the Jewish People

So How Many Are We?

World Jewry's number is stagnant. Whilst 650,000 Arab refugees have multiplied by a factor of six to nearly four million in the last 50 years, we have stood still. Furthermore, there has been a dramatic shift in where we are.

Intermarriage, low birth-rate, assimilation and migration have played havoc with *Am Israel* in the last half century. Fifty-two percent of American Jewish women between the ages of 30 and 35 are childless. Anglo-Jewry, down to 285,000, is reducing itself by 2,000 per annum. Eighty percent of World Jewry lives in two countries: Israel and the USA. One-third lives in two towns: Tel Aviv and its satellite towns (2.6 million) and New York (two million).

There were 1,800,000 Jews in the former Soviet Union in 1979; now there are less than 450,000. Over 1.4 million emigrated: 900,000 to Israel, 300,000 to the USA and 200,000 to other countries – mainly Germany.

There are today 13.3 million Jews in the world. The figures quoted here are based on the research of the world's leading Jewish demographer, Prof. Sergio Della Pergola, who is based at the Harman Institute of Contemporary Jewry of the Hebrew University, and were published in the 2002 edition of the American Jewish Year Book. They are supplemented by explanatory notes sent to me by Sergio, a friend of many years' standing (his father, Massimo, was Chairman of Maccabi Italy for 30 years).

The aggravated tragedy of the Holocaust is that apart from the six million who were slaughtered, an additional 15 million, who would have been born by this most fecund part of the Jewish people, never saw the light of day. World Jewry today would number some 33 million had there been no Hitler. This is the view of our leading demographer.

Examining the composition of the 13 million plus, we find an extraordinary shift in the location of primary Jewish centres, a seismic burst of increase and decline unprecedented in our history or that of any other people.

In 1937, there were 9.6 million Jews in Europe, including the European part of the former Soviet Union and the Balkans. Today, the comparative number is 1.6 million, a post factum victory for Hitler.

So where are we today?

Israel	5,025,000
North America	6,064,000
Central/South America	412,000
Asia	45,000
Europe	1,583,000
Africa	88,000
Australia/New Zealand	103,000
	13,320,000

Let us examine some of these numbers in different parts of the world, on the principle of *mihaklal el haprat* – from the general to the particular – according to an old Gemara principle, recited in our daily morning prayers.

Israel: Thirty-eight percent of world Jewry now lives in the Holy Land. The population growth slowed down dramatically during the intifada. According to the Central Bureau of Statistics, it dropped to 1.4 percent. The long-term demographic outlook is not good. While the Israeli-Arab's birth-rate has fallen from 87.5 percent per family to about 4.5 percent, it is still more than double the Jewish secular majority's rate of reproduction. In the year 2000, 4.9 million Jews lived west of the Jordan River compared to 3.9 million Muslims and 200,000 Christians. If the concept of "Greater Israel" was ever realised, that is Jewish sovereignty from the Jordan to the Mediterranean, there would be an Arab majority within the next two decades. This would be the end of the Jewish state, unless non-Jews were disenfranchised or "transferred." It is hard to imagine that the rest of the world would tolerate either eventuality.

United Kingdom: There are an estimated 285,000 Jews according to Jewish Policy Research's Expert, Marlena Schmool of the British Board of Deputies, a dramatic decline from 410,000 in the immediate post-war era. Anglo-Jewry continues to shrink. Only four provincial towns have more than 5,000 Jews: Glasgow, Leeds, Manchester and Brighton.

The symptoms manifested in the rest of the Diaspora apply equally in the United Kingdom. Intermarriage, emigration and deliberate dropouts are an ongoing haemorrhaging process at the rate of 2,000 per annum. A consoling factor is that the community has never been so vibrant, with an increasing number of Jewish schools and educational facilities.

France: has the largest number of Jews in Europe. In excess of half a million, they are confronted by ten times that number of militant Muslims. Aliya has doubled to more than 2,000 per annum due to the increasing number of anti-Semitic incidents.

Germany: is the exception. The number of Jews has doubled in the last 25 years to over 100,000, mainly due to immigration from the former Soviet Union. What an irony of fate that the only country in Europe where the number of Jews is increasing should be Germany.

Austria and Poland: The Jewish populations in 1937 were 191,000 and 3,250,000 respectively. Today the relevant numbers are 9,000 and 3,500 – not so far from being *Judenrein*.

South America: Here too Jewry has suffered a dramatic decline. They may total only 363,000. In 1960, Argentine had 310,000 Jews; today there are no more than 195,000. Rampant anti-Semitism, a powerful Catholic church, corrupt governments and regular economic disasters have led to mass emigration.

South Africa: The Jews now number some 80,000 with an ageing population. Their aliya has been mostly to Australia and, to a lesser extent, to Israel, Canada, USA and the UK.

Australia: The Jewish population is burgeoning. It has doubled itself in the last four decades to over 100,000, mostly due to immigration from South Africa and the former Soviet Union.

USA: Finally, we come to the modern equivalent of Babylon, with a hitherto self-confident, assertive, prosperous and yet diminishing number of Jews. Theirs is the most examined, dissected and analysed segment in the world of Jewish demography. In the 1960s, Philip Klutznick, the eminent world president of B'nai B'rith, objected to Ben Gurion's description of American Jewry as part of the Diaspora. Although Klutznick was a great benefactor of Israel and also a leading investor, he objected to being categorised as a *galut* Jew who should make aliya.

Alas, those halcyon days are over. The American Jewish Committee's annual survey of 2002 showed that American Jewry considered growing anti-Semitism as the greatest threat to Jewish life today – more dangerous to continuity than inter-marriage. Incidentally, only 37 percent of American Jews have visited Israel, including 20 percent who have been there only once.

The latest available figures show 5,340,000 core Jewish population (American Jewish Identification Survey). The numbers are necessarily imprecise, being based on a variety of surveys, estimates and calculations by professional demographers, complicated by a substantial internal migration. The trend, however, is clear. The core Jewish population is declining whilst the non-core is rapidly increasing. The latter includes mixed marriages and their offspring. Only 18 percent of children of mixed marriages are raised as Jews.

On present indications, it is only a question of time when Israel will overtake the USA to become the largest Jewish population centre in the world. If we are to be blessed with peace and the embassies return to Jerusalem, this could come much sooner than one dares to hope at present.

This article was originally written in the 1990s. The figures have changed to some extent since then.

Post-Zionism Combat Fatigue

Apart from its unprecedented external pressures, Israel is preoccupied with an internal debate which will affect its very existence. Many haredim do not recognise the state, created by man without the specific authority of the Almighty.

Eighty percent of the Jewish population in Israel are secular – that is they send their children to non-religious schools where, judging by results, the teaching of our sources and traditions has been appalling. Patriotism has given way to consumerism. The heroes of Entebbe have been superseded by young dotcom millionaires.

Already in 1993, the then minister of education, Prof. Amnon Rubinstein, appointed a Special Committee of Inquiry under the chairmanship of Prof. Aliza Shenhar. Although both Rubinstein and Shenhar defined themselves as secular Jews, they, as well as the rest of the country, were shaken by the conclusions of the committee, which were devastating. Youngsters, who knew the basketball league tables by heart, had barely heard of the Ten Commandments.

I had the opportunity of discussing the report with Prof. Shenhar some five years later in Moscow, where she was the Israeli ambassador. She expressed deep disappointment that her recommendations had been largely ignored and that the follow-up by subsequent coalition governments was conspicuous by its absence. Now, in 2001, another secular education minister, Limor Livnat, has again taken the initiative to change the deplorable state of affairs, in the face of mixed reactions from both the Right and the Left. She said in the Knesset:

> What I would like to see is that there is not a single child in Israel who doesn't learn the basics of Jewish and Zionist knowledge and values. Today, there are children, Jewish children, who reach Bar/Bat Mitzvah age, sometimes older, without ever having seen *tefillin* (phylacteries for morning prayer). They need to know about it, that is all. The prayer book, the *siddur*, they should also know what that is. I don't want them necessarily to put on tefillin or a *kipa*, but they need to know about them. I also would like them to learn the Bible in a way that will make them love it and be familiar with it. We

are the People of the Book. Not everyone need observe the *mitzvot* (commandments), but we should know what they are, to know our basic values. Afterwards, everyone can do what they want, make their own decisions. By providing this basic knowledge, we are, in essence, providing everyone with a right to choose their way of life.

The issue came to the fore last year with the publication of an epoch-making book, "The Struggle for Israel's Soul," by a young Jerusalemite academic, Yoram Hazony The head of the right-wing Shalem Center and a former speech-writer to Prime Minister Netanyahu, Hazony lays the blame for the present malaise on the founding professors at the Hebrew University.

He maintains that the influence of Martin Buber, Franz Rosenzweig, Gershom Scholem and particularly Yehuda Magnes – its president for many years – all protagonists of a bi-national state, were responsible for the moral decay of the present professors of the Hebrew University who were their pupils. In other words, the *yekkes* (German-born Jews), whose humanistic instincts were over-reacting to the extent of potential self-destruction, had sown poisonous seeds.

Hazony quotes from the latest text books for 15 and 16-year olds in secular schools. These books, authorised by a special committee under the chairmanship of Professor Israel Bartal of the Hebrew University, represent a complete change from previous editions. The changes were discussed at length in a Knesset debate in November, 2000. I quote some examples: The new textbooks contain pictures of Hitler, Roosevelt and the Beatles but not of Ben Gurion. The photograph of the Declaration of the State of Israel has been omitted. A map of five thick black arrows showing the 1948 invasion by five Arab armies has been superseded by a map of Palestinians fleeing in five directions. The Entebbe rescue mission, admired by the Western world, is not mentioned at all. There are two issues here: One is the culpability of the Hebrew University. In this day and age, it is complete nonsense. There are at least as many right-wing professors today as there are peaceniks, and to suggest that the whole of the faculty is still under the malignant influence of the old yekkes is mere propaganda.

The second issue remains relevant, namely that the enthusiastic confidence in the rightness of the cause of the old pioneers has largely evaporated. The phenomenal success of the Israeli high-tech industry and the American McDonald/Coca Cola invasion has created an unhealthy atmosphere of greed at the expense of social concern. The growing reluctance to serve in the army is another manifestation of the creeping disease.

Whilst this so-called post-Zionist Revisionism still has its defenders who decry jingoism and chauvinism, and who maintain that Israel today is mature enough to face its past sins, there is now a groundswell of popular revulsion against this very dangerous trend. A country whose physical existence is threatened by its neighbours is, alas, not in the same situation as, say Sweden or Holland, where extravagant soul-searching and self-denigration are luxuries which do not affect their very existence.

The good news is that there is now an intensive drive to teach the teachers of the secular schools to bring back the Torah into the curriculum and that Minister Limor Livnat is withdrawing the offensive textbooks. The Hebrew University, through its Revivim Department and the Hartman Institute, under the leadership of Rabbis David and Donniel Hartman, are pioneers in this field and they are teaching 60 principals of schools at any one time what they should have learned at elementary school. Having witnessed some of these seminars at the Hartman Institute, I found nothing more moving than finding a secular teacher in front of a Gemara with tears in his eyes stating "why was I not taught this before?"

What are our Priorities?

Zionism has become a pejorative word; anti-Semitism has become legitimate again and world Jewry is under siege, reflecting the isolation of the state of Israel.

How has this dramatic change come about in less than two decades? The authorised version, accepted in facile fashion by many, is the transformation of the State of Israel from being the underdog to an aggressive expansionist state, keeping its Arab minority under ruthless military rule.

The creation of mythology in one's own lifetime, flying in the face of demonstrable facts, is a highly-skilled public relations operation, carried out by generously rewarded professionals. Yet the uncomfortable questions remain. Why should governments and the media who know the facts prostitute themselves by tendentious selective reporting, by ignoring atrocities carried out in Moslem countries whilst giving headline treatment to minor incidents which would certainly not be mentioned if they took place anywhere else. The rot set in with the power of the oil weapon. The world's financial reserves shifted gradually from the control of Wall Street to the sands of Kuwait and Saudi Arabia. The economic pundits of the free world are surprised by the depth and length of the recession. Yet the writing was on the wall as long as ten years ago, clearly visible to all those who did not wilfully close their eyes.

The phenomenal accumulation of the world's spending money in the hands of a few corrupt rulers, who have been projected from archaic desert tent life to high finance, electronic gadgets and the micro-chip in a breathlessly short period, is a tragedy of historic dimensions which augurs ill for the future.

A man who gives his wife 100 pounds per week housekeeping money and then cuts it to 60 in the face of rising costs, knows that he cannot expect to maintain his standard of living. He must go and borrow, or sell his remaining assets or sell himself into slavery.

The world queues up for the so-called recycling of Arab money. Nations vie with each other to sell their real estate, their industry, their media, to the Arabs who often disguise their ownership through willing local nominees, usually emanating from the financial elite of the country concerned. Yet vast amounts remain on useless, unproductive short-term deposits, the hot money of the world, following greedily the lure of the highest interest rate, rushing from sterling into dollars, from yens into euros, leaving millions of unemployed, social unrest and shattered national infra-structures in their wake.

The Times wrote on 10th March: "About 65 percent of OPEC's total foreign assets are accounted for by just two countries – Saudi Arabia and Kuwait – whose governments between them command some $250 million worth of overseas investments. But the ways in which these two countries' funds are deployed reflect important differences in their attitudes to foreign investment and its ultimate purpose. The Saudi philosophy is that its foreign investments are "temporary" and that the country's wealth is held abroad only until it can be used productively at home. The absorptive capacity of the Saudi economy is still limited, but the massive development plans now being implemented will, it is hoped, create better opportunities for the country's oil revenues to be invested domestically. This is the real cause of the world's economic difficulties and nothing individual governments can do will bring about a return to their former prosperity and economic independence.

Four thousand princes of the Saudi royal family have a minimum personal income each of one million dollars per annum. Many have scores of millions every year. This perverse state of affairs results in such vast spending power that it dwarfs the GNP of more than half the UN member states. One might think that the temporary oil glut has brought an improvement. Not at all. The so-called free world will sell its soul for trade. The oil bonanza has lasted long enough to give the OPEC countries colossal purchasing power. Their highly paid international advisers have taught them to combine economic clout with political blackmail. Statesmen, newspaper editors, deans of universities and even curators of museums see it as their duty to protect their particular infrastructure by entering into a game of make-belief. They use weasel words, they compromise their personal integrity, they abandon old friends – all under the euphemism of weathering the economic storm. It must be understood that in the face of these realities anything which Israel does or does not do is only of peripheral importance. If Mr. Begin were to resign, if Israel would withdraw behind 1967 frontiers, and if there were a PLO-dominated Palestinian state in the West Bank, the pressures would not cease. Moreover, Iran has tremendous oil reserves which pay for the development of nuclear weapons capability.

Every president or prime minister receiving a delegation is briefed by his specialists, who will acquaint him with the likely views of those who seek his help. Only those who can be relied upon to exercise independent judgement can be of true value in furthering the long term interests of the State of Israel. Yes, the debates matter. Not so much because of *ma yomru hagoyim* ("What will the Gentiles say?"), but because of our own Jewish self-respect. A beleaguered world Jewry cannot be muzzled. We need to communicate, primarily with each other, on the basis that the centrality of Israel is a sine qua non.

Our polarisation proceeds apace. The assimilationists go about their way quietly and disappear. The Yavneh complex on the extreme right represents another challenge. Yavneh is a concept which lays the main emphasis on the continuity of the Jewish religion as an ongoing historic force, regardless of the survival of the State of Israel. When the Second Temple was destroyed in the year 70 AD, Rabbi Yochanan Ben Zakai pleaded with Vespasian, the Roman general "Let me have a yeshiva and its wise students!" There is little doubt that the establishment of Yavneh ensured the survival of Judaism at that time when there was a distinct danger of its obliteration. There are some yeshivot today which have turned their backs on what they consider to be a sinful secular state. They concentrate on a totally inward-looking perception of perpetuating the Torah from Sinai for a chosen few. There are others who would not forgive God a second time for allowing another Holocaust through the destruction of the State of Israel. Where does this leave us? It leaves us with an enormous educational challenge. Our survival – physical and spiritual – is in our own hands. Our falling birth rate, accelerating assimilation and growing ignorance of our heritage combine to sound a shrill warning note. Is anybody listening?

The fund-raising cake is getting smaller. The conflicting claims of Israel and Diaspora institutions are getting bigger. Here we have the seeds for future conflicts. Nothing, but nothing should be allowed to diminish the over-riding importance for the claims of Jewish education in Israel and even more so in the Diaspora. We lack schools, we lack teachers, we lack suitable audio-visual materials. Where there are outstanding schools such as Ramaz in New York City, its fees of over $5,000 per annum make it difficult for parents to finance the cost of sending their children.

Great strides have been made in the United Kingdom since the re-activation of the Jewish Educational Development Trust under the aegis of the Chief Rabbi. Some 25 percent of Jewish children go to Jewish schools, although there is still an imbalance in favour of primary schools. But some 50 percent receive no Jewish education at all and are totally unprepared to face the anti-Israel and anti-Semitic onslaught which meets them on university campuses. Hillel is fighting an uphill battle to keep them within the fold and to slow down the erosion based on the ignorance of their heritage. Parents must be made to understand that they are deeply involved. Our traditional priorities need complete re-appraisal. We shall ignore the problem at our peril.

The Jewish Quarterly

Israel and the Diaspora – is there a Dialogue?

Herman Wouk, the author of "The Caine Mutiny," "This is My God," "The Winds of War," recently came out with another book "Inside/Outside." It is partly autobiographical and deals with an American Jew who leads his life both inside the Jewish community and outside it as an advisor to the president.

Inside/Outside – the classical Jewish dilemma. He starts with an evocative scenario. Wouk's alter ego is not quite sure why he has been invited to join the president's staff as a speech writer. All he knows is that he has precious little to do, so he takes a volume of the Talmud with him to the White House. There he sits, *kipa* on head, learning his daily page of Gemara. Unexpectedly the president walks in. He is naturally intrigued, asks questions and comes to the conclusion that a man who does this sort of thing as a hobby can probably be trusted more than most. It is a poignant little illustration of a situation in which a Diaspora Jew can find himself.

What about the problem of "dual loyalty?" Ben Gurion had no doubt that it existed. He wrote in 1952: "Even with the best of intentions, the Jew in the Diaspora can never be exclusively a Jew, and in fact he is a Jew very little. Whether they recognize it or not, Diaspora Jews live in a permanent condition of exile. I mean that they are always a minority and thus dependent on a majority beyond their capacity to control. They are born in never-ending conflict between a desire to preserve their Jewish status, which keeps them separate, and the assimilationist pressures of the social structure..." Winston Churchill held contrary views. He said, "It is a poor man who only has two loyalties. I have my loyalty to my country, to my family, to my church, to my mother's country, to my regiment and so on..."

Does the conflict of interest prevent a meaningful dialogue between Israel and the Diaspora? Let us in the first place define what we mean by Diaspora. This word creates a special resonance and produces different echoes from various parts of the world. Diaspora means Dispersion.

The American Jews acknowledge that they are in the Diaspora. They would vehemently deny, however, that they are in the *Galut*, which means Exile. Russian Jews who want to emigrate are in the Galut. American Jews, who have no intention of going to Israel, feel very strongly that they are not only the largest but the most influential sector of the Jewish people, the modern Babylon with yeshivot and seminaries to rival those of Surah and Pumbedita.

At the time of the Second Temple there were some four million Jews living in the Land of Israel and a similar number outside. Today, there are some 13 million Jews in the world. Three and a half million are in Israel and nine and a half million in the Diaspora which will continue to decline to eight million by the year 2000 and possibly to only six million by 2025, according to the demographers of the Hebrew

University. On the other hand, even without aliya, Israel's population will grow because of the far more positive birth/death ratio.

Certain ground rules seem to have established themselves in relation to the dialogue between Israel and world Jewry. It is a sine qua non that there can be none as far as the security of the state is concerned. This may seem an uncontroversial statement surely accepted by everybody. It will be seen, however, that anything in relation to Israel is not as simple as it may first appear. There are double standards. At one level, the Diaspora is called upon to close its ranks. No public criticism of Israel must be made; this could be of comfort to the enemy. If you have anything to say that is not favourable, then direct it to the appropriate Israeli authority in the hope that it will not get lost in its bureaucracy. On the other hand, Israelis in their free and democratic country can say, print, broadcast and televise their views which more often than not are far more critical than anything the Diaspora might offer. There is a tacit understanding that the enemy does not read the Israeli press and that if the late Sir Sigmund Warburg or the Chief Rabbi expressed themselves in public, deploring certain aspects of the war in Lebanon, that this was harmful, whereas had they emigrated to Israel and expressed identical views through the columns of the Israeli press, this would have been perfectly acceptable.

There is a second level. The Lubavitch Rebbe, in the midst of the conflict in Lebanon, came out with a clear and unequivocal statement which had the most far-reaching strategic implications and thus impinged on the security of the state. He called upon the Israeli government not to give an inch and quoted halakhic sources. When a symposium on "Jewish Terrorism" was held at Yeshiva University, New York, a subject which many considered a contradiction in terms, 27 Orthodox rabbis came to the conclusion that the Jewish terrorists who were condemned by an Israeli court were not guilty of a moral crime and should therefore be immediately released.

It was strange, but not entirely unexpected, that there was no outcry from the usual quarters against this blatant interference in internal Israeli affairs. The vociferous right welcomes this kind of Diaspora involvement as perfectly legitimate if it strengthens their political beliefs.

This poses a very great moral dilemma for our leaders in the Diaspora and in particular our rabbis, whose silence on all and every occasion will be taken as tacit consent by the rest of the world. Indeed, there is no denying that world Jewry looked upon the silence of the pope and other church leaders during and after the Holocaust as a severe dereliction of their duties, preferring self-interest to their obvious moral obligation.

There is yet another dilemma. Israel is no ordinary state. The word "Zion" has a most evocative deep-seated place in the Jewish psyche. The Jew's soul has yearned for two millennia for a Zion from which goes forth the Torah. Yet we have the extraordinary phenomenon that many of those who pray three times a day and turn their faces in the direction of Zion, despise the state and look upon it as an affront to the Messiah who has not yet come, whilst others who are far less religious have no difficulty with the credo based on the centrality of Israel as the focal point of their lives.

Israel is one of the few democracies in the world in which religious parties have consistently formed part of the government. When we talk about the word "dialogue" we are not, therefore, dealing merely with political and cultural issues, but also the far more intractable religious ones; issues on which Jewish solidarity has splintered since the exodus from Egypt. Religious dissent in Israel (e.g. "Who is a Jew?") affects every Jew in the Diaspora.

In the eyes of the world, rightly or wrongly, Israel speaks for World Jewry. The maxim that all Jews are responsible for each other is clearly accepted by the Gentile world. All of us have had the experience of being congratulated (and did we not walk seven feet tall?) at the time of the Entebbe rescue. "You people put up a splendid show," or alternatively "Your army should never have entered Beirut." The fact that this may be addressed to a seventh generation English Jew who has never been to Israel in his life is quite irrelevant. In politics illusion is often stronger than reality. There is, therefore, this quite extraordinary responsibility on the government of Israel, not only vis-à-vis its own citizens, but also in relation to the Jews in the Diaspora.

If Jews are killed in a synagogue in Turkey, the Israel government swears vengeance. If Israel sneezes, world Jewry catches a cold. It would seem natural, therefore, that Israel should call the tune and Diaspora Jews should be seen as uncritical supporters but not heard.

However, recently there has been a subtle change, a minor revolution by the Diaspora leadership of the World Zionist Organisation and the Jewish Agency. There is a new spirit of independence in the air. Gone are the days when the non-Israeli members of the WZO rubber-stamped the decision of their Israeli colleagues and when the swelling number of bureaucrats in the offices of the WZO and the Jewish Agency remained unchallenged. A series of traumatic exposés of these bodies were featured in the Israeli press.

The new scenario has a number of consequences. On the religious level, 85 percent of American Jews (i.e. those who are not strictly Orthodox) do not accept the "Who is a Jew?" definition of the Israel rabbinate. On the financial level, the Federations as the American regional central funding bodies are called, now decide by themselves how much of their funds stay in America for local needs and how much is sent to Israel.

In view of the increasing demands for Jewish education, from senior citizens and from social services, the percentage has changed in some localities from say, 60:40 in favour of Israel to a reverse ratio.

A permanent, self-reliant Diaspora used to run contrary to established Israeli thinking. On the occasion of the centennial celebrations of David Ben Gurion's birthday, Shimon Peres wrote: "He [Ben Gurion] condemned the Diaspora: Diaspora, dispersion, the ghetto mentality seemed to him a sad rift in the life of the Jewish people. The Third Temple should have followed the First and Second. Only the nation's colossal spirit enabled it to endure 2,000 years in limbo without creative existence. The Diaspora is anti-history. History itself demands renewal in the place where it began."

Not so, say some Diaspora leaders with new-found confidence. "Let us see how many Nobel prize-winners, how many Maimonides, Spinozas, Baal-Shem-Tovs, Marx, Einsteins and Freuds, the State of Israel will produce before our history is being denied to us." One comes to the reluctant conclusion that meaningful dialogue is not possible. Dialogue presupposes a modicum of equality in the standing of the participants. Of course, there can be a dialogue between master and servant, general and private, employer and employee, but the more slanted the relative gravitas of the two parties, the less likely that equal listening time will be given.

Are there any equal parties in Israel and the Diaspora? Apart from the so-called partnership in the WZO and the Jewish Agency, one cannot think of any. What about the rabbis? Aye – there's the rub! There is so much non-recognition between the different factions that even the title "rabbi" is no longer a generic nomenclature. Even if we were to confine ourselves to those rabbis who operate on the strict basis of *halakha* from Mount Sinai, we look at colour ranges of greys, blacks and ultra-blacks, each of whom believes that those standing on his left are not to be recognised as representatives of true Judaism.

Essentially, however, dialogue with Israel will fail because one party is politically enfranchised and the other is not. Politics is a power game. "How many battalions has the Pope got?" Actually, that rhetorical question posed by Stalin is no longer as relevant as it was when first asked. Religious parties in government do not need armies to assert themselves. Fundamentalism has moved from a religious concept to an explosive force in politics. Rabbis, who form part of the government of Israel, will not agree to de-politicise religion. No-one is willing to participate in his own demise in this power game.

Having dealt with what at first glance might have appeared as the most likely candidates for a meaningful dialogue, and having reached a negative conclusion, who else is there? Could it be leaders of voluntary organisations in the Diaspora or powerful individuals who have made a name for themselves in commerce, science, philosophy or even local politics?

The reality must be faced. These individuals do not have the clout of the Israeli politicians who can make things happen. We may develop a new kind of Court Jew – a prominent American lawyer who may have a special relationship with this or that Israeli cabinet minister, an oil tycoon who because he controls billions, commands some attention, but essentially they can be no more than *eitses-gaybers* – advice givers – whose suggestions may be accepted or rejected.

Even the fund-raisers are losing out. As their contribution diminishes year by year as a percentage of Israel's gross national product, (it is already less than two percent), their influence may last longer with certain institutions such as the universities and museums, but that is not the basis of our definition of a dialogue.

Would the writers who so often express the conscience of the community in which they live provide a channel of communication that could be enlarged? Judging by a symposium of Israeli and Anglo-Jewish writers organised by the *Jewish Quarterly* in London in December, the answer, alas, is a categorical "No."

There was a dissonance, a dichotomy, a gulf that widened as the discussion proceeded. Diaspora writers were labelled as insecure, rootless and living nervously between two cultures. When Danny Abse, the Jewish poet from Wales, asked whether Israeli writers present felt safe in the shelter of their homeland, a new dimension of inside/outside angst was revealed.

"The Well of the Past," as Thomas Mann defined our history, demonstrated the frighteningly short period of the second Jewish commonwealth. The unity of the dream, before the state was created, was rudely shattered when reality took over or, as Bruno Bettelheim put it, "the fabric of the dream was torn from the children of the dream."

Israeli visitors felt that continuous exposure to rift and danger drained their energy. In visiting Jewish north-west London, they were reminded of soldiers returning to luxury from the battlefields. They felt isolated and predicted that the Israeli/Diaspora divergence would grow. "Look at New York," they said. "There you have a Jewish Diaspora and an Israeli Diaspora and even there the two don't mix." Are we, therefore, bound to witness a growing polarisation, an ever-widening gulf between Israel and the Diaspora?

Are we doomed to the pre-ordained fate outlined in the prognosis of the demographers? Is there no alternative to the steady decline of our people? Sam Goldwyn said: "Never prophesy, least of all as far as the future is concerned." Winston Churchill put it more elegantly: "The future, though imminent, remains obscure."

Let us look at the analogy of a prosperous family which lived in a large mansion from which they also carried on their business. In their comfortable lifestyle they gave generously to the under-privileged. Unfortunately the house suffered from dry rot. The inevitable major repairs were put off from decade to decade until one day the mansion collapsed. That was the end of the family, their livelihood and their charity. They had even neglected to take out an insurance policy.

Demographic forecasts are largely based on past and present behaviour. Is it possible to make a radical change? While we still have 13 million people it is not too late. If a clarion call went out from the lay and religious leadership in Israel and the Diaspora, that the Jewish education of our young must take absolute priority on which our shrinking financial resources must be concentrated, we still have a chance.

If we create schools which become centres of excellence, a teaching profession which attracts our most brilliant students, a rabbinate which relates to the mass of our people, then our problems will gradually become less insuperable. Hebrew would become the lingua franca, universities would give credits for time spent in Israeli educational establishments and there would be a new-found pride in our heritage. Identification with *Am Israel* – the People of Israel – would reduce assimilation and intermarriage. There would be aliya and a continuing crossing of bridges between Israel and the Diaspora and the generations to come would be free from the intolerance and *sinat hinam* – baseless hatred – within the contemporary Jewish scene.

Utopia? The alternative is that in 2087 there won't be anybody with whom to have a dialogue.

A Letter to Professor George Steiner

Fred and Della Worms met Professor Steiner, the eminent European-born American literary critic and, philosopher who lives in Britain, over dinner at the home of Chief Rabbi Jonathan Sacks in October, 1999. The dinner sparkled with provocative thoughts which set off a lively exchange of ideas and opinions. Following the dinner, Fred sent the following letter to the professor, who telephoned in reply.

When you told me that you were about to visit your friend, the professor of the Law Faculty at Tel Aviv University, and that you deeply regretted that there were no Jews left in Israel, I was naturally intrigued by your remark, bearing in mind that according to the latest count there are 5,619,000 Jews in the country.*

You explained, with your proverbial courtesy and patience, that these are not your kind of Jews; you consider them nationalists, oppressors and deviants from the prototype of the Diaspora Jews who formed the seedbed of Nobel prize winners.

"Where are your Nobel prize winners in Israel?" you ask. "Not at the Weizmann Institute, not at the Technion, not at the Hebrew, Tel Aviv or Bar Ilan Universities" – a clear sign, you thought, that something has gone radically wrong.** Unlike Isaiah Berlin, who was often ambivalent about Jewish issues, but was perfectly clear that the Jews were entitled to their own country so as to be somewhere in the majority, you apparently maintain an attitude that all nationalism per se is to be condemned and that the Jew's home remains his typewriter. Do I misinterpret what you said?

I suggested that you had something in common with the late Professor Yeshayahu Leibowitz who, although a strictly Orthodox halakhic Jew, considered the Israeli army to be equivalent to Nazi storm-troopers. You confirmed that you had discussed this on several occasions with the late professor in his magnificent library and that on this particular point you were ad idem.

Incidentally, tiny Israel's own Silicone Valley is producing an extraordinary number of scientists in various fields of information

---

* Ed. Today the number is 5,901,000 (eve of 2012), out of a total of 7.836,000.

** Ed. It is worth noting that since this letter was written, six Israeli scientists have received Nobel prizes: Daniel Kahaneman (Economics, 2002), Aaron Ciechanover and Avram Hershko (Chemistry, 2004), Robert Aumann (Economics, 2005), Ada Yonath (Chemistry, 2009) and Daniel Schechtman (Chemistry, 2011.) This in addition to Shmuel Yosef Agnon (Literature, 1966), Menachem Begin (Peace, 1978), Shimon Peres and Yitzhak Rabin (Peace, 1994).

technology some of them world leaders in their fields, all alumni of Israel's universities.

I then asked you for examples of the ideal Jews in our history who could serve as role models for the younger generation. You mentioned Spinoza, Freud and I believe Karl Marx. Now I am totally at a loss. Baruch Spinoza was placed under a *herem* (edict of boycott) in 1656 when he was 24 years old, the very year in which Menasseh Ben Israel prevailed upon Oliver Cromwell to re-admit Jews to England.

The insecurity of the rabbis and the church at that traumatic period, shortly after the 30 years war and the havoc caused by the false messiah Shabtai Zvi, was not conducive to non-fundamentalist criticism of the Bible.

Unlike Freud, Spinoza was not an atheist. His definition of a pantheist God was somewhat opaque, but so is the God of the Old Testament who is sometimes anthropomorphic and at other times in the inscrutable *ehyeh asher ehyeh* "I am who I am."

To some extent Spinoza merely followed the exegetical explanation of Ibn Ezra that not every word in the Torah was dictated by God and that its final composition was probably undertaken by Ezra in the 5th century BC.

Today, Spinoza would be a respected Reform rabbi. Indeed, he is not all that far from Rabbi Louis Jacobs, the eminent Talmudist. The fact that Spinoza took a total rational approach and eschewed Aggada and Midrash is highly commendable, considering the times he was living in.

Sigmund Freud was a militant atheist. In his book "Moses and Monotheism," he makes the fanciful assertion that Moses, an Egyptian prince, was murdered by the children of Israel in the desert who then returned to polytheism until Jethro the Midianite priest brought them back to the straight and narrow. Even loyal followers of Freud – and they are rapidly diminishing – have found it difficult to find out what this theory is based on. Freud was certainly no Ahad Ha'am.*

---

* Ed. Pen-name of Asher Ginsberg (1856-1927), the Zionist writer and philosopher.

If my ageing memory serves me right, you also nominated Karl Marx as one of our all-time greats. Whilst he was undoubtedly brilliant with an encyclopaedic mind, he was Jewishly illiterate. He was baptized at the age of 15 and became a practising Christian. In reality he was a self-hating Jew who poured out scurrilous anti-Semitic libels *Stürmer* fashion in his essay "Zur Judenfrage" and in "Das Kapital." This did not help him. The aristocracy he married into looked upon him as an atheist Jew and under the Nazis, Marxism became synonymous with evil Judaism.

We have here three examples of Jewish geniuses, deeply unhappy and frustrated men who presumably could have only flourished in the Diaspora.

My question is this: Is it reasonable to demand of the Jews that they should be the only people in the world condemned to permanent exile in a hostile environment, in order to produce the occasional genius? Is it realistic to give up national aspirations in a world in which nationalism continues to be the principal power factor? Why should only the Jews conduct themselves as though the Messiah has already arrived in his benign glory.

I would be most grateful if you would let me have your guidance.

Fred S. Worms

Rabbi Menachem Hacohen

The following letter was received from Rabbi Menachem Hacohen, MK, who had been Chief Chaplain of the Israel Navy, the moshav movement and later ambassador to Romania, following an interview in The Jerusalem Post *in which he was highly critical of certain trends within the Orthodox community in Israel.*

November 3, 1981

My dear Mr. Worms,

I was delighted to hear again from you within one week, and naturally I am gratified that my interview in *The Jerusalem Post* aroused positive echoes, especially with such an eminent Jewish communal leader as yourself. It was really most encouraging that an observant Jew like yourself should take the trouble of writing to me expressing his support and of having further contacted the Chief Rabbi, my esteemed friend Rabbi Jakobovits in this connection.

I do think that the time is overdue when the forces of sane Judaism should combine to curb the wave of neo-Khomeinistic fanaticism which threatens to engulf the Jewish world.

I am obliged to you for conveying to me the Chief Rabbi's letter, for as you probably know I am an admirer of his forthrightness and courage. However, I beg to differ with him on the issue of the disestablishment of the Israeli Chief Rabbinate. We see it through different prisms perhaps. In the United Kingdom, the Chief Rabbi is accepted as the spiritual head of the Anglo-Jewish community, not by virtue of any secular law adopted by parliament as the result of bargaining between the parties, but by virtue of his personal authority and his acceptance as the supreme spiritual leader by his Jewish community. There is no element of coercion by secular law as is the case in Israel.

I would also add that the rabbis of Agudat Israel and other extremist sects in Israel and the U.K. only have a hold on their own congregations. The nub of my interview with *The Jerusalem Post* was that the constant intervention in politics of the Chief Rabbis of Israel must involve the reduction of their authority to that of followers of the religious parties. Hence my warning that their word would no longer hold for the general community

I will be pleased to accept your invitation to become a trustee of the new B'nai B'rith World Centre in Jerusalem, largely because you are at the head of that body. I do hope we can meet on your next visit to Jerusalem.

"A Taste of Freedom"

Fred Worms interviews Natan Sharansky.

Anatoly Shcharansky, the best known of the Russian refuseniks (those whose immigration was denied by the Soviet authorities), was arrested and convicted on a trumped-up charge of spying for the West and was incarcerated in a Soviet prison in 1977. He was released in February 1986 and immediately made aliya to Israel, changing his name to Natan Sharansky. He served in several ministerial positions in Israeli government and since 2009 has been Chairman of the Executive of the Jewish Agency. The following interview was conducted at Passover, 1992, when Sharansky had been in Israel for six years.

FW: The last year has seen tremendous changes in what was the USSR. Many of our brethren were allowed to leave and go to Israel. But what of the Jews who are left in Russia? What facilities do they have? Will there be a renaissance of Jewish life there? What influence do you think the refusal movement may have had over the years in bringing about the ultimate collapse of the Communist system?

NS: There is no doubt that the human rights movement played an essential role in accelerating the demise of the Communist system and bringing about what is now known as *Glasnost'* and *Perestroika*. Initially, *refuseniks* were the most prominent ones who kept the West acquainted with human rights violations in the Soviet System and this led to crisis after crisis which found its climax with the ascent of Gorbachev.

Now, if you look at the human rights movement, there were many different components, each one with its own agenda. There were national movements, religious movements, ethical movements like that of Andrei Sakharov and ethnic movements. Most of all there was the Jewish movement which pressed for emigration. The most dangerous to the Soviet authorities was the Zionist movement which went against everything the old system stood for. It insisted on free emigration to the Jewish state. Its message was simple and clear.

Surprisingly, the only mass movement in terms of tens of thousands was the Soviet Jewish or Zionist movement. Others had a few thousand but not many were willing to go to the barricades as the Zionists were. There was enormous pressure on us, particularly from the Israeli authorities, that we should make it clear to the Soviet authorities that we had nothing against their system but were mainly concerned about freedom of emigration of the Jews to Israel. In other words, to make the Zionist movement more kosher than the others. The Soviet leadership, and in particular the KGB, understood very well how dangerous it was to call for an opening of the gates. Freedom of emigration was completely contradictory to everything the Soviet Union stood for. The Soviet system was based on the acceptance that people are told what to read, what to think, and where to live. A little bit of freedom was too dangerous; as it proved to be. The moment you opened the door by a fraction it was impossible to close it and the system could never go back to where it was before. There is no such thing as partial freedom.

FW: So, whilst the Jews had their own agenda they played the major part in the liberalisation of Soviet society. I assume that one cannot possibly conceive of a return to any kind of Communism, but is there not a distinct danger that after last year's failed coup and the ensuing economic chaos, some reactionary force may take over?

NS: There is no possibility whatsoever of a return to Communism. Communism as a political movement or as a theology is dead. There are remnants of the Communist party in various countries, even in Russia, but they mainly consist of people whose careers depend on it. Communism as an ideology has no chance of recovery. The Communists at the height of their power understood very well that their system was based on fear. Total control over everybody was essential to the system. That is no longer possible. People have changed. To create such an atmosphere of fear and total submission, Stalin had to kill millions of people. Without this all-consuming fear the system would not have worked as long as it did. A few thousand political prisoners kept under abominable conditions reinforced the system of fear, and served their masters well. Seven years ago people caught the virus of freedom; that virus is in their bodies and cannot be removed.

On the other hand, some system of dictatorship, especially in some of the republics, is not only conceivable but possible. The truth is that Communism has left no deep roots within Soviet souls, so people are looking for new roots, their nationalism, their religion, something which identifies them with their past and the past of their forebears. Jews don't have this dilemma because they have something to identify with. The Jew understands today that he has really no chance of becoming a true Ukrainian or Latvian, Lithuanian or Estonian. Those people look upon him as a Jew, and he will never have a permanent place as a Ukrainian.

FW: This reminds me of the old pre-war days in Germany when there was a large organisation consisting of assimilated Jews which was called the Central Council of German Citizens of the Jewish Faith. German citizenship came first. It so happened that these particular citizens were not Catholics or Bavarians, they happened to be Jews, but that was considered of minor importance.

NS: That is very interesting. I was not aware of that. In this connection it's very interesting to note that local governments in traditionally anti-Semitic places like Ukraine, Latvia and Lithuania, have leadership today that is very sympathetic to the Jews. There are several explanations for this. They believe that world Jewry has great influence on the West and they see Soviet Jewry as a potentially important bridge to the West. Secondly, there is this enormous personal contact. The new leadership and the refusenik Jews were fighting together, they were on the same side of the barricade. They were in prison together. I still have close personal contact with some of them whom I was able to assist because I got out a little earlier than they did. We have a lot of sympathy for each other but there is an enormous amount of difference between the intelligentsia on the one hand and the man in the street who is now returning to a kind of primitive nationalism.

He is a person who has always been taught to believe in the limitless potential of the unitary Soviet Power, and is now suffering badly from economic deprivations. He would like a kind of a Nuremberg Trial of all who are guilty, but he cannot point a finger at the entire leadership. He needs a specific person or group whom he can blame, a scapegoat who will carry upon its back the sins of the government. He notices amongst the leadership in the provinces a significant number of Jewish names, and turns those people into the scapegoats for which he has been searching. This is the reason why, at the grass-roots level, anti-Semitism inevitably grows and is strengthened and feeds upon itself.

FW: Are you so sure that all the Jews wish to emigrate? Are there not many who will fall into the same trap into which we have fallen so often in our long and tortured history when we thought that a change of regime would bring about better conditions?

NS: You are right, many of our Jews have long traditions in their respective countries. In Ukraine they go back for generations, they have deep roots, and if conditions are reasonable they would like to stay. However, life is going to get more and more difficult for them, and the worse the economy the greater the anti-Semitism and they are beginning to feel that already. There are no pogroms, but there is a deteriorating atmosphere.

The first lesson each generation of Jews must learn is that although their ancestors may have been hundreds of years in a particular locality, they are not looked upon as equal citizens. This they will find out to their cost. The second thing they must learn is that there is probably no alternative to emigration and there is only one place which will accept them and that is Israel. They will not come out of Jewish idealism, they will come out of fear and, of course, Israel is unique in that it offers all Jews a place of refuge.

FW: In view of what you have said, is it worthwhile for world Jewry to invest in a Jewish infrastructure in the Soviet Union? Is it worthwhile building Jewish schools, yeshivot, teachers' seminaries etc., which a normal community would require for its survival? I would like to remind you that many years ago the late Nahum Goldman, and later on our Emeritus Chief Rabbi, Lord Jakobovits, said: "Let My People Know!" That slogan meant that apart from the right of emigration, it was equally essential to ensure that those who would stay in Russia should not be cut off from their Jewish faith, their tradition and their history both in terms of ethnic and religious expression.

NS: I am convinced that in spite of the three or four hundred year-old tradition of Russian Jewry, within a generation or two the vast numbers that we have known will be down to under a hundred thousand. The Russian chapter of Jewish history will rapidly come to an end. What it will be in one hundred years I cannot tell you. We are seeing unique, historic and demographic changes in the history of Soviet Jewry. The vast majority will leave Russia and its independent former satellites. So, of the scarce resources of world Jewry, I think some money should be put into the system as has been done by Lubavitch, the Steinsaltz Yeshiva and so on.

FW: Would you start new Jewish schools?

NS: Yes, on a limited scale. Nothing like we had in the olden days of the last century. I would also discourage a permanent Jewish infrastructure which might encourage Jews to stay in the Soviet Union. It would not make much difference in the long run but thousands might miss the boat.

FW: In other words, you would rent but not build; leasehold but not freehold.

NS: Precisely. I would not try and recreate the Vilna Ghetto. I would not put many millions of dollars into a permanent structure. I think it would be a great mistake. I would do everything in my power to keep Jews Jewish in so far as this can be done on a basis that does not seek a perpetuation of their stay in Russia. I would send professors, lecturers, groups, sports teams – anything to remind them of their Judaism, teach them their heritage and to keep them identified with world Jewry, but that is all.

FW: Give me your candid opinion about whether or not the many Jewish movements that have endeavoured to establish themselves in Russia and the former Iron Curtain countries are making an impact. I refer to B'nai B'rith, Maccabi, WIZO and others.

NS: First of all, let me tell you, that Lubavitch was the movement which kept channels open in the 1950s and 1960s when it was extremely dangerous. At the time it was of tremendous importance. Today, anybody who supplies knowledge and education is playing an important part and should be encouraged. Anything which gives our youth some link, some identification with the Jewish people is of great importance. They stand by and watch other peoples retrace their roots, identify with their churches, their different nationalities, and they are bewildered. Therefore, anything that gives them pride in their Judaism is of the utmost importance. Here, sport may play an important role. For some, sport may be more important than the Bible. Sport has a unique way – *lekarev otam* – of bringing them back. The moment a Russian Jewish boy plays football in a blue and white shirt with a Magen David on it, he has taken an important step towards Judaism.

May I remind you that during the last Maccabiah, Bank Leumi gave a reception for the Russian team and you spoke for Maccabi whilst I spoke for the Russians. I made the same point at the time. I consider Jewish sport a vital entry point for Russian Jewish youngsters who would otherwise stand apart from the community.

FW: I am delighted to hear this. The Maccabi movement has for decades used sport as a means to an end to bring non-committed youngsters back to Judaism, and in this we have been successful. May we now come to the very difficult and delicate subject of religion. We have seen on television how the Russian people have flocked back to the churches, back to religion which one thought the system had completely driven out of them. There has, undoubtedly, been this deep yearning in the Russian soul to return to the Mother Church. Is there no similar urgent instinct within the Jewish soul?

NS: The Russian people were forced to eradicate their roots. Their history had been cancelled. Churches were closed, priests were killed. Communism was the only religion. The one faith, Communism, which was instilled into them, has failed. People are looking for alternatives. The churches and the mosques have been successful in providing such an alternative. The Church gives them integrity of the soul, a sense of belonging, a return to their history. Unfortunately, this is not the case with the Jews. There, Communism has been much more successful in driving out any remaining yearning for the old. Jews often identified with the system and were happy to make Communism their true religion. There was much less problem amongst the Jews when their synagogues were closed than there was with the Russians when their churches were closed. Since the *haskala* period of the Enlightenment, religion has played a diminishing role. Furthermore, the Jews did not have quite the same identity crisis. They had something to identify with, a Judaism which was not necessarily religious. Today, there are many thriving cultural organisations in Russia which are of a Jewish nature but not of a Jewish religious nature. One of the strongest alternatives for the Jews was Zionism, the return to Israel.

FW: I understand that non-Orthodox sections of the American Jewish establishment are trying to get a foothold in Russia. Do you think they may have a chance?

NS: I do not think there will be a demand for a network of synagogues. In so far as synagogues become a social and cultural centre there may be a chance. However, Soviet Jews should be afforded a choice of pluralism in Judaism.

FW: Let us now come to the influence which the Russian aliya may have on Israel. Can the Russian immigrants form a political party of their own and thus become the balancing factor which is what the religious parties have been since the inception of the state?

NS: Whilst I believe that Russian Jewry is going to have an enormous influence in changing Israel, I am opposed to the formation of a political party consisting of Russian Jews.[*] I am all in favour of uniting people on the basis of a common political belief. To unite them under an ethnic banner is dangerous, ridiculous and undesirable.

FW: But is this not precisely what the Arabs may do one day?

NS: Yes, but that's completely different because they have a common political interest, whereas the Russian Jews have the same range of interests as the rest of the Israeli Jews.

FW: Would you say that Russian Jews are a reflection of the whole of the Israeli political spectrum? The picture one has of the typical

---

[*] Ed. Nevertheless, Sharansky established a Russian immigrant party Israel Be'Aliya *in 1996 which gained seven Knesset seats. He subsequently left it and joined the Likud party.*

Russian immigrant is that he is well educated, not religious and very likely to vote Likud for the simple reason that he is opposed to anything to do with Socialism.

NS: You are right. Most Russians are unlikely to vote for Labour, which is deemed to be a Socialist party. On the other hand, they very quickly discover the inefficiency of the Likud in so far as absorption and employment are concerned. They see in the Likud a reflection of the Russian system, politicians in power, undue influence, jobs for the boys, and they do not like it. They do not like bureaucracy. Also, they distrust the Arabs because they feel their lives are endangered by them. Their tendency to hang on to the territories is not dictated by any biblical mandate but purely by security reasons. They would be attracted to a new party that is pledged to electoral reform, that would provide jobs, improve the economy, and if such a party would be willing to negotiate on the territories, they would go along with it, provided there would be proper peace and security. There is, therefore, a unique opportunity for a new generation of Likudniks or even Labour Party people to take advantage of this, to infuse a new spirit into politics and they could capture the Russian vote.

FW: I believe that some 90 per cent of the children of the Russian aliya go to secular schools. Do you think that in the long run this could have an effect on the composition of future governments, and lead to a diminution of the power of the religious parties?

NS: Unless you change the electoral system this will take a very long time. But I do want to say that when the Russian Jews come here they are not anti-religious, they are simply not observant. They often react sympathetically and very positively towards religion. There is a yearning for knowledge. For instance, my wife Avital gives lectures on the Jewish religion to Russian immigrants, and that kind of work is spreading. This in itself is remarkable. One of the reasons why the Russians will not send their children to religious schools is because they believe, rightly or wrongly, that not enough importance is attached to the sciences – mathematics, physics and chemistry, which in their opinion are an essential part of education. Furthermore, there is a growing antipathy to the ultra-religious parties.

FW: You may not wish to answer this, but may I ask you, will you send your children to a religious or a secular school?

NS: There is no question, my children will go to a religious school.

FW: Did you come to this conclusion yourself or is it because of Avital's influence?

NS: No, I would have taken precisely the same initiative on my own. To my mind the religious schools – the modern Zionist religious schools – produce a more rounded Israeli, somebody who has a much clearer all-round Jewish identity.

FW: You said Zionist, modern, Orthodox schools. Would you send your children to a school which produces boys who wear black *kipot*?

NS: I think they all have a part to play, but as far as I am concerned, my family and I identify with the knitted kipa, the *kipa seruga*, like the one I am taking out of my pocket right now.

Jerusalem

Interviews with Teddy Kollek

The following interviews with the iconic mayor of Jerusalem, Teddy Kollek, were conducted over the period November 1987 and January 1988.

FW: Teddy: 40 years of Israel, 20 years of Jerusalem; what are the achievements of these last 20 years?

TK: The greatest achievement is that with all the difficulties, with individual terrorist acts, the tension between the Jews, we have held the city together. People prophesied in 1967 that there would be daily clashes between Arabs and Jews. I know people who were planning to move away from Jerusalem because they were afraid of what would happen to their daughters. The city improved from an architectural point of view. It has become a green city. There were very few trees around. Now it is full of flowers and parks. We have a green belt around the Old City and a larger green belt around the entire city. We have restored many ancient monuments and sites for all religions. It is a pleasant city to live in.

FW: Would the Arabs agree with this?

TK: In 1948 East Jerusalem had 70,000 Arab inhabitants. After 19 years of Jordanian rule, East Jerusalem still had 70,000 Arabs. Since 1967 East Jerusalem's population has doubled. We now have more than 140,000 Arabs who have prospered.

FW: What are your disappointments?

TK: The municipality has no power. I would like to change the whole structure. We still live under the same colonial system which the British introduced in 1934. Everything we want to do has to go through at least two government departments. No other city in the world has that kind of problem. I cannot even put up a traffic sign without permission from the government. This is the reason why we are behind in our educational plans. We are short of school rooms, both for Jews and for Arabs, and in particular we ought to give a better infrastructure to the ultra-religious Talmud Torah schools. It is very difficult to run such a diverse city under such conditions.

FW: How diverse really is the city?

TK: We have 103 different kinds of Jews here with 103 different backgrounds. What does a Jew from England, like you, have in common with a Jew from Afghanistan or a Jew from Ethiopia? We have 40 different Christian denominations, all of which have venerable ancient rights and they are not always attuned to each other. 25 percent of our population are Moslem Arabs who regard themselves as the real owners of the city. They listen every day to anti-Israel propaganda on their radios and television beamed to them from several Arab countries.

FW: Did the December and January riots in East Jerusalem come as a shock to you?

TK: You cannot find peace in Jerusalem if you do not make progress on a national scale, but it took 11 days of rioting in Gaza before something happened here. What happened here was not nice but should not be exaggerated. Stones were thrown; some of our banks in East Jerusalem had their windows smashed and some furniture was burnt. Nobody was hurt; nobody was killed. All the city schools remained open and 90 percent of the Arab workers showed up. We meet with Arab colleagues on frequent occasions. One of these was the regular annual Christmas/Hanukah party at City Hall. The next day we were the guests of the 40 different Church denominations when many Arabs and Jews turned up. A number of Arabs came over and said: "We specially came in large numbers to make a statement through our presence." We had meetings with school teachers and heads of various villages within the Greater Jerusalem area. They were apologetic. "It is only the children. We could not hold them back."

FW: Have you been invited to any Arab-sponsored gatherings since?

TK: We built a health centre in Sheikh Jarrah five years ago. We did not know whether the Arabs would come there. Today it has 700 to 800 Arab patients a day and 22,000 members of the Kupat Holim health fund. At that same time we opened a new eye clinic there and the attendance was tremendous. We also held a party celebrating their five years of existence. It was a most joyful gathering. It all depends on what you expect. You could also draw the opposite conclusions. I am sure at the forthcoming municipality elections allegations will be made by whoever will stand, that Teddy's policy of co-existence has failed. If there is progressive legislation we shall learn to live together.

FW: Is Jerusalem becoming like New York with some no-go areas for Jews?

TK: Forty years ago people went to Harlem for supper and dancing. Today it is a purely black area into which whites do not venture in the evening. I know there is apprehension in Jerusalem. I walk through the Old City alone and I personally feel no difference.

FW: If your Jewish citizens prefer to go to the Hebrew University via Ramat Eshkol rather than through Sheikh Jarrah, how does this reflect on the political indivisibility of Jerusalem?

TK: Well, you know England best. Today, you have a heterogeneous citizenry, which you did not have 40 years ago. The people who come from the West Indies or Pakistan or Kenya are gradually becoming anglicized. The Sikhs preserve their distinctiveness but even their children will speak English and not the language of the Punjab. Here things are different. You have a population that wants to stay different out of principle. We have a mosaic. Moslem Arabs will continue to speak Arabic and go to Arab schools; Armenians will go to Armenian schools; the Christians to Christian schools and so on. As I said before, this is a difficult city which will only survive if tolerance continues to be shown with the same passion that nationalist fanatics or the ultra-Orthodox fight for their particular point of view. It is a city which is the heart of the Jewish people and it will remain so but this can only be achieved if we show the same consideration for others that we demand for ourselves. This is why we allowed the Mormons to build their university here. We don't want to be told by anyone in any part of the world that you cannot build a synagogue here because you do not allow us to build in Jerusalem. The treatment of our minorities is under a microscope.

FW: Is there a political solution along the lines of cantonisation, where Arabs have a modicum of self-government?

TK: We are on our way to that. We started three or four years ago to designate certain areas for some local self-government. We have ten such areas which cover 150,000 people – about one third of our population. They have between 10,000 and 25,000 people each with directly elected representatives on their councils, and so far the success is outstanding. Within an indivisible Jerusalem we shall pass on increased regional responsibility. Of the ten local councils, three are Arab. They have a feeling that they are represented and they can do things for themselves. This will have wider political repercussions one day. If you rush too much into this we shall be attacked that this is just a device to draw up new lines for Jerusalem, which is certainly not the intention.

FW: A few years ago there was talk about the danger of polarisation between the Ashkenazim and the Sephardim. Is this still the case?

TK: Not all Jews who come from Islamic countries are Sephardim. In Jerusalem 69 percent of all Jews came from Arab countries. In Tel Aviv they are 25 percent and in Haifa 16 percent. When they came they knew nothing about Israel. Israel was a strange name to them but they had all heard of Jerusalem and that's where they wanted to come to. That was the place their parents had prayed for. So we have a much greater problem with housing and with schools. They came here penniless and without skills. When I became mayor 20 years ago two percent of them went on to university. Now 20 percent go to university and they play a prominent part in the government, in the Knesset, in the army and in business. There is still some resentment which expresses itself from time to time, but this is a rapidly diminishing problem.

FW: How do you feel about Ariel Sharon moving into the Moslem Quarter?

TK: This is a considerable and very expensive irritant, a move strongly objected to by the Arabs who interpret it as a step to drive them out, and criticised by much of the Israeli press. In principle everybody should be able to live wherever he would like to. In practice it does not work out like that, particularly as far as the Old City is concerned. There is an Armenian Quarter, and no-one other than Armenians live there. In 1967 when we entered the Jewish Quarter we saw what the Jordanians had done to it over a period of 20 years when they occupied it. They eliminated all evidence that Jews had lived in it. All the synagogues were totally destroyed. Well, we transformed the Jewish Quarter into what you see today, but we also delineated it very clearly. There were several thousand Arab refugees from Hebron and other places who were settled in it by the Jordanians. We told them to leave. There was no question about this. It was the Jewish Quarter, and although in the past several Arab families had lived in it, we expropriated the whole of that area. On 12 June, 1967, Prime Minister Eshkol, together with Menachem Begin, called a conference of all the heads of the various religions. They jointly assured the Moslems and the Christians that whatever rights they had in the past they would continue to have in the future. We would not touch them. Today there are several yeshivot who feel that by their presence in the Moslem Quarter near the Western Wall they will speed up the coming of the Messiah. Nobody can judge whether the Messiah needs that sort of support but the Arabs are convinced that all this is part of a plot to drive them out.

FW: There was a letter in *The Jerusalem Post* written by one Rabbi Bar Chaim in which he states that it is not a problem of Ariel Sharon moving in, but of 140,000 Arabs living in Jerusalem where they should not be in the first place.

TK: I come back to my basic position. If we will not treat the Arabs as you would like Jewish minorities all over the world to be treated, there is no hope for our retention of an undivided capital. We will not be able to hold on to it. This is not a question of our willpower, but it is a question of what can be achieved in a modern society. There are people who say nothing can be achieved in co-operation with the Arabs. That is quite wrong. After months of quiet negotiations we renewed the mandate of the Jerusalem Electricity Corporation until the end of the century. They will continue to supply electricity to the Arab districts. This is one of several examples. Provocative acts at this stage are counter-productive.

FW: It is claimed that 18,000 yeshiva students of military age never serve in the army. Is it conceivable that if they have their way we could have an upside-down pyramid in Jerusalem where everybody studies Torah and nobody minds the shop?

TK: I am not so pessimistic. Of course it creates a great deal of ill-feeling that they sit and study whilst others defend the country. But put yourself in their shoes. The haredim sincerely believe that they and they alone have maintained the continuity of the Jewish people. They do not believe in the State of Israel. They do believe in an inward-looking ghetto. If we followed their line, the Jews will become a tiny, extreme sect and the Jewish people as we know it will disappear. We are now confronted with violence within the Jewish community introduced by the ultra-Orthodox. They wish to enlarge the status quo agreement. This is based on a letter which Ben Gurion wrote in 1947 giving certain assurances to the ultra-Orthodox. At that time, 400 young men claimed exemption from army service. Under the status quo agreement soccer games have always been played on Saturday afternoons but for the last 15 years the ultra-Orthodox have prevented us from building a soccer stadium which the city greatly needs and which is to replace the small one opposite the King David Hotel. There are two local teams in Jerusalem; one has its home ground in Tel Aviv. 15,000 of their fans travel to Tel Aviv every other Saturday and if this is not a desecration of the Sabbath I don't know what is! The prime minister, acting as temporary minister of the interior, under ultra-Orthodox pressure and against government regulations, refuses to sign the formal approval to build the stadium in an area which is nowhere near any Orthodox population.

FW: Would you consider Israel to be a secular state?

TK: It is becoming increasingly clear to most that what we need is co-existence, pluralism and tolerance, confirming each community's right to live according to its customs. Jewish fundamentalism and Islamic fundamentalism disturb peaceful co-existence. Religion should be entirely detached from politics. Alas, this is not likely so long as our government under the present electoral system needs the religious vote.

FW: Are you optimistic in the long run?

TK: I am convinced, as I have said before, that we shall all learn to live together. The century started with many great concepts, few of which survived. Socialism, Communism, wars to end all wars, Esperanto to end nationalism, the welfare state, the United Nations – it is a long list of failures. I am firmly convinced that history will look upon the creation of the Jewish state as the great success story of the 20th century. So what if it takes us 100 years to settle down? It took Germany and Italy even longer.

Rabbis of Rejection

In the wake of Teddy Kollek's defeat in 1993, as mayor of Jerusalem, in an article in The Jewish Chronicle, *London, Fred Worms considers the worrying implications of the Secular/Orthodox divide.*

Jerusalem and Teddy Kollek have been synonymous for 28 years. And Teddy's defeat in this week's mayoral election raises new problems at an inopportune time.

[The new mayor] Ehud Olmert owes his victory to the strictly Orthodox. The extent of the debt remains to be seen but the conquest of the city by the haredim, who are extending into different neighbourhoods, will be accelerated. Teddy's modus vivendi vis-à-vis the 160,000 Arabs living in East Jerusalem, his manifest sense of fairness, will be a hard act to follow, particularly with the peace process in a delicate state of health.

In the country as a whole, there is no real euphoria, and no illusions, but there is an indefinable change of atmosphere. Peace – that ephemeral, messianic concept – seems no longer an impossibility. Jerusalem, the settlements and the refugees are but three time-bombs which must be defused. "Better the Golan without peace than peace without the Golan," remains a popular slogan. And there is hatred that divides families, kibbutzim, neighbours and friends.

Amid all this, the strictly Orthodox, whom the majority of Israelis have tolerated over the years, are giving religion a bad name. Too many rabbis have come out categorically against the peace agreement. No ifs and buts, just total condemnation. Former Chief Rabbi Shlomo Goren said: "The signing ceremony in Washington is a day of mourning for the Jewish people and one must tear one's clothes for the destruction of Eretz Israel." Lubavitch, always short of funds, has found a reported $1 million to mount a campaign which proclaims that the peace agreement is against *halakha*.

In the meantime, some wise men are looking beyond tomorrow. "Suppose" they say, "that Shimon Peres' dream of open borders, a Middle Eastern Common Market, a prosperous Gaza and West Bank, is realised, that genuine peace will prevail, what will this do to the ethos of the State of Israel?"

From the Babylonian exile onwards, two-and-a-half millennia of Jewish history have demonstrated that we have survived because of outside pressures. There appears to have been an immutable law that assimilation proceeds in direct ratio with pressure reduction. Give the Jews total freedom from persecution and discrimination, and they will self-destruct, as demonstrated by the 65 per cent intermarriage rate in North America.

The argument that the Diaspora is phasing itself out and that continuity of the Jewish people rests entirely with Israel, suddenly takes on a whole new dimension. A peaceful Israel, prosperous but overwhelmingly secular could, within a couple of generations, lose its Jewish character. Holidays in neighbouring countries, joint ventures, business and high society intermingling, could undermine and destroy the Jewish qualities of the Jewish state more drastically than any external enemy could have done.

During the Rosh Hashanah/Succot period, more than 200,000 young Israelis flocked to the Michael Jackson and Madonna concerts, a display of Western moral decline, unthinkable before the Six-Day War. Does the future, therefore, lie with the haredim whose withdrawal from the realities of modern life make them dependent on *Shabbes goyim*? Is that part of the *yishuv*, whose sons do not serve in the army, going to be the saviour, though congenitally unable to function on its own?

A strictly Orthodox or a strictly secular state – is this to be the stark choice facing Israel as it battles for peace? All of a sudden Israel faces a challenge that hitherto was uniquely a Diaspora problem. Secular Judaism is a contradiction in terms. It will lead inevitably to our disappearance. On the other hand, governments which include religious partners whose main objective is to put money into yeshivot, are morally tainted.

Never has there been a greater need for a tolerant modern Orthodoxy of the kind taught, for example, at Bar-Ilan University. Unless the educational system in Israel can put the Torah back into the secular system, the Jewish character of the state will be endangered.

What an irony of fate if, after 2,000 years of waiting and praying, we will have proved that a Jewish state with a truly Jewish ethos can be realised only after the Messiah has come.

The Jewish Chronicle, 5 November, 1993

The Teddy Kollek Award

The Teddy Kollek awards given for significant contributions to the City of Jerusalem have been given each year since 1999, by the Jerusalem Foundation, to persons who have strengthened Jerusalem's status as the capital of Israel and who have excelled in their support of an open, tolerant and modern city which embraces people of all religious, national and ethnic backgrounds. Fred Worms was given the award in 2011 in the Knesset. The award citation reads as follows:

"Fred Worms, born in Frankfurt, Germany, moved to Great Britain as a young refugee. While he pursued a successful career in business, he devoted much of his life to the Jewish community.

In Britain, he chaired the B'nai B'rith Hillel Foundation, which created a network of Hillel Houses that strengthened Jewish life on university campuses and he chaired the European Jewish Publication Society, an organization that treasures Jewish history and culture. He co-founded Immanuel College, a Jewish secondary school in London, and assumed a key leadership role in the Jewish Educational Development Trust.

In recognition of his services to the elderly in Britain, Mr. Worms was awarded the Order of the British Empire by Queen Elizabeth II.

He is an active member of the Hebrew University Board of Governors and received an honorary Doctorate of Philosophy from the University. He is a Trustee of the Rothberg International School and the guiding spirit behind the Scopus Student Village on Mount Scopus, where a seven building hi-rise accommodates 1,800 students.

Mr. Worms is a supporter of culture in Jerusalem and is an Honorary Fellow of the Israel Museum, where he was responsible for bringing the Cochin Synagogue from India to Israel. He is also a former President of the Maccabi World Union and a co-founder and Honorary Life President of Kfar Hamaccabiah.

In the field of education, he has made an indelible imprint on the Pelech Experimental Girls High School, the Efrata Elementary School, and the Hartman Institute.

Nearly every part of modern day Jerusalem has been touched by Mr. Worms: the Gilo Community Centre, the Beit Yisrael synagogue, Beyachad, the Cinemathèque, the Counselling Centre for Women, the Botanical Gardens, the Jerusalem Symphony Orchestra, the Jerusalem College of Technology, the Konrad Adenauer Conference Centre at Mishkenot Sha'ananim, Meitarim, Melitz, Nitzanim School for Special Education, Reut School, Pardes Institute for Jewish Studies, Sha'are Zedek Medical Centre, Yad Sarah, The Tali School in Bayit Vegan, Yemin Moshe, and more.

Mr. Worms and his wife Della, who has been actively involved in all of his activities, live in Jerusalem. They have three children and 11 grandchildren."

The Mount Scopus Campus

The location is awesome. The magnificent amphitheatre carved out of Jerusalem stone faces east. The setting sun in the west shines upon the distant Dead Sea, now a dark streak, underlining the blue horizon. No one can compare with the Almighty in dramatic landscape painting. A gentle breeze has followed a scorching hot day. We have assembled for the annual conferment of Degrees of Honorary Doctorates and the award of two special prizes.

Some 73 years earlier, almost a quarter of a century before the establishment of the Jewish state, there was another convocation. On 1 April, 1925 on this very site, the Hebrew University was founded in the presence of Lord Balfour, Lord Allenby, Chief Rabbi Abraham Isaac HaCohen Kook, Sir Herbert Samuel, Prof. Chaim Weizmann, Chief Rabbi Dr. Joseph Hertz, Haim Nachman Bialik and Ahad Ha'am.

Today those to be honoured include some of the world's leading academics and a 1997 Nobel Prize Winner. Israel's Chief Justice

Aharon Barak speaks on behalf of the honourees. I say a quiet prayer to myself, the *Shecheyanu*, to have been privileged to be included in such august company.

At the same time one is deeply troubled by the unusual number of security men with their earphones and sunglasses standing around conspicuously. Why? There is no apparent threat from the Arabs. Evidently they are there to protect Jew from Jew, or more specifically, to safeguard the life of the Chief Justice who, in common with other Justices of the Supreme Court, has received a number of death threats from haredi quarters.

The tragic history of the last few years, culminating in the Rabin assassination, forces the authorities to treat these threats seriously. Chief Justice Barak speaks of his understanding of the definition of democracy. Just as the late Sir Isaiah Berlin concluded, "there is no such thing as absolute freedom (one man's freedom may encroach upon another man's privacy)" so democracy has its limitations. A majority rule which is not benign, but suppresses minorities, is not acceptable in a civilised state. An independent judiciary is the ultimate safeguard to protect the rights of all citizens.

One would have thought that this was a sine qua non but the shrill demands of the ultra-Orthodox to have their nominees appointed to the Supreme Court, to apply the law in accordance with their interpretation of *halakha*, would sound the death knell to democracy.

A few days earlier the deputy minister of religious affairs, Yigal Bibi, stated in the Knesset that, "if Chief Justice Barak does not stop being overly interventionalist in the decisions of the religious courts, there will be no choice but to change the way the judges are chosen." This statement was immediately condemned by President Ezer Weizman, and – wonder of wonders – by a joint statement of the government and the opposition.

It is unusual for the attorney general to respond in public to the remarks of a cabinet minister, but on that occasion Elyakim Rubinstein warned on Israel Radio "that these [haredi] threats are undermining the very fabric of democracy. I do not think there is another country in the world where such unrestrained attacks are made on the judicial system."

I mention this incident, not because it was an extraordinary occurrence but because, in the verbal warfare between the ultra-right and the rest of the country, it is no longer extraordinary. Under the law of physics every pressure produces counter-pressure. It is not easy to prevail upon the extremists of the religious right and the secular left to moderate their language. Irresponsible words, as we have seen, lead to tragic consequences. A minority which tries to enforce its way of life on an unwilling majority achieves the opposite. It creates fear, contempt and hatred.

The Independence Day festivities, on the other hand, demonstrated how far the secular majority has been brainwashed into accepting the unacceptable. In the official celebrations of the 50th anniversary of the foundation of the State, the only religious message was given by the American vice-president, Al Gore, who pronounced the *Shecheyanu* blessing in flawless Hebrew.

One of the highlights of the evening was to be a ballet performance by the Batsheva Dance Company. The pièce de résistance was to be a dance to the accompanying words of a choir singing the text of *echad miyodaya*. "One – who knows?" from the Passover Haggada. With each question a garment was to be removed by the performers until finally they were to dance in their underwear. One would have thought that such a display would be generally considered unsuitable for the half century celebration of a nation that has survived in spite of overwhelming odds, overcoming untold tragedies. Considering that this ceremony was viewed by millions all around the world, the very idea of including a semi-striptease should have been dismissed with contempt.

The cacophony from the secular left when the performance was cancelled was overwhelming. How the mighty have fallen! We need a long quiet period of contemplation and more respect for our fellow men. We need a long quiet period of less religiosity and more courtesy. When the quiet central majority of non-extremists will assert itself, Israel will become the *Goldene Medineh* – a "Golden State" indeed.

Sunday, 7 June, 1997

The Hebrew University Dormitory Village

The Hebrew University has some 23,000 students of which only 6,000 are residents of Jerusalem; the other 17,000 need to sleep somewhere. Many make their own private arrangements, while a very large number look to the university for accommodation. What has been available hitherto is pitifully inadequate both in terms of numbers and quality.

In the 1980s it was pointed out at the annual Board of Governors' meetings that the tens of millions of dollars required for even a partial solution was simply not available and the crisis has been a continuing one ever since. The financial situation was not helped by the astonishing omission of the creation of a pension fund for retired academics and other tenure holders. In the early years, the 1930s and 1940s, this was not a serious problem, since there were relatively few retirees, but the situation deteriorated dramatically during the last 20 years, when pensions had to be paid out of annual revenue.

This was a problem which was bound to grow year by year and threatened the very future of the faculty's research programmes and the employment of young professors. No wonder, therefore, that dormitories were not among the first priorities.

Over ten years ago, I suggested at a Board of Governors' meeting that there was a relatively simple solution to the perennial dormitory headache. One should follow the example of some English universities, which had entered into a quasi-sale and leaseback arrangement with leading property developers who would build and provide finance, often in conjunction with a bank. The university pays an annual rental which shows a reasonable return for the entrepreneur and includes a modicum of capital repayment. After 25 years the freehold reverts to the university.

My proposal was considered to be unrealistic and based on wishful thinking, and some of the leading American governors and principal fundraisers told me that it was positively harmful since it would interfere with the billion dollar campaign in which the university was presently engaged. Unrepentant, I explained that the rental from the students plus holiday lettings would enable the university to service the annual payments to the developer and allow for maintenance; that the leisure and commercial centres which would be included could ultimately become a source of revenue and that the new "village" could become a most interesting part of the fund- raising campaign by having various buildings endowed by individual donors.

Thus I repeated my mantra year after year, making myself unpopular with a number of my fellow governors. "Here he goes again, flogging a dead horse. Why does he not shut up?"

When Menachem Magidor became president of the university some five years ago, he took me on one side. "Fred, I am going to solve two problems during my term of office – pensions and dormitories." With the enthusiastic cooperation of the energetic director-general of the university, Moshe Vigdor, both targets were achieved.

The plans prepared by the university's architects in 1999 provided for 1,800 single rooms in 380 apartments, housed in 11 tower blocks of eight or nine floors each, plus ancillary facilities, at an estimated cost of $45 million. Invitations to tender were sent out. 14 developers applied including two from Britain. By the time the three centimetre-thick bill of quantities had been analysed, five interested parties remained.

Bureaucracy is rampant all over the world but nowhere more so than in Israel. A public body requires government permission to borrow money on real estate involving a number of overlapping ministries. This was no easy task but not as complicated as getting planning permission for developing the 80 dunams (20 acres) of land situated between the Scopus campus and Hadassah Hospital. The Israel Land Authority is responsible to the nation via the Knesset to ensure the most beneficial use of this scarce resource. They do not release land easily.

Ultimately, after years of patient negotiations, agreement in principle was reached with the Africa-Israel Company and the Minrab Company as the chosen developers. One's patience was sorely tested. Every time signatures were to be appended to the contact, another negotiation ploy reared its head.

On Friday, 27 December, 2002, President Magidor telephoned. "Fred, *Mazal Tov*, we have just signed and we are drinking *lechaim*." I replied quoting from the Hallel prayer, *ze hayom asa adonai; nagila venismecha bo*. ("This is the day the Lord has made. We will be happy and rejoice.") Instantly Magidor completed the text: *even ma'asu habonim hayta lerosh pina.* ("The stone which the builders rejected has become the cornerstone of the building.") to which I added jokingly, "Yes, but rather in Jerusalem than in Rosh Pina."

Moshe Vigdor emailed me, "Thank you for your continuous support. You have always been *halapid shelifnei hamahaneh* ("the torch leading the camp"). Now we have to build it together."

The truth is that in these troubled, uncertain times, when the intifada is going on, when a war may be fought in a few weeks time, when the economy is at a low ebb, this is an enormous act of courage proclaiming faith in the future of Israel and especially Jerusalem. The people of Israel owe a great debt of gratitude to the energetic and farseeing current management of the Hebrew University.

June, 1997

"*Yerushalayim shel Zahav*"

I hope and pray that, by the time this is published, peace will have returned to our Land of Israel. All is not golden, in the words of Naomi Shemer's *Yerushalayim shel Zahav* in Jerusalem, the city which I love and where we spend many months every year. It is only mentioned once in the Torah, rather indirectly as "Salem" *(Genesis 14:18)*. The Aggada, in which it is referred to more than 1,500 times, states that: "of the ten measures of beauty in the world, Jerusalem took nine." It has an indefinable magic which some call the *shechina* ("Divine Presence").

What is often forgotten is the city's phenomenal growth in 150 years. In 1865 its population was 18,000 of whom 9,000 were Jews. In June 1948 on the eve of the War of Independence, there were 264,000: 199,000 Jews, 54,000 Muslims and 11,000 Christians. Today, the total population has increased to 710,000, of whom 466,000 are Jews, while under the wicked Zionists, the Arab population increased to 232,000 Muslims and 12,000 Christians (figures supplied by the Jerusalem Municipality). In other words, its population has more than doubled in the last 40 years. From the demographic point of view these figures are only partially encouraging. The Arab birth rate is more than twice that of the Jews except for the ultra-Orthodox haredim, but their number is too small to make a vital difference.

There is a modicum of antagonism between the ultra-Orthodox and the rest. The ever-smiling and optimistic haredi mayor, Uri Lupoliansky, is genuinely doing his utmost to bridge the gap as far as his rabbis allow him to. The leader of the opposition, a secular young multi-millionaire, Nir Barkat[*] has ambitious plans to deal with Jerusalem's shortcomings. It is, per capita, the poorest city in Israel (one-third of all households including the Arabs live below the poverty line). Its property tax (*arnona*) is a fraction of what it ought to be. This is due to the many educational establishments – but particularly a proliferation of yeshivot. Barkat is full of ideas to make the town prosperous but alas, he and the current mayor, Lupoliansky, are not talking. I am on first name terms with both and have tried to bring *shalom bayit* (domestic harmony) to the municipality but have not succeeded.

What Jerusalem needs is an industrial infrastructure to provide employment, which in turn would generate a positive cash flow. The Hebrew University has created an industrial park whose small units develop inventions of a scientific and medical nature that are developed by the University's science departments on the Givat Ram campus and the agricultural departments in Rehovot. From these small acorns already some healthy trees have grown with the aid of venture capitalists.

Why is there an exodus of young people from Jerusalem? This is mostly due to lack of employment opportunities, but that is not the only reason. Secular youngsters find the town too religious and they prefer the night life, the restaurants, bars and clubs and the job opportunities in Tel Aviv. There is, incidentally, a rather tenuous relationship between

---

[*] Ed. Since the elections of 2008, the mayor of Jerusalem.

Tel Aviv and Jerusalem. During the last Intifada, people from the north looked on Jerusalem as being too dangerous. Jerusalemites looked down upon Tel Aviv as a sinful city, far removed from religious tradition. However, when Saddam Hussein sent missiles during the 1991 Gulf War, none was aimed at Jerusalem with its mosques and large Arab population. That was when the Tel Avivians remembered their families in Jerusalem, whom they had rarely visited before!

Why do young haredim also leave the city? Property prices in Jerusalem have risen enormously. Young people have no chance of getting on the property ladder without family support, hence the exodus to satellite towns such as Beit Shemesh, Beitar and Modi'in Ilit – the last two, beyond the Green Line. Those who are prepared to live beyond the Green Line can get a four-bedroom house with garden for under $200,000, which in Jerusalem would barely buy a two-bedroom apartment.

Now let us look at the positive aspects. Jerusalem is a beautiful city. Virtually all buildings are of Jerusalem stone – some polished, others rough-hewn – under an edict from a Governor of Jerusalem during the British Mandate, Sir Ronald Storrs. There is a building boom, partly caused by French Jews whose sense of insecurity is leading them to purchase a second home in Jerusalem for immediate or eventual aliya. High-class, expensive apartments are going up in Mamilla; there are major developments in King David Street, in Baka'a, by the Binyanei Ha'ooma Convention Centre and near the Haas Promenade in Talpiot. We have seen houses built by American millionaires with ten rooms, gym and swimming pool, which are only occupied for a month or two each year.

Ben Yehuda Street and Zion Square used to be the most popular shopping and entertainment areas. Perhaps due to the Intifada, the town centre has lost some of its appeal. Emek Refa'im, the main street of the German Colony starting at the Liberty Bell Gardens, has become the preferred upmarket street in the capital. There are no less than 25 cafés and restaurants, supermarkets and speciality shops within half a mile, adjacent to the elegant old Templar houses. Emunah had a kindergarten next to the Liberty Bell Gardens. This was sold and in its place there are plans for a ten-storey hotel and even higher apartment blocks. The neighbourhood is furious and is trying to have the planning permission reversed – a sure sign of civic pride.*

The Jerusalem Foundation, started by Mayor Teddy Kollek in 1966, has raised over one billion dollars for cultural and physical amenities in the city. Enormous efforts are being made to promote co-existence. Very recently, the Rayne Foundation of London has given two million pounds for a modern school for Jewish and Arab children. It is hoped that with examples like this – and there are many others – the hatred of the unknown will give way to trust among school friends.

It is not often appreciated in the Diaspora how many cultural facilities there are in Jerusalem. There are no less than 12 museums, three theatres, a cinematheque, five music centres and an ever-growing number of children's playgrounds. The Israel Museum alone is a world-class attraction with its youth wing, archaeology department, and its tremendous collection of paintings and sculptures ranging from the earliest Greek period to contemporary artists. One has a choice of going to half a dozen talks and more formal lectures every day or evening often sponsored by synagogues, many of which also serve as cultural centres.

There are many outdoor attractions, such as the University's Botanical Gardens, the Tisch Family Biblical Zoo, the Jerusalem Forest and the Wohl Rose Garden. Flowers bloom everywhere, including along the central dividers of the main roads.

Della and I are closely involved with The Hebrew University and its 1,800-bed new Student Dormitory Village, probably one of the finest in the world, (see page 111), Hillel, Emunah, the Jerusalem Foundation, The Israel Museum, the Botanical Gardens and the establishments of Rabbis Steinsaltz and Hartman (see page 40).

There is a very strong English-speaking community (known in Israel anachronistically as "Anglo-Saxons") with many university professors, bankers, entrepreneurs, and senior civil servants. I know some elderly people who in 40 years have never learned Hebrew and who still manage in English.

---

* Ed. Since then, the plans have been heavily modified.

To be a conscientious Jew in Jerusalem is easy. One feels at home and has the choice of the many attractions, only some of which I have outlined above, to provide intellectual stimulus and physical wellbeing within a social circle of your choice.

August, 2006

Since this article was written, the new mayor, Nir Barkat has also begun to contribute in a very significant way to the general life and appearance of the capital, especially in the field of culture. Among events inaugurated on his watch, is the Jerusalem Marathon, in which over 15,000 runners participated this year, 1,500 of them from abroad, as well as 4,000 soldiers.

Isaiah Berlin

Zionism and Sir Isaiah Berlin

Hundreds of obituaries were published all over the world after the death of Sir Isaiah Berlin in November, 1997. Other biographies may be written but none are likely to equal in authority and perceptiveness, Michael Ignatieff's magnum opus.[*] He is the only one who was nominated by Sir Isaiah Berlin himself to become his official Boswell and he spent ten intensive years on the preparation of this book which had only one qualification placed upon it by Berlin, namely that it should be published posthumously.

No one will be able to write in future with any authority on any subject impinging on the life of Sir Isaiah Berlin without reference to Ignatieff's biography, and I too am indebted to him. Professor Henry Hardy of Wolfson College is the literary trustee of the Berlin Estate, and has acted in that capacity for some 23 years. Had it not been for his single-minded devotion, the majority of Berlin's writings would not have been published. Hardy unearthed drafts of lectures, faded copies of articles, *festschriften*, and so on, which were carelessly dumped by Berlin into suitcases. In some instances, scientific methods had to be employed to reconstitute missing papers, just as some Geniza manuscripts have been deciphered with the magnifying capabilities of the computer. Professor Hardy used, inter alia, the latest laboratory techniques so as to reconstruct old dictabelts which provided missing pages of important manuscripts.

---

[*] "A Life – Isaiah Berlin" by Michael Ignatieff. Chatto and Windus, London, 1998.

In this essay, I propose to deal with the not uncomplicated issue of Sir Isaiah Berlin's Zionism, which was predicated on his own particular brand of Judaism. I was privileged to enjoy his friendship. We had been exchanging letters for many years (see pages 136-173). Let us repeat a conversation which I had with Berlin in July 1991 at the Athenaeum Club in London, which, in addition to the lobby of the King David Hotel in Jerusalem, was his preferred meeting place, and where he entertained his London friends.

IB: You mentioned anti-Semitism. There are two types. The acceptable and the non-acceptable. Very few people are free from it. It becomes unacceptable when it becomes threatening. We owe anti-Semitism quite a lot. Without it, it is doubtful whether we [Ed. the Jewish people] would have survived. Complete freedom accelerated assimilation. Persecution makes people draw together and this maintains identity.

FSW: Are you religious?

IB: I do not believe in God. I don't know what God means. Is he a man with a beard, an anthropomorphic figure? If God is a force for good, for morality, then this is simply man's invention of a concept.

FSW: Are you an agnostic?

IB: No, I am religiously tone-deaf. What I mean to say is that a deaf person cannot appreciate music. That is my position vis-à-vis God. I go to synagogue from time to time because I wish to identify myself with the traditions of my ancestors which I would like to see continued.

Isaiah Berlin claimed a blood relationship to the Lubavitch Rebbe who predeceased him and who he disliked intensely. However, as we will see, there is no basis for this claim. The original Isaiah (Shaye) Berlin was an immensely wealthy member of a Hassidic sect. He married Chayette Schneerson, the daughter of a prominent rabbi, who was the third Lubavitch Rebbe. Isaiah and Chayette were childless. He took a certain Mendel Zuckerman, son of Dov Behr Zuckerman and his great nephew, into his business at the turn of the century and sent him to a German high school where the young man excelled, opening doors with German businessmen that had so far been closed to Shaye. It was then that this Isaiah Berlin decided formally to adopt Dov Behr as his son and Mendel as his grandson, when they changed the family name to Berlin. Mendel was Sir Isaiah's father who named his son after his adoptive grandfather.

This name change has an ironic twist. The name Zuckerman was to haunt Berlin at the apex of his career when Sir Solly Zuckerman, the Labour government's chief scientific advisor, and a trustee of the Wolfson Foundation, fought tooth and nail against the establishment of Wolfson College in Oxford, a fight which Berlin won only by asking Harold Wilson, the prime minister at the time, to intervene. The argument was that too much money was being spent on elitist universities and not enough on the red brick universities which were (and are) the majority.

Sir Isaiah Berlin's Judaism was in fact far more deeply rooted than he cared to admit. Lord (Noel) Annan, in his address at the memorial service for Berlin at the Hampstead Synagogue in January 1998, said:

> But there was one public issue on which he left no one in doubt. Above all, Isaiah was a Jew, and never forgave those who forgot to conceal their anti-Semitism, the nastier ways of snubs, pinpricks, acts of exclusion which we Gentiles inflict upon Jews, and in so doing defile ourselves. He was a Zionist precisely because he felt that however well Jews were treated and accepted by the country they lived in, they felt uneasy and insecure. That was why they needed a country of their own where Jews could live like other nations.

As Berlin lay dying, he declared that partition of the Holy Land was the only solution to give Palestinians rights to their land and Israel Jerusalem as its capital city with the Moslem holy places under a Moslem authority, and an Arab quarter under United Nations protection. He never felt the smallest difficulty in being loyal to Judah and loyal to Britain. When he worked during the war at the British Embassy in Washington, he told American Zionists that he was the servant of the British government – but its servant, not its conscript. At any time he could resign if he decided British policy was unforgivable. He was proud to belong to Britain, to the country which Chaim Weizmann had praised for "its moderation, dislike of extremes, a human democracy."

Berlin's mother kept a kosher household. Their family Seder on the eve of the Passover festival was famous throughout London and later at Oxford. He fasted on the Day of Atonement and was an irregular visitor to Hampstead Synagogue. He detested dogma and abhorred agnosticism.

In one of his letters to me he wrote (see page 150), "Stone-dry atheists don't understand what men live by." Berlin's modesty, like that of Moses, was famous: "I have been over-estimated all my life… still, it is extremely nice to get more than one's due." Yet, when his personal integrity or that of his Judaism was challenged, he would retaliate furiously. He was my predecessor at St. Paul's, a leading London school, but was 11 years older. In response to some laudatory remarks in an issue of the Old Pauline Magazine that I sent him, he replied: "As for myself, I was not in the least 'confounding and dazzling' – I was never top in any form at St. Paul's and had very moderate success academically and never did better until my last year at Oxford; so I think this is purely imaginary. Did I ever tell you the row about St. Paul's and Jews which I had? – it became an Affaire do ask me about it next time we meet."

What was this affair? Evidently it referred to when St. Paul's introduced a quota for Jewish boys. Following this, Berlin cut all connections with the school.

Another classic example of Berlin's militancy when Jews were attacked was his controversy with the poet T. S. Eliot. Eliot had said in a lecture at the University of Virginia in 1934, that "one ought to place the Jews beyond the borders of the city because their critical and discontented spirit jeopardised the uniting of European Christian civilisation." Although in a letter to Berlin, in November 1951, Eliot apologised, Berlin was not prepared to accept his apology. Eliot wrote again: "From the Christian point of view, the Jewish faith is finished because it finds its continuity in the Catholic faith. Theoretically the only proper consummation is that all Jews should become Catholic Christians. Berlin was furious. He did not reply. Their friendship was permanently fractured. This controversy strengthened Berlin's conviction that a Jew could only be truly free if he lived securely within a Jewish culture and this was, therefore, a crucial theme in his attitude to Zionism. This was a recurrent theme in his long life.

When he sat in mourning for his father in 1953, he cherished the age-old custom of the Jewish religion which kept him and his mother occupied for the seven-day *shiva* ritual mourning period. This was another indication of the basis of his Zionism. He wrote "for a community to be rooted in its own territory is as vital as food or shelter."

In this he reminds me of the Shunamite woman who replied to the prophet Elisha, *(2 Kings 4:13)* who wanted to reciprocate her hospitality: *Betoh ami anohi yoshevet* – "I dwell among my own people." The implication is clear. If you have a secure family background and that family is anchored within a certain culture, only then do you become a complete human being. The rootless cosmopolitanism of a George Steiner was anathema to Isaiah Berlin.

He would have no truck with the Reform Movement in contemporary Judaism. In his mind, observance had to be traditional and authentic. In a letter to Lord Jakobovits, (the Emeritus Chief Rabbi of Great Britain) he expressed his reservation on the concept of life after death:

> For myself, I should be very happy if I thought that there was the Other World, *haolam habah*. In spite of fears for my own fate in it, I should like to believe that there is this world after death. I even want to hope that it exists. But I cannot persuade myself that it does. I realize the teaching of our sages demands some kind of leap of faith – not rational argument; and if I suddenly found that I had made this leap and began to believe that there is a life after death, I should be happy to be in that state – but at present I am not.

Berlin was perfectly clear in his own mind that for the total believer, religion transcends morality. This is not the place to deal with his philosophy but this article would be incomplete without referring to some of his thoughts on liberty. In his essay, "The Proper State of Mankind," he referred to imprisonment by conformism and that there was no absolute liberty. Liberty for the wolves is death for the lambs, with the clear implication that unchecked capitalism is not acceptable.

For him the notion of the perfect whole was unattainable. "Liberty, equality and fraternity – beautiful but incompatible," he said in a lecture given in the United States in 1949.

Sir Isaiah Berlin received honorary doctorates from Oxford, Cambridge, the Hebrew University of Jerusalem, Harvard, Yale, Athens, Toronto and several other universities, but nothing pleased him more than the award of the Jerusalem Prize for the Freedom of the Individual in Society, in 1983.

He had first visited Palestine in 1934. During that visit, he played his usual roll of detached observer. He found the noise, the excitement, the irritability and the frenetic pace of the pre-state community to be wholly disagreeable. The country seemed to him to be an "exotic oriental bazaar." He was amused by the German Jews, who had recently arrived in considerable numbers, who were rushing around "with little portfolios under their arms complaining that the bus was late." Mornings were spent sight-seeing with the high commissioner and his staff; the governing establishment. Afternoons were dedicated to family – his mother's two sisters, Ida Samunov and Eugenia Landber.

He had a love/distaste relationship with the burgeoning Jewish community. After all, was he not, at the age of 23, the first Jewish Fellow of Balliol, the most exclusive college of Oxford, the breeding place of the English power elite?

Berlin's father had always been ambivalent to the concept of a Jewish state, whereas his mother, Marie, was a Zionist from her youth. One has doubts whether Isaiah Berlin would have carved out for himself an equally successful career had he immigrated to Eretz Israel. He was not a Gershom Scholem, nor a Martin Buber. As a perennial outsider, his delicate roots were nurtured through his quintessential English university life. It was not too difficult for him therefore, to resist the blandishments of Chaim Weizmann, Moshe Sharett, David Ben Gurion, Abba Eban and Teddy Kollek. He was simply not prepared to exchange the Olympian calm of Oxford academe with the noisy birth-pangs of a state to which Jews had immigrated from 120 different nations. He later stated that to choose Oxford may have seemed unpardonable egoism, but that was the milieu that he needed for his work.

While Zionism as a concept was a sine qua non for him, he was not prepared to make the ultimate decision to live in Israel. As a trustee of the Rothschild Foundation, he was deeply involved in Israel's academic and cultural affairs, although he had considerable distaste for the policies of the Likud-led governments.

Berlin was much concerned with the question of whether the Allies could have done more in the Second World War to save the Jews. In particular, was the leadership of American Jewry guilty by default? This subject was dealt with in a long exchange of letters between us in 1995 (see pages 136-173).

Berlin reserved an ice-cold contempt for some of his famous Jewish acquaintances who were embarrassed by their faith. He called them Otags – "Order of the Trembling Amateur Gentiles" – and he awarded honorary membership to the banker Edward Warburg, to Arthur Hays Sulzberger of the *New York Times* and to Walter Lippmann, the influential journalist. At a lecture at the Anglo-Israel Association in 1953 he said, "Israel allowed Jews to escape their history of martyrdom. They had a right to normality."

He did not suffer from *weltschmerz*. "I am happy because I am superficial," he said to Michael Ignatieff, belittling himself, as was his constant practice. He was also constantly surprised by the mere fact that he should have lived so peacefully and so happily through so many horrors.

Apart from his last wish that Israel should find a way to live in peace with its neighbours, he made one further request as he lay dying. He wanted the *tahara*, the Jewish ritual cleansing of the body after death. He died on a Thursday night and special arrangements had to be made to receive the body in time for the funeral which took place on Friday morning, 7 November, 1997, in Oxford.

Sir Isaiah Berlin was the embodiment of the Hebrew phrase *sameah behelko* ("contented with his lot"). He did, indeed, live a life of contentment. He found the ideal companion in Aline, a remarkable lady whose grandfather, Baron Horace de Gunzburg, was the founder of the Jewish technical education network, ORT, in St. Petersburg in 1880. She provided him with serene surroundings in considerable luxury. At their mansion – Headington House in Oxford, and at the Albany Club in London – Isaiah Berlin was cosseted by a loyal staff. He followed the recommendation of Ecclesiastes: "Go thy way, eat thy bread with joy and drink thy wine with a merry heart, for God had already accepted they work ... Enjoy life with the wife whom thou lovest ...for that is thy portion in life."

This article was originally published in 2000 in Ariel: the Israel Review of Arts and Letters, *and is reproduced here by permission.*

Isaiah Berlin: Personal Impressions
Hogarth Press, London, 2001

A review by Fred Worms

This is a splendid book. It is a modern "Hallel," a song cycle consisting of 12 hymns of praise of men whom Isaiah Berlin admired. His approach is the very antithesis of that of C.P. Snow. There are no jaundiced, back-biting university dons soured by frustrated ambition. Here we have paeans of praise composed by a man of a most generous character, who would rather follow the school of Hillel than of Shammai.

Isaiah Berlin is a polymath. His interests include philosophy, history, languages, politics, music and literature of an immense range in five languages. He is secure in the niche he has carved himself in Academe and lives happily with a variety of loyalties which include his Russian-Jewish ancestry, his admiration for the United Kingdom and his qualified devotion to the State of Israel.

Lord (Noel) Annan wrote the introduction. This is not a hastily-dictated perfunctory going-through-the-motions effort, but a sympathetic and astute tour de force. To read it, is to begin to understand what makes Sir Isaiah tick. The last chapter, "Meeting with Russian Writers," deals largely with encounters with the writer Boris Pasternak and the poet Anna Akhmatova. The author conjures up the claustrophobic mood of Russia in the immediate post-war years, in the grip of a megalomaniac who stultified artistic creation. Artists like Pasternak fought a continuous battle for survival. Many of their colleagues were executed or imprisoned. Yet Pasternak remained a Russian patriot who deplored his Jewish origins. He wished the Jews to assimilate, to disappear as a people. When Isaiah Berlin mentioned Palestine to him, it caused him visible distress. Against this background of unrelieved gloom there is one surrealist scene; the awe-struck young Isaiah succeeded, after much effort, to gain access to the revered Anna Akhmatova who had never met a prominent foreigner before. After initial diffidence, she began to recite her own poetry. Suddenly an insistent voice was heard shouting, "Isaiah, Isaiah." It was Randolph Churchill who had just arrived on a journalist's assignment. He had traced Isaiah Berlin by most amazing coincidences and now wanted him to come back to the hotel and act as interpreter so that Randolph could buy some caviar.

The main part of the book consists of profiles of Churchill, Roosevelt and Weizmann – three politicians of contrasting styles; a chapter on Einstein and his relationship to Israel, and essays on academics whom Isaiah Berlin met in those halcyon days of the last 1920s and early 1930s when Balliol and All Souls were the foci of debate elevated into an art form.

Lewis Namier and Felix Frankfurter were of a more mature vintage. Namier's father, who was called Bernstein, had converted to Roman Catholicism. Namier decided to return to the Jewish community and he became an ardent Zionist and a colleague of Weizmann. His overpowering personality and acid tongue made him few friends. When he converted back to Christianity, Weizmann broke with him. Isaiah Berlin, who never indulges in the simplest of prose, once submitted an article to him. Namier commented, "You must indeed be a clever man to understand what you write." Other contemporaries were J.L. Austin, the philosopher who would have rather been an engineer; J.P. Plamenatz, the outstanding teacher of political theory, and Maurice Bowra, one of the strongest personalities who left a deep imprint on Oxford on his and subsequent generations, a veritable primus inter pares. Auberon Herbert, Aldous Huxley, Hubert Henderson and Richard Pares – an academic sui generis, complete the cycle.

The most penetrating essay, not unexpectedly, is on Weizmann: "the only statesman of genius," he knew. "An activist whose intervention made the improbable happen." Even his shortcomings are defined in such a subjective way that they seem like virtues. The mixture of triumph and tragedy is described with compassion. Weizmann's ruthlessness in discarding former colleagues is glossed over or justified, as in the case of Namier. When I visited a broken Professor Selig Brodetsky in Jerusalem in 1950, he told me that Weizmann's attitude in virtually ignoring him during the preceding five years, was the second greatest tragedy in his life.

Isaiah Berlin: Flourishing: Letters 1928–1946
Published by Random House, London, 2009

A review by Fred Worms

This is a combined book review and essay, dedicated to Isaiah Berlin, who was one of the towering figures in the academic world from the moment he went to Balliol in 1928, aged 19, until his death in 1997.

The letters, which he wrote between 1928 and 1946, are a tour de force. It is a pity in some respects that one never sees the correspondents' replies or their letters, eliciting his response, to complete the often-intriguing subjects.

I write as a personal friend of many years' standing. It is extraordinary that a man who led a very busy academic and social life found time almost daily to write these many letters to his friends, many of which could form the basis of a Ph.D. thesis. He loved gossip. "Sit down Fred" he would say, either in the King David Hotel lobby in Jerusalem or at the Athenaeum Club in London. "Let's talk a little *rechilut* (gossip)."

Isaiah was born in Riga in 1909, after his mother had given birth to a stillborn girl. His father was a prosperous timber merchant and his mother was a domineering, well-educated woman. Isaiah was the apple of her eye. His parents adored their *wunderkind* and thoroughly spoiled him. The Berlins were related to the Schneerson Lubavitch family and, in fact, the late Lubavitcher Rebbe was a cousin.

His father, Mendel, brought the family to London in 1921, and in 1922 Isaiah was enrolled at St. Paul's School, where he stayed until 1927. In his last year at school, he wrote an essay called "Freedom." It is of the highest academic standard and could have been written by an Oxbridge don. He went up to Balliol, Oxford, from 1928 to 1932 and to All Soul's from 1933 to 1940. He was an expert in classical music, was consulted by Covent Garden and visited the festivals at Salzburg regularly.

His letters from Oxford can be put into two categories: firstly, correspondence with fellow-academics or people he considered worthy of sharing his wisdom; and secondly, letters to his parents. I find the latter most moving. He signed all letters ''Shaya.''* This close attachment to his parents manifested itself by their frequent meetings in London or in Oxford, quite apart from on-going correspondence between them. His *Yiddishe Mama* continually enquired after his health (he was a bit of a hypochondriac and in the end on one occasion he found this rather tiresome and sent a one-word telegram "flourishing." In another letter:

> I am well, healthy, wealthy, busy, happy, versatile, perpetually mobile: on excellent terms with everyone owing to my continuing absence of ambition, which not even the passionate local competition has to my regret done anything to stimulate. If one is born emotionally vegetarian the sight of blood makes one more not less so. Enough of these pensées approfondies.

---

* Ed. Shayah is a Yiddish diminutive of Yeshayahu – Isaiah in Hebrew

Isaiah became a don at 23 and merged effortlessly in the academic world, where he developed personal friendships with such eminent personalities as Freddie Ayer, Maurice Bowra, Lord Cecil, Richard Crossman, John Foster, Roy Harrod, Douglas Jay, Ben Nicolson (the artist), Goronwy Rees and Stephen Spender. He loved corresponding with married women, with whom he had a platonic relationship. Examples are Elizabeth Bowen, the novelist; Mary Fisher, Principal of St. Hilda's College; Sheila Grant-Duff, the journalist; Rosamond Lehmann, the novelist; Lady Daphne Straight, the civil servant; and Rachel Walker, one of his upper-class pupils who desperately wanted to marry him. He confided his innermost thoughts and insecurities, which he would not share with his parents or male academics. Here is a extract from a letter written to Cressida Bonham-Carter from Dublin in 1938:

> An enormous sense of leisure is my conception of 19th century Russian small gentry, which is what I really mean by saying I like Russians so much, not the genuine aristocracy which is most horrible & really corrupt & dull. Which brings us to Herzen, I am very glad indeed that you like it. Do you find it at all dull? You see, if one, for example, really prefers French or Latin literature generally to the Russo-Germans, how can one not find it dull? At least in long patches? I admire French inquisitiveness & sharpness & a certain unsentimental appetite for first hand experience etc. very much, as e.g. in Diderot, Balzac, Maupassant, but really I feel fearfully unsympathetic to it on the whole: I can't bear so much cut out, such linearity & anxiety to come to the point, to say it once, & then to move on. Whereas the Russians (& up to a point the Germans in general) except Dostoyevsky, describe long, solid emotions & characters, on & on, which inevitably involves moralizing & irrelevance, but on the other absorbs one, so that, unlike one's attitude when reading e.g. Henry James or Flaubert, one is not, all the time, aware of how good it is, or how well expressed, page by page & description by descriptions; but proceeds at some submarine level, at which what (one) reads is absorbed & expanded, & it does not occur to one to note the quality of the water; or even to note that one is in fact in water, or how deep. I am sorry; this is like a Sunday newspaper.

One would love to see the lady's reply. The reason why these letters have taken such a long time to make their appearance is Professor Henry Hardy's editorial efforts. Virtually every page has extensive footnotes on the background of the names mentioned in Isaiah's letters.

Isaiah was accepted rapidly into high society due to his conversational charm and his capacity for making friends. Lord Victor Rothschild, in particular, cultivated him and on one occasion, when Isaiah was pressed for time, sent him back to Oxford from Cambridge by private plane.

Isaiah was often accused, both during his lifetime and posthumously, of a lack of commitment, too much sitting on the fence and not coming down on one side or the other.

He first visited Palestine in 1934 and although an ardent Zionist all his life, he writes as the detached observer, preferring the company of the High Commissioner's select crowd to his own struggling relations. I quote from some of his sardonic observations:

> Tel Aviv incredible, like my conception of the Klondyke, full of gold-rush, built on sands in every sense, with more telephone calls per person per day then even New York, only 100,000 strong, with the tempo of a town of 600,000, hot, sticky, the sea so full you cannot see it, the German refugees swarming about with little portfolios under their arms doing business everywhere – in cafés, in buses, in bathing huts, in the sea, everywhere save their offices, the policeman checking traffic with a stick which he lashes with like a conductor's baton, using Hebrew when cool but loud and passionate Yiddish when excited, the car-drivers all shouting advice, cursing, laughing like Greeks or Syrians, already levantinized, suddenly checked by a long caravan of camels, very beautiful & like a tourist advertisement, led by a little Polish Jew in a black bowler hat making suitable Arab noises to the camels, learnt overnight, followed by a group of official intellectuals, poets, editors & the like, a peripatetic academy arguing about the possibility of coining a new word, etc. etc. etc. unbelievable it is, like the performance of Pergolesi's 'Serva Padrona' in Hebrew in the University theatre overlooking the Hills of Moab & the Dead Sea.

...the German Jews, as soon as they arrive, of course begin by buying a Fahrplan of the omnibuses: Fahrplan is the first thing they think of. They come at 10 a.m. to the place, no bus. They ask whether there will be a bus soon, the Jew in charge say no, no bus, no hope of bus. The Jew begins "aber im Fahrplan..." the other interrupts & says '

"Weil en Jid will machen gutes geschaft und verkauft aich a Fahrplan, missen wir fahren wie er wittl!" [Ed. German-Yiddish: "Just because a Yid wants to do good business and also follows a timetable, it doesn't mean the bus will come"].

Perhaps the most interesting period covered by his letters is his wartime stay in America. Since he could not join the regular forces due to his damaged arm, he volunteered for the Ministry of Information and the Foreign Office. He was sent to New York and Washington, first by the Ministry of Information and then as a regular attaché to the embassy in Washington. His tasks were two-fold: to let the American public, to whom the early war years were remote, know of the valiant battle which England was fighting against overwhelming odds; and to send confidential reports of the inner political circles that had an influence on the conduct of the War. He was commuting between New York and Washington, with access to the rich and famous and getting immersed in the Zionist activities of his fellow Jews: Felix Frankfurter, Henry Morgenthau, Bernard Baruch, Stephen Wise and Abba Hillel Silver. The White House let it be known loud and clear – despite extensive Jewish pressure – that the priority was to win the war and nothing was allowed to deflect from this overall aim. When news of the death-camps filtered through, a number of Jewish leaders, in particular Rabbi Stephen Wise and Abba Hillel Silver, agitated for some direct action but their appeal fell on deaf ears. The "softly, softly" school was led by Chaim Weizmann, whereas the activists were influenced by Ben Gurion's militant attitude. Isaiah adored Weizmann and agreed that England, which would not allow refugee ships to land in Palestine, should not be attacked for their callousness. "I cannot afford a breach," said Weizmann, "and must keep negotiating doors open," although "to American Zionists I must have appeared as a compromiser." In the event, Weizmann lost the long-term strategic battle when the Hagana and the Irgun took up arms and became a major factor in the British abandoning Palestine in 1947. Isaiah Berlin wrote:

> Terrorism in Palestine enormously diminished all chances of co-operation. The horror of the Nazi death-camps transformed American, and indeed world opinion. Attlee and Bevin adopted the White Paper policy in its entirety and, by making Arab consent a necessary condition for immigration, shut all doors to the Jews. This radicalized the Zionist moderates overnight. By 1947 we were all at one: Weizmann and Silver, Frankfurter and Emanuel Neumann, Goldmann and Ben Gurion, and those to the left and right of them – indeed, every Jew with the faintest sympathy for Zionism – all were moulded in a united whole. The Labour Government's flat rejection in 1946 of the American proposal to admit a hundred thousand refugees into Palestine made total resistance to its policies unavoidable.
>
> About this Ben Gurion's instinct proved sound. It was mass enthusiasm in America and the discipline and the strength of the yishuv itself, not the British connection in which I so strongly believed, that were decisive in the creation of the mood in which Palestine Commissions were set up, Britain reappraised its strategic position and abandoned Palestine, the United Nations vote took place, the war of 1948 was won.
>
> The hopes and fears of 1942-45 which I have described are now a mere historical memory. It is for historians to say whether the beliefs and policies of those who followed Weizmann – the men of the centre, amongst whom I count myself – were written in water, built on shifting sands.

His official transfer from the Ministry of Information to the Foreign Office materialized only in January 1945. *Time* Magazine wrote:

> After three years in the Washington bivouac, rumpled, tubby, articulate Isaiah Berlin had left the British Embassy staff last week and gone home to London. As one of the Embassy's First Secretaries, he had for a time contributed more than any other one person to official British knowledge of the current US.

Isaiah, who had wanted to be attached to the Moscow Embassy all these years, at last achieved this in September 1945. His famous visit to the poetess, Anna Akhmatova, is recalled in detail in Ignatieff's biography. From Russia there were no long letters of political significance since Isaiah Berlin was fully aware of the ruthless censorship. As it was, when this meeting was Akhmatova leaked out. Stalin was furious which led to more intensive anti-Jewish legislation.

Isaiah was self-critical and continuously analysed himself, for example: "I really do apologise for the extreme scarcity of letters from me lately but I have almost completely got out of the habit of writing with my own hand, preferring the greater joy of dictation. I have become quite a good spontaneous composer of official documents; my pomp and stiffness in official communications cannot be exaggerated."

He was right in classifying himself as a very fortunate person indeed, molly-coddled by his parents and spoiled by his friends. The best years of his life were after his marriage to the aristocratic Aline from the de Gunzberg family, which only took place in 1956 and which brought him wealth; a mansion in Oxford; a London apartment in The Albany; and a summer house in Italy. He was indeed flourishing, which will become manifest when the letters covering that period are published.

Also included in this fascinating volume is the Jacob Herzog Memorial Lecture delivered by Isaiah Berlin in 1972, entitled "Zionist Policies in Wartime Washington." One is not surprised by the choice of this subject. Isaiah was sensitive to the criticism that, with his influence amongst the movers and shakers in Washington, he could have done more for the rescue of European Jewry. He maintains that, as a follower of Weizmann's "softly, softly" approach and as a representative of the British Government, his hands were tied. I have a letter from him written in 1990's on this very subject.

One is privileged to share these epoch-making letters. Those who give them quality time will be richly rewarded.

Correspondence with Ephraim Halevy, former head of the Mossad and a nephew of Sir Isaiah Berlin

25 October, 1999

Dear Mr. Halevy

It was a great pleasure meeting you and your wife in Rome and exchanging some nostalgic reminiscences on Isaiah Berlin and other mutual friends. I conducted extensive correspondence with Isaiah extending over a period of 15 years and some of this has been featured in various publications. I am enclosing one which appeared in *Ariel*, not only because it will be of particular interest to you but also because of the additional correspondence attached hereto. If you could lend your weight and influence to the campaign which some of us are conducting it would be extremely helpful.*

Della and I hope that our paths will soon cross again as we spend a lot of time in Jerusalem.

Fred. S. Worms

■ ■ ■

---

* Ed. The reference is to the threat by the Israel Foreign Ministry to cease publication of their flagship journal Ariel: *The Israel Review of Arts and Letters*. A long list of writers, artists and public figures joined a petition to save the magazine. It eventually ceased publication in 2003 after more than 40 years.

14 November, 1999

Dear Mr. Worms,

Many thanks for your letter of 25 October and its attachments. I found the exchanges so fascinating and they reminded me of many of my encounters with Isaiah over the years. As time goes by and Isaiah's unique and personal "brand" of Judaism and Zionism comes into perspective I have often regretted his inability and that of others so close to him to make their message "relevant" to the Jewish masses in Israel. As I live through the rough and tumble world of modern day Zion, with its numerous irreconcilable dialectic contradictions, I yearn for a voice of wisdom and sanity and I mourn our inability to imbibe the non-religious Jew at the turn of the century (or for all that matter at the turn of the millennium!) with a sense of real identity. There is of course one aspect of Isaiah's background which I believe had more to do with his emotional and intellectual make-up than he would admit. However much he rejected messianism, he was nevertheless a descendant of Lubavitch; as such I think this was a measure of *Ahavat Yisrael* in much of what he did. This was an element that Isaiah the scholar could not shake-off.

I have noted your concern over "Ariel" and have spoken to a couple of people; let us see what happens.

It was a pleasure making your acquaintance in Fiuggi and Hadassa and I do hope we can stay in touch. I come to London from time to time and my son is presently working there as a lawyer in one of the leading international law firms (White and Case) so there is a personal reason for my coming back "to the scene of my youth."

All the very best to you,

Ephraim Halevy

■ ■ ■

The Berlin and Worms Correspondence

For over 16 years, Sir Isaiah Berlin and Fred Worms carried on an intermittent but far-ranging correspondence, in addition to regular meetings in London and Jerusalem. The following is a selection from this exchange of letters beginning in September 1981 and ending in February, 1997, a few months before Sir Isaiah's death.

22 September 1981

Dear Mr. Worms,

It was exceedingly kind of you to write to me – it was something that was read in the interval of a Prom, was it not? I have no idea what the extracts from my original lecture may have been. The entire lecture lasted well over an hour, the bit about Akhmatova, I suppose, half-an-hour. I agreed to let the BBC make what cuts they wanted, and I was abroad at the time and did not hear it. But if you thought well of it, perhaps it wasn't too bad. One often thinks of writing to authors when something they have done pleases one, but one sometimes does not bring oneself actually to do it. It was very generous of you to write, and I am truly grateful.

IB

■ ■ ■

30 December 1987

Dear Mr. Worms,

I read with interest your account of Frankfurt. Who are the Jews of Frankfurt today? Are they the children of the Jews of yesterday who survived, are there those who returned after the war and are now very old (like Erich Warburg in Hamburg, who, to my horror, flew the swastika flag on his yacht in the mid-thirties when racing somewhere in Scandinavian waters between Kiel and Skaggerak)? Are there Israelis who have come to make money? I realize that the Breuer community must be over – whatever its faults, at least they did not set themselves to disrupt existing communities, as the Hassidim – my cousins – am I not a second cousin of the present Lubavitch Rebbe, and 6th cousin of Yehudi Menuhin? – are disrupting the community of Rome – and indeed, of Milan too, to the despair of poor Rabbi Toaeff. Nor would they perhaps have said that the holocaust was sent upon the Jews by a vindictive deity to punish them for efforts at assimilation, as was said recently by you know who[*]. Is the community of Jews in Germany vanishing? Static? Or growing? Don't bother to answer these questions – next time we meet I shall put them all to you again and you will tell me. In the meanwhile, thank you for sending me that most interesting piece.

IB

■ ■ ■

6 January 1988

Who are the Jews of Frankfurt? They can be generically referred to as *Zugelaufene*.[**] You will find very few genuine German Jews amongst them. They are a mixture of *yordim*[***] and survivors from the camps. This is, of course, apart from some genuine *yekkes*[****] in the old age homes. I doubt whether they have a future. 30,000 of them spread over half a dozen towns does not appear to be a viable proposition. The Warburgs have always been sui generis.

---

[*]   Ed. This is obscure. Possibly a reference to a fanatic haredi rabbi.
[**] Ed. German: A hanger-on – probably unwanted.
[***] Ed. A person who has left Israel. The reverse of aliya.
[****] Ed. Somewhat derogatory term for German-born Jews. Evidently from the jackets they were said to wear even in Israel's hot summers.

I learn with great interest that you are a second cousin of the Lubavitch Rebbe. With great respect the good that his followers do by their extrovert activities is, in my opinion, completely undone by the cult-like worship with which they revere him. He sits in New York and instructs the Israeli Government not to give up an inch. The haredim in Israel today are probably as big a menace as the Arabs. I refer to this in the enclosed article which may be of interest to you and which has been commissioned by my local Synagogue paper.

FSW

■ ■ ■

17 May 1988

Dear Mr. Worms,

Thank you ever so much for that most interesting offprint from the Old Pauline. I remember Rupert Martin well – unlike Tom Martin, he was a very nice man (an Indian once reported to me that Tom Martin said to him, "I remember Isaiah Berlin in my form, he really was not much good at anything; he has had quite an academic career since, I can't imagine how"). And of course I remember John Bell very well, he was very kind to me. H.A.M. Tyson, the father of the eminent musicologist now a Fellow of All Souls, taught German and was quite awful, but Leslie Matthews, "the spectacled, wrinkled, gnarled old Classic" was genuinely inspiring, and I owe him a great deal. I remember Langham, but never knew he was called Bo. Young was no good but quite nice, and Pullinger was a terrible martinet. I had a terrible disaster with Gilks, when he was High Master – he invited me to deliver the Milton Lecture, and I referred to him throughout as the Sur Master, which I thought he was – very ill-received, and I was never asked again to this do.

As for myself, I was not in the least "confounding and dazzling" – I was never top in any Form at St. Paul's, and had very moderate success academically and never did better until my last year at Oxford; so I think this is purely imaginary (I wish he read the Bible and did not mis-spell my name). Martin Flett, son of the Astronomer Royal, was a great friend.

Did I ever tell you the terrible row about St. Paul's and Jews which I had – it became an Affaire – do ask me about it next time we meet.

IB

■ ■ ■

7 June 1989

To have become a legend in one's own lifetime, to have a host of friends but no enemies, to be at ease with princes, philosophers, musicians and the working man are rare achievements, but the most astonishing thing is that you are so genuinely surprised by the accolades that are being heaped upon you.

FSW

■ ■ ■

15 June 1989

Dear Mr. Worms

Thank you ever so much for your over-generous letter. I am not so sure that I have no enemies at all – although perhaps fewer than others – if you read *The Times* of two Saturdays ago you would find a very vicious attack on me by one Roger Scruton – it may be caused by the fact that I did say to a number of people, some of whom probably knew him, that I did not wish to be in the same room with him, as I disliked and despised him so much. But I won't go on about that. All I wish to say is that your letter was marvellously generous, extremely moving to me, and I should like to thank you most sincerely for writing in the terms that you have, which I value greatly, for you know my opinion of you – and there is nothing like loving friendship in the world.

IB

■ ■ ■

24 August 1989

I do not know whether you have followed the Adin Steinsaltz controversy. It is an appalling indictment of the prevailing atmosphere and a milestone in what seems to be an unstoppable march of progress of black fundamentalism at its worst. You may note that your name is mentioned in one of the articles as one of his illustrious friends. Should not everyone with some influence lift up their pens and strengthen the back of this eminently sensible Rabbi who, for reasons which have not yet been sufficiently explained, has chosen to apologise to the powers of evil?

FSW

■ ■ ■

27 September 1989

Dear Mr. Worms,

I am appalled by your enclosures about Steinsaltz. I do not think I have met him, and I have never written about him. I have no objection to my name being mentioned as one of his friends, since I certainly sympathise with some of the things that he is doing; but I admit that I regard his excessive addiction to the doctrines of my relatives, the followers of the Sage of Lubavitch as deplorable – but what he is doing in the Soviet Union is, I am sure, important and worthy. The task he has taken upon himself of translating both the Babylonian and the Jerusalem Talmud seems to me too heavy for anyone's shoulders – I wonder whether he really thinks he will accomplish it. As for the "black" religious pall which hangs over Israel, I could not sympathise with you more strongly, as you know.

IB

■ ■ ■

25 October 1989

Many thanks for your letter of the 22nd September which awaited my return from Israel where we spent a whole month.

Incredible as it may seem, the publication of the translation of the Steinsaltz Babylonian Talmud is apparently due to take place within the next six months and the American publishers have had such an enormous demand that they are going to print the unprecedented quantity of 20,000 sets. My information is that Steinsaltz is so preoccupied with this enormous venture which involves him in travelling through the US and coast to coast interviews on a variety of television stations that he just did not have the time to fight the haredim.

FSW

■ ■ ■

Notes on a meeting with Sir Isaiah Berlin at the Athenaeum Club, London,

Wednesday, 10 July 1991

IB: I knew Arthur Koestler well. I crossed swords with him when he came out with his outrageous statement after the State of Israel was formed and he called upon World Jewry to assimilate or emigrate. A preposterous proposition which he knew perfectly well was impractical and wholly untenable. He was very clever but he did have a habit of stabbing in the back whatever organization he had latterly joined. He started off as a Communist and finished as a Revisionist. Remember his books – Thieves in the Night, and Promise and Fulfilment – violently anti-British and strongly pro Irgun.

FSW: Nevertheless, he had a flair for explaining complicated issues and in retailing anecdotes. I recall in one of his early books he described how, in his Communist phase, he was taken to Russia on a VIP tour. They wanted to show him how far their education had advanced. He was taken to a class which was learning German. As he entered the classroom the whole class got up and shouted in unison "A gitten Tog." Both the class and the teacher thought they were studying German, whereas all the teacher knew was Yiddish.

IB: You mentioned anti-Semitism. There are two types. The acceptable and the non-acceptable. Very few people are free from it. It becomes unacceptable when it becomes threatening. We owe anti-Semitism quite a lot. Without it, it is doubtful whether we would have survived. Complete freedom accelerated assimilation. Persecution makes people draw together and this maintains identity. What do I mean by acceptable anti-Semitism? T.S. Eliot – whom I knew, was not a bad fellow, but he indulged in a bit of anti-Jewish poetry. Hilaire Belloc and G.K. Chesterton, incidentally another Old Pauline, were worse.

FSW: We started talking in Jerusalem three weeks ago on the problem facing the Chief Rabbinate. In the meantime we have had this fracas with the Chief's injudicious interview when on the front page of the *Evening Standard* he was quoted out of context.

IB: There is no objection to what Lord Jakobovits said. There is every objection to the criticism levelled at him by a man who calls himself a communal leader who is beneath contempt. You told me that the Chief Rabbi has shown you the letter which I sent him expressing these views.

FSW: Yes, I faxed him from Israel along similar lines.

IB You asked me about Jonathan Sacks. He is a bright young man but I am deeply disturbed that he has become a follower of the Lubavitcher Rebbe.

FSW: Why does this trouble you?

IB The present Lubavitcher Rebbe is a distant relation of mine. Both Yehuda Menuhin and I go back six generations to the same ancestor. The Rebbe is not a lineal descendent but a nephew of the last Rebbe. None of his predecessors had messianic pretensions. I think the harm he does outweighs the good. His interference in Israeli politics and strategies is wholly unacceptable.

FSW: Are you religious?

IB I do not believe in God. I don't know what God means. Is he a man with a beard, an anthropomorphic figure? If it means a force for good, for morality, then this is simply man's invention of a concept.

FSW: Are you an atheist?

IB: No.

FSW: Are you an agnostic?

IB: No, I am religiously tone-deaf. What I mean to say is that a deaf person cannot appreciate music. That is my position vis-à-vis God. I go to Synagogue from time to time because I wish to identify myself with the traditions of my ancestors which I would like to see continued.

FSW: I am surprised you use the analogy of music. You have a reputation of an excellent ear and to be an expert in classical music.

IB: As far as pop and jazz is concerned I am tone-deaf.

FSW: Even if Alfred Brendel played it?

IB: I saw him last night at Covent Garden. He is an old friend. He would not. There are only four great pianists alive – Brendel, Richter, Lupu and Pereia.

11 July 1991

The choice of being clamped in the West End or being held up on the Northern Line is an odious one. It seems to me that like the two sections of American Jewry that cannot intermarry because one section contains so many intermarried offsprings, there will soon be two classes of Londoners. Those who lead wholly self-contained lives in the suburbs and those who live or venture into the West End. It is getting more and more difficult. Thank you for being so understanding. I hate being late for an appointment.

As promised I am enclosing Richler's book herewith. It may take some little time to get over the initial chapters but the man has remarkable insight into all strands of society. The Bronfman family is being skilfully libelled and I would not be at all surprised if Sir Hyman Kaplansky was not based on Solly Zuckerman.

Alas, our time together is always too short. I hope there will soon be another opportunity of continuing our conversation.

FSW

■ ■ ■

12 July 1991

Dear Mr. Worms,

I, too, enjoyed our conversation greatly – only a man of the most utter scruple would apologise for being ten minutes late – when I think of my own habits, I am put to shame.

What you say about the Chief Rabbi is genuinely worrying – I think a delegation of Jews and Christians, old-world moderates, will have to call on the Chief Rabbi and the Archbishop of Canterbury jointly, to beg them to desist from the wilder shores of mystical commitment.

You ask about the other two pianists – none, so far as I am concerned, but if you wish to add to them, I will not deny the merits of Michelangeli and Pollini.*

Thank you very much for Richler – I shall read that, I am sure, with the usual malicious pleasure one gets from this kind of roman à clef.

IB

■ ■ ■

16 July 1991

I do not think a delegation calling on the Chief Rabbi and the Archbishop of Canterbury will have the desired effect. Who ever admits that he has bad breath?

There are two points that trouble me following our recent conversation. Is secular Judaism not a contradiction in terms? If its continuity is deemed desirable, is religion not a necessary concomitant? Is religious practice without belief in God feasible for the majority?

The second issue is of a more light-hearted nature. Whilst I quite understand that you are tone deaf as far as God is concerned, I simply cannot believe that you have given jazz a fair trial. As for pop, I am also tone deaf, but jazz can be very beautiful, moving and elegiac along classical lines. Have you never heard the late Leonard Bernstein play a classical piece of music on the piano when, with some skilful syncopation, he would start swinging it? Victor Rothschild used to do the same. In the old Fantasia film – not the dreadful rehash which they made recently – there is an evocative scene in which the orchestra, whilst waiting for Stokovsky to arrive, breaks into an impromptu jam session. Finally, Louis Armstrong on his trumpet and Fats Waller on

---

* Ed. Maurizio Pollini, the Italian pianist.

the piano (both of blessed memory) have delighted thousands, if not millions, of classical music enthusiasts. Give them a chance!

FSW

■ ■ ■

18 July 1991

Dear Mr. Worms,

Let me try to reply to your letter of 16 July.
1. Secular Judaism is a contradiction in terms: religion must be a necessary concomitant. Religious practices without belief in God cannot be accepted by the majority. In this respect I find myself in a probably small minority, whose outlook is not likely to commend itself to many people. Consequently my example is of little use – we must continue to plod our lonely way as best we may, and support – without hypocrisy but with some degree of ambivalence – the traditional Jewish faith.
2. I am afraid no good. My hatred of jazz began when I was ten or eleven, even "the original fox-trot" and "Felix Keeps on Walking" horrified me: hence I refused after a bit to take dancing lessons. I heard Victor Rothschild imitate Fats Waller, and could scarcely bear it. Moreover, I have a deep antipathy to all the works of the admirable Bernstein. So you see, I am a hopeless case – lonely path again.

IB

■ ■ ■

18 February 1992

I spent the weekend on "conversations with Isaiah Berlin" and I was exhilarated, stimulated and, as one would expect from a layman, occasionally perplexed.
Could I make the following observations?
I believe there are two typographical errors.

On Page 89 the word *Anerpennung* should be *Anerkennung*. On page 122 the word *wenden* should be *werden*.

On page 83 you state that "in the Jewish tradition there is no merit in work as such. It is a necessity." This is in complete contradiction to the "Ethics of the Fathers" Chapter 2, Verse 2, where it states that "the study of the Torah without working is futile and leads to sin." This, incidentally, is an injunction more ignored than followed by the excessive number of Yeshiva Bachurim [Ed. students] who are staying in Kollel all their lives.

In any case, the curse placed by God upon Adam that by the sweat of his brow he would have to make his living was given by a non-Jewish God to humanity, according to David Hartman, the respected American Israeli philosopher. God only became Jewish at the time of Abraham!

Another intriguing thought that you have triggered is the possibility of a similarity between Marx and your distant cousin, the Lubavitcher Rebbe. It seems that both believe in historical determinism. Marx's theory has been disproved; the other one is waiting for the Moshiach now.

When you say (on page 47) that there is nothing more destructive of human lives than fanatical conviction about the perfect life allied to political or military power, should one not add the evils of the certainty of religious fundamentalism?

Pascal said that humanity's misfortunes are due entirely to man's inability to sit quietly in a room. This seems to be in conflict with Heine who warned "against ignoring the humble professor in his study. He has considerable power." Who is right?

What happened to Christianity which you describe as "the humble religion" with its subsequent triumphalism of the Crusaders and the Inquisition?

One would have liked your views on a number of aspects with a particular Jewish angle. For example: Is Judaism with so many variations still a monotheistic religion? You said to me once that as far as the existence of God is concerned, you were tone deaf yet you feel a deep commitment to the continuity of our people and you occasionally visit a synagogue. What about the Revelation on Sinai, Moses Maimonides, Spinoza (from the Jewish angle) and Steinsaltz, who had the courage to paint our forefathers – warts and all – only to be condemned by the ultra-Orthodox for blasphemy?

You have known and worked with Churchill, Weizmann, Simon Marks, Israel Sieff, Isaac Wolfson, Ben Gurion, Sharett and the Rothschilds and your pen portraits of some of these contemporaries, most of whom are, alas, no longer with us would be fascinating.

Incidentally, I was intrigued to learn that you consider Stravinsky a pure genius but Prokofiev, who is one of my favourite 20th century composers, not to be in his class.

What is all this leading up to? Hopefully another interview with Isaiah Berlin, a relaxed chat with a specific Jewish angle. During our occasional conversations I was amazed at your modesty and the astonishment which you expressed that your views should cause such passionate interest. Believe me when I say that it would be a tragedy if your public portrait would go down to posterity without a fuller exposure to the Jewish side which only surfaces with the occasional obiter dicta on Zionism and its precursors.

Could I come and see you, either in London or in Oxford, with my tape recorder? Over the years I have interviewed some of the leading Jewish thinkers for the *Jewish Quarterly* and *L'Eylah*. The practice has invariably been that the double-spaced draft is submitted to the interviewee for correction and approval.

I do hope you will say yes.

FSW

24 February 1992

Dear Mr. Worms,

Thank you for your fascinating letter of 18 February: I shall try and answer your points one by one – all of them seem to me interesting – the cap fits.

You are right about the typographical errors – there are, I am afraid, others too: I have done my best to eliminate them from the American edition, and if the thing ever goes into paperback that will be a more correct version too. But although I am sorry about the misprints (there are some real mistakes too), for reasons which I will not go into I was helpless, or nearly so, in the matter.

The Jewish tradition and work. No doubt you are right – the quotation from the "Ethics of the Fathers" is very relevant, and I did not remember it, if ever I took it to heart. But the question arises: what about not merely the Yeshiva Bachurim, about whom of course I agree, but about all the learned rabbis totally immersed in the study of the Talmud, the later interpreters, or even the mystical writings, who have certainly never done (or regarded themselves as obliged to perform) any other work whatever? Since dedication to the Jewish tradition and religion does not count as "work," I do not think that is what the quotation you adduce can refer to. I still, perhaps too obstinately, stick to my view that work in the ancient world was not much thought about: and that *laborare est orare* (Ed. "To work is to pray") is a Christian innovation, which no doubt penetrated the Jewish tradition as well, including the quotation you adduce. But one could argue about that for a long time. As for the curse placed on Adam, I cannot accept Hartman's doctrine – for Jews there is only one God, the Creator of the Heaven and the Earth; consequently, any act of His is binding – it may be on all mankind, but certainly upon Jews; the curse was placed on our original ancestor – no Jewish sage has ever maintained (so far as I know, and I am, of course, pretty ignorant) that Adam or his descendants or Noah or Shem were not Jews and presumably for the most part in Paradise. So I fear I must reject this piece of modernism.

You are quite right about Marx and the Rebbe – we must wait and see. The fact that Marx's grandfather and uncle were both rabbis is perhaps not entirely irrelevant.

Now to p. 47. I entirely agree with you, as you know, that religious fundamentalism leads to all kinds of evils – but I do not think that by itself it is nearly as effective as it is when combined with political clout (*vide* Israel now); consequently, although every kind of fanaticism is included by me, I think that without political or military power it is relatively ineffective.

You speak of Pascal and Heine. True, Heine did say this about the humble professor; but of course, that was in connection with the disasters which poor Kant is accused of – since it is Robespierre whose bloody arm performed the task which, according to Heine, Kant stimulated. So maybe there is some truth in Pascal's saying, although I never actively defended it, I merely used it as an illustration of something or other. Pascal was giving a recipe for a life without misfortunes, Heine a recipe for philosophically-inspired violence.

Where do I describe Christianity as "the humble religion" – it may have so started, but you are quite right about its later career – do I actually say that? On which page? Is it perhaps one of the errors in the text which will have to be eliminated?

The Revelation on Sinai, Moses, Maimonides, etc.: all I know about them seems to me sometimes profound and important, sometimes unacceptable. I simply believe what I believe: having been brought up as a Jew, no doubt what I am and believe is deeply affected by that – to what degree, and in what ways, I cannot begin to realise or express. But my original statement is, I fear, correct: I have no idea what is meant by "God." I wish I did. But I do believe, as I think I may have said in my piece, that stone-dry atheists don't understand what men live by; that understanding of religious feeling is essential to fully-developed human consciousness.

You speak of all these men with whom you say I worked. I never worked for Churchill, nor Marks, nor Sieff, nor Wolfson, nor Ben Gurion, nor Sharett – so what can I say about them which is not generally known? You would like me to talk into your tape recorder. I have done far too much of that; and it exhausts me totally; and I have very little to say about the topics which you have brought up. I do not believe that the views which you seek from me would be of any real interest to the readers, whether of the JQ or anything else. If you are set on doing it, do let us allow at any rate a year to pass. Perhaps if I am alive in 1993, or better still 1994, you could perform this task, by the proposal of which I am deeply flattered. But believe me, it is not false modesty, it is pure realism which makes me say that there is nothing of value which I could say into your machine – although no doubt we could have a conversation of interest to people who know us both.

IB

■ ■ ■

3 December 1992

Dear Mr. Worms,

Thank you for your enclosure about Abraham. I agree with all you say. I still remember the pleasure with which I re-read the *Akeda* – I suggested it to Stravinsky for a cantata, which surprisingly enough he wished to dedicate to the State of Israel. He wrote it, Hebrew words and all, dedicated it, I went to Jerusalem to hear it – it was badly performed – the entire Israeli Government, headed by the President Ben Zvi, was there – the audience was totally foxed and puzzled by the entire thing, even more than by the Berio, which you must have heard, which again was my fault. But still – it enters the *oeuvre* of the great master, and therefore does Israel proud, as it was meant to do. The reason for this, I won't enlarge on here – he was a terribly mean man, Stravinsky, and did everything for money – in this case he charged nothing – and had not the remotest relation to Israel – that, too, demand explanation, which I think I can give next time we meet.

Now to the subject. You are quite right: Abraham does seem to have acted badly, both in the case of the Pharaoh and of Abimelech. He could have acted differently and got away with it, without sacrificing his poor wife; and the fact that she didn't object merely shows that that was the kind of relationship between an Arab sheikh – which is what I imagine Abraham in some sense to have been like – and his subservient wives. The story of Hagar is notoriously awful (what did Isaac do in imitation of the wicked act of his father? I can't remember – do tell me): why did the commentators not utter the faintest word of criticism? Because everything that holy men do is right – not for us to ask – God alone can understand the human heart and motives and reasons and the way men and things are – that is what faith means – not to ask the question why, not to apply the kind of rational criteria that you do. I remember Herbert Samuel once wrote in a book that the Jewish religion did not oblige one to believe anything which reason was against. That is absurd. Faith, blind faith, is what is enjoined upon us; and that is true of every truly religious religion – the imitation religions, liberal churches, Reform synagogues, diluted Buddhism and the like are not the genuine article, and Kierkegaard is right – only totally commitment and no questions asked is the truly religious attitude, the rest is a modification which is perfectly fulfilling and noble (or can be) for those who profess it, but not what the Bible demands. Hence my sceptical attitude about these things, inasmuch as I was never favoured by this act of total commitment, which I think Jehovah surely demands, all this demands, all this despite my Hassidic origins.

The age of Ishmael is a genuine puzzle. There are all kinds of contradictions in the Bible anyway, which the highest critics seized upon with a certain degree of glee – and so did Bertrand Russell in one of his typically rationalist essays in which he attempted to dismantle religion. That is not the way to treat what religious beliefs mean to those who hold them.

To go back to the Akeda: I do not believe Kierkegaard. I do not believe that Abraham knew that in the end, because the Lord had promised him that his seed would multiply, etc., it would in fact not cause him to kill Isaac. After all, the Lord could have given him another child at whatever age, for He can do anything, Sarah could have been 200, if the promise was to be fulfilled. No, I believe that Abraham fully believed that if need be he had to sacrifice his son, and that that is the whole point of the "trial" – that what the Lord commands has to be done no matter how deeply it offends against natural morality. That, I think, is what religion dictates – the rest is human morality which, however much it may follow from certain commandments of the Lord, is nevertheless something which must be intelligible to, and explicable in terms of, human faculties. But direct orders from on high, if they occur, brook no much analysis – they must be obeyed no matter what they are, that is what words like "absolute" must mean.

Or do you disagree? Or does this shake your faith? I do trust not.

IB

■ ■ ■

8 December 1992

I appreciate the trouble you have taken in commenting in such a wide-ranging fashion on my letter concerning the enigma of Abraham.

Are you saying that reason and faith are incompatible? With respect (and I do not use these two words as the usual cliché) such a dictum comes more easily from someone who is tone deaf as far as the existence of God is concerned.

No, you have not shaken my faith, for what it is worth, but I follow in the footsteps of Rav Soloveitchik who feels that unless we continuously wrestle with the problem we have not begun to understand our religion. When Jacob's name was changed to Israel it was precisely because he was wrestling with a super-natural force.

The great challenge to Christianity, Islam and Judaism is to reconcile the old religion with the present age. This is what I would have hoped halakha would have done for us but, as Yeshayahu Leibowitz indignantly shouts from the rooftops, halakha has stood still and is unsuitable for modern man and even more so for the State of Israel.

To answer your specific question "What did Isaac do when he repeated his father's sin?" Chapter 26 of Genesis tells us that when there was another famine, God told Isaac not to go down to Egypt; instead he visited the same Abimelech, King of Gerar, with whom his father Abraham, had the wife/sister/charade. Isaac, too, said of Rebecca "she is my sister" and he was only found out when Abimelech saw them *mezachek* with each other. This, incidentally, is the same word which was used when Ishmael abused Isaac, much to Sarah's annoyance. It is interesting that the word "laughter" could have such sexual overtones.

Why do I still think that Abraham was confident that he would not have to murder his own son? Because on three previous occasions God had promised him that through Isaac he would be make great. Even to the fundamentalist God cannot have it both ways.

I have just written a critique of Yeshayahu Leibowitz for *L'Eylah*. Alas, not very flattering. Would you like to see it?

FSW

■ ■ ■

19 December 1992

Dear Mr. Worms,

Thank you for your letter of 8 December. Indeed I am not saying that reason and faith are incompatible – though they may well be. As for the tone-deafness of which you speak, I may indeed in the end have to plead guilty. My difficulty about the existence of God has always been not that of atheists or agnostics, who understand what it means but deny or doubt it; but an inability to understand what it does mean.

However that may be, my impression of our Bible is that all the heroic figures spoken of in it have moral faults, which are not slurred over in the text; all, I think, save for Jonathan, who appears totally blameless. Your difficulty seems to me to be to reconcile Abraham's, Isaac's (thank you for Isaac) and indeed Jacob's conduct with the canons of accepted human ethics as advocated in the Bible, and indeed in other religions also, and surprise that the commentators should not have dealt with this. Indeed, Jacob and his sons' conduct at Shechem in the terrible episode about Dinah, not to speak of the mess of pottage, seems particularly reprehensible. It is the humanity of these characters, and the refusal of any attempt to disguise them, that seems to me one of the great strengths of our tradition, as opposed to those of e.g. Christianity or Islam. A tradition in which even saints and heroes can behave badly is unique, I think, and I am prepared to take some pride in this. Do you disagree?

As for the question of reconciling an old religion with "the present age," once one is set on that path, dilution and trendiness set in; and so, heretic as I undoubtedly am, I believe that one must either choose the really traditional religion or depart from it altogether – but not adapt and adjust. In that sense, I agree with my impossible friend Isaiah *(sic)* Leibowitz; Impossible, but noble.

IB

■ ■ ■

7 January 1993

Here is the most amazing coincidence. Having recently moved into the penthouse at Highpoint which Lubetkin built for Gestetner in the 1930s, his then junior partner, John Allen brought me a package of material. I understand from John, who now acts for me, that you were one of Lubetkin's heroes and all the underlining was done by him.

I do not know who Aileen Kelly is but she is certainly very impressive except that I am allergic to the words "final solution," not only because of the connotation but because they are rarely final. One wishes that every country would have a few Isaiah Berlins and Herzens whose tolerant pluralism stands in clear contradiction of the political and religious extremists whose unflinching certainly is causing so much damage.

FSW

■ ■ ■

11 January 1993

Dear Mr. Worms,

I have never seen this piece in this form in my life. Aileen Kelly is a great friend of mine, and did me the favour of writing an Introduction to the volume "Russian Thinkers" of my collected essays. But I had no idea (or perhaps I have just forgotten) that it was printed separately in the TLS.

I agree with you about "final solution."

I have just received a letter from the Chief Rabbi, to whom I sent a very critical piece on Lubavitch, which appeared in "The New Yorker," with approving comments, and a faith in many opinions, openness, pluralism, liberalism, etc. I hope he means it.

IB

P.S. I had forgotten the interesting fact that Lubetkin – a man of whom I had only vaguely heard in the thirties as an architect, and did not even know what he had built – approved of what I wrote about the Russians. One is always pleased by pleasing other people who are respected – Lubetkin is now being written about with great regard, and I am most grateful to you for digging this out and sending it to me.

■ ■ ■

14 February 1994

It was a great pleasure seeing you again at Harry Woolf's house the other night. Bearing in mind that the ladies at the JIA luncheon, which was held on the same day, drank a toast to the guest speaker, Madame Sadat, and another one to Egypt, I wondered whether our daily prayers were not due for some revision.

The enclosed text speaks for itself. If the roles were reversed I could imagine the ADL creating a special protest lobby.

I think we have agreed in previous conversations that religion should be practiced in moderation, faith does not bear examination and Triumphalism should be taboo.

FSW

Encl. Copy of the triumphal victory song celebrating the drowning of the Egyptians in the Reed Sea after the exodus from Egypt. This is included in our daily morning prayers.

■ ■ ■

21 February 1994

Dear Mr. Worms,

Thank you for all those admirable transcripts from our Prayer Book. I think it is just all right: after all, the ancient Egyptians have not survived, the modern Egyptians don't really think they are descended from them – they're semites, not hamites. The only people who claim descent are the Copts – the name comes from Aiguptos – and they, I don't think, are in a position to protest against anything much – unless, of course, the Secretary of the UN, who is one, rises in his wrath.

About religion, faith, triumphalism – I agree most strongly.

IB

■ ■ ■

18 March 1994

Dear Mr. Worms

I read your account of the Rothschild celebration in Frankfurt with great pleasure and some amusement. The only conspicuously absent

Rothschilds were Evelyn and his family – I am sure you know the reason – and Miriam, Jacob's aunt, who refuses to go to Germany on any account. Your description of the whole thing brings it to life, and I get a far more vivid impression of it than from Jacob's own account to me.

The only thing that slightly surprised me was your reference to the fact that Napoleon blew the ghetto apart in 1796: surely at that time he had not yet attacked any part of German-speaking countries, and had not yet gone to Egypt? I imagine you meant 1806. But that is a very excusable misprint.

Thank you ever so much for sending me this account.

IB

■ ■ ■

1 June 1994

Dear Mr. Worms,

Warm congratulations on your Honorary Fellowship of the Israel Museum – it is a very well-deserved compliment; and Yekutiel Federmann is a good man – the rest I know nothing about.

IB

■ ■ ■

16 June 1994

Thank you so much for your letter of the 1st June. The Israel Museum is getting better and better. Whether it will retain its momentum once Teddy will no longer be on the scene is problematical. We shall be celebrating its 30th anniversary next year. There cannot be many other institutions in the world which have accumulated so much in so little time. Della and I felt privileged to play a small part in its development by bringing over the Cochin Synagogue.

We stayed on in Jerusalem for the Board of Governors Meeting of the Hebrew University. Six years ago it had 16,000 students and the total number of university students in Israel was 65,000. Now the HU has 22,000 and the national total has grown to 100,000. This is largely due to the Russian aliya. Naturally every department is bursting at the seams and there is great rivalry between the different faculties for funding. I am told the quality of research has not suffered and from the little that I have seen that claim appears to be justified.

Whilst I am sure that you have seen your brief and quite inadequate profile in the *New Yorker*, you may not have had an opportunity of looking at Ken Auletta's remarkable research on Edgar Bronfman Jr., the *angeheiratete* [Ed. Relative by marriage] member of your wife's family. It makes interesting reading.

Della joins me in sending you our heartfelt congratulations on your 85th birthday. Since you detest hyperbole I will not add to these sentiments other than by saying: *veyimtza chen vesechel tov be'eynei elohim ve'adam –* [Ed. So shalt thou find favour and good understanding in the sight of God and man – *Proverbs 3:4*].

FSW

■ ■ ■

17 June 1994

Dear Mr. Worms

Thank you ever so much for your exceptionally nice letter of 16 June. Interesting about Jerusalem, and encouraging: Israel looks like being en route to South Korea, Taiwan, etc.

The Profile in the *New Yorker* was originally written by a friend of mine in Israel, but they rejected it because of lack of anecdotes, mockery, etc. – hence the piece you read; the photograph is beyond words appalling, I look like a pathological murderer about to savage his prey.

Thank you for the piece on Bronfman – I will read it with interest, so will my wife.

Your words in the Holy Tongue naturally go straight to my heart, as intended – I can only reciprocate by offering the same to yourself and your wife.

IB

■ ■ ■

21 March 1994

Three points in your most welcome letter of the 18th March call for some comment.

The first relates to Evelyn, who was in China whilst we were in Frankfurt. When I sent a letter of thanks to Jacob I wrote as follows: Henry V summed it up on St. Crispin's Day before the Battle of Agincourt. "…and all gentlemen in England (or in China) now a-bed shall think themselves accursed they were not here."

Secondly, Miriam – who as you say refuses to go to Germany – has asked Della and me to visit her in the country when we return from our trip to Israel, Budapest and Prague on which we shall be embarking tomorrow.

Finally, you are surprised that 1796 was the year in which Napoleon blew the ghetto apart. This may be a terminological inexactitude but it is numerologically correct. It was in 1796 that General Kléber and his army virtually demolished the ghetto. I enclose relevant photocopies from two history books. It was not until 1811, however, that the Jews obtained equal rights and became citizens of

Mayor Ehud Olmert with Fred and Della in their home, 2002

Chief Rabbi (now Lord) Jonathan Sacks and Fred with Rabbi Adin Steinzaltz, 1997

Rabbi David Hartman

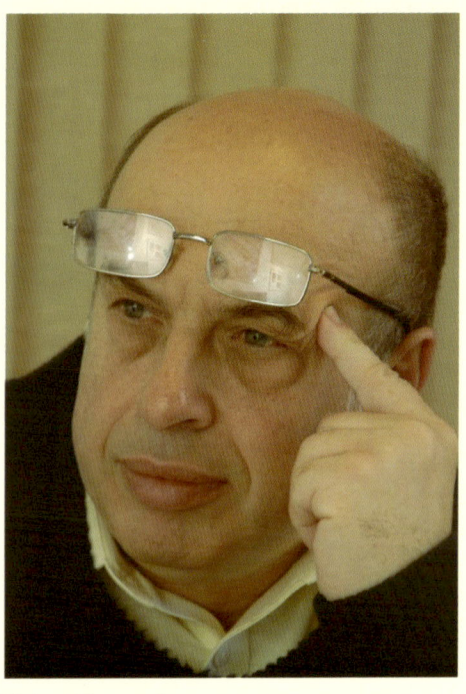

Natan Sharansky

Professor Yeshayahu Leibowitz

Rabbi Immanuel Jacobovits

Sir Isaiah Berlin, OM

Fred and Della with industrialist Stef Wertheimer at the Tefen High-Tech Park

Dedication ceremony of the "Living Water" section, part of the new Childrens' Discovery Trail at the Jerusalem Botanical Gardens, 2012 (see page 12)

The Worms Family Thespians at the 230th anniversary celebrations (see page 17)
Left to right: Zohar, Noam, Kinneret, Amir, Shira, Sigal, Ido, Maayan, Roi, Barak, Maor, Matan, Tal

Photo courtesy Eugene Weisberg

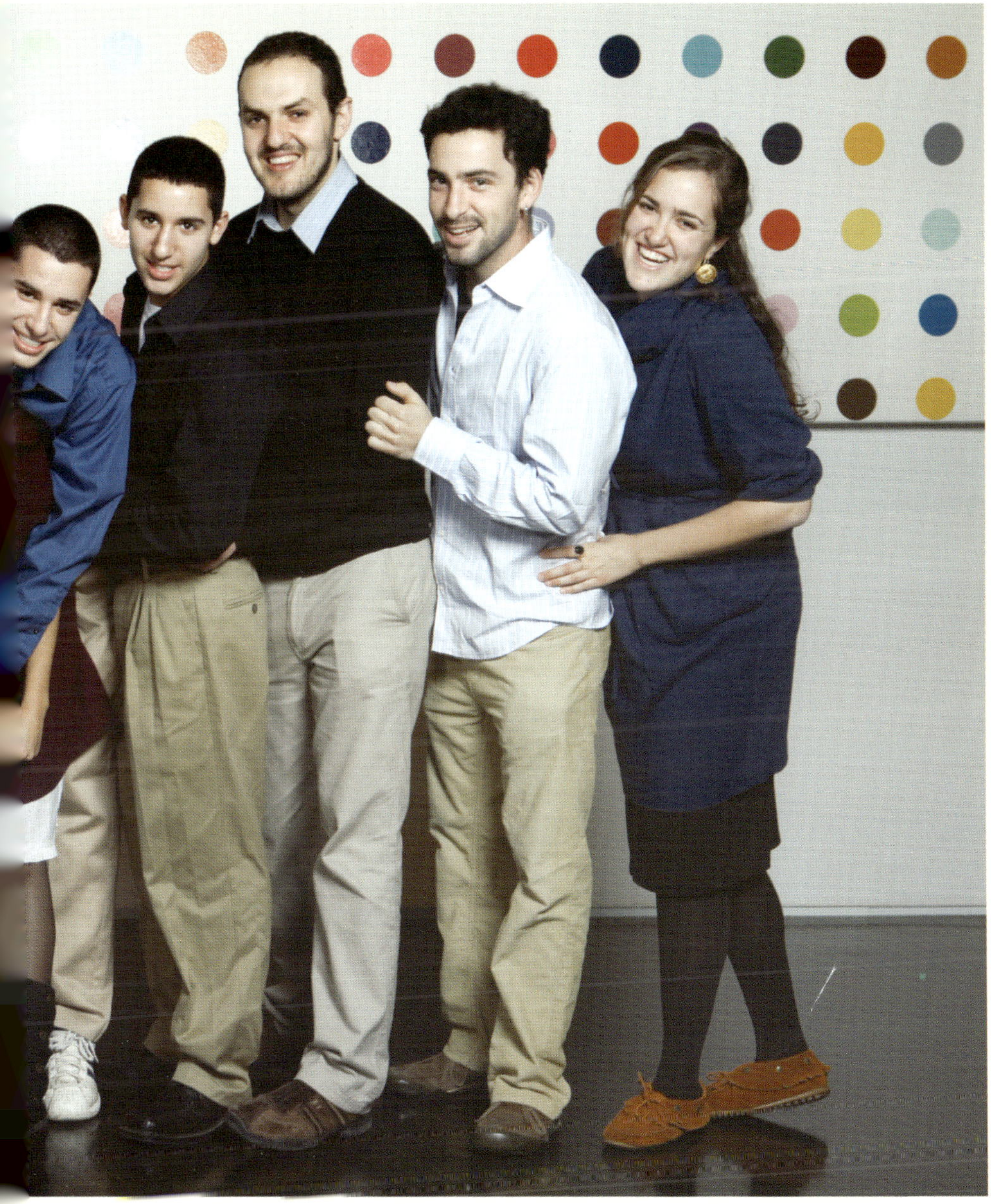

Fred and Della with Minister Dan Meridor

Fred introduces Chief Rabbi Lord Jonathan Sacks (right) guest speaker at the annual B'nai B'rith "Jerusalem Address," 2010

Left: Mick Davis of the United Jewish Israel Appeal, Ron Prosor, Israel's ambassador to the United Kingdom, and Fred

Fred and Della with Dennis Ross, President Bill Clinton's special Middle East coordinator

Jerusalemites, 2012

Frankfurt. This decree was cancelled in 1849 and was only reinstated in 1864. In 1867 Baron Mayer Carl von Rothschild became the first Jewish representative in the Prussian Landtag.

FSW

■ ■ ■

4 January 1995

I suppose it is in order to wish you a healthy and contented New Year. In fact, I do not see why such beneficial sentiments should not be expressed at regular intervals, regardless of special dates in the calendar.

A friend of mine, an American constitutional lawyer, has retired to Israel and is now one of my neighbours in Yemin Moshe. He has spent the last few years on researching the attitude of American Jewish efforts in connection with the rescue of German Jewry and subsequently the rescue of Polish, Hungarian and Rumanian Jews. For some reason best known to himself, he has asked me to go through the manuscript, which I have done with considerable interest and indeed, I was able to be of some positive assistance.

He refers to an incident in which you were involved. He writes that in the beginning of 1944, Nahum Goldmann came to the British Embassy in Washington and saw Isaiah Berlin who found him more gossipy than usual. The purpose of the visit was to sabotage the activities of the Bergson Group. The American Jewish Committee, in due course, condemned the Bergson Group and the Washington Post ran a three day campaign from October 3rd to the 6th against their activities. This apparently was deduced from a note which you sent to a Mr. Hayter at the British Embassy. At the time, Bergson and his Irgun cronies were, of course, thoroughly unpopular but with hindsight, one wonders whether ultimately they were not more effective than Stephen

Wise, Nahum Goldmann and others who were terrified lest they offend the White House in general and Roosevelt in particular.

We hope to make the official launch announcement of the European Jewish Publication Society in the next four weeks.

FSW

■ ■ ■

10 January 1996

Dear Mr. Worms,

Thank you for your good wishes for the New Year – may I reciprocate them warmly, to you and your wife.

You ask me about Nahum Goldmann and Mr. Hayter. I think I can throw light on all this. Nahum Goldmann was the principal representative of World Zionism in America. From time to time he used to come and see me in the British Embassy, and chatted about the latest policies of the American Zionists, and similar topics. On this occasion, he came in order to say that the official Zionist organization disapproved of the demonstrations organized by Bergson (the son, or grandson, of *the* Rabbi Kook) – Bergson organized something which was known as "The March of the Rabbis" – marches to Washington to demand the opening of the gates of Palestine, steps towards the rescue of the Jews in the Nazi-occupied territories. He explained that the reason for disapproval was that the Zionist organization believed in cultivating good relations with important persons in the US Government, Congress and other influential bodies. They had had considerable success in this regard by the time he came to see me.

He knew that Roosevelt was infuriated by these marches, which denounced the American Government, the British Government, etc., for their failure to do anything about European Jews. He and the other Zionist leaders took the line that there was nothing which either America or Britain could do to alleviate the state of the Jews – it was clear that the Nazis intended to destroy them in one way or another (I cannot remember whether the crematoria were already known about at this time, I think probably they were), and demonstrations of this kind, while quite natural expressions of indignation and despair, antagonized a good many influential persons whom it was in the interests of Zionism to make allies, in order to secure their help in creating what at this time was known as the "Jewish Commonwealth" – the word "State" was never used. This, in a sense, was reasonable. Of course there was something awful about the fact that Jews in America didn't cry out as they could have done about the horrors in Europe – it is true that Roosevelt persuaded Stephen Wise not to spread information about the terrible events, which had been reported by the World Jewish Congress representative in the Geneva by the end of 1942 (I think).

What arguments the President used I do not know, but Wise was convinced that Jews, and in particular Zionists, had nothing to gain by demonstrations against American authorities (the British, of course, talked about the likelihood of this to excite the Arabs, whose acquiescence the Anglo-Americans needed) and had something to lose. In a sense this was an intelligible policy. What could the British or Americans in fact have done? It was quite clear that the Nazis were determined to exterminate the Jews – they wanted this more than any other single thing. If you remember, in even 1945, by January, February, March, when Soviet troops first entered Auschwitz, and British troops liberated Belsen, such Nazis as were still in charge of camps went on killing Jews. It is clear to me that they wanted to kill Jews more than they wanted to win the war – it was the centre of the entire Nazi enterprise, more than any other single objective.

Given this, what could the Allied governments have done? Protests were obviously useless; the two minutes' silence which Eden, as Foreign Secretary, asked the House of Commons to observe as an expression of grief and indignation at the persecution of the Jews, was no doubt a dignified act but had no practical significance.

There was a great deal of talk about the need to bomb the trains which carried Jewish victims to the gas ovens. I never myself believed in the utility of this (I think I was in a minority in this view), because if a train was bombed no doubt 300 Jews and 30 Nazi guards might be killed; but the trains would be rebuilt immediately – the entire policy of bombing traffic in Germany didn't work too well, and in this case the passion to keep the traffic to the camps going was overwhelmingly strong, so that I do not see that this could have done much good – as a demonstration, as a piece of symbolic action, perhaps – but whom was it intended to impress?

There is no doubt that the State Department was one hundred percent anti-Zionist – anti-Semitism played its part, of course. The same is true about the Foreign Office. There were, however, three members of the FO known to me who were not anti-Zionist – I knew of no others – they were my friend the late Sir Anthony Rumbold (son of one of the British ambassadors in Berlin at the beginning of the Nazi period), William Hayter (then a First Secretary in the British Embassy in Washington, later, as Sir William Hayter, British Ambassador in Moscow, then Warden of New College – and still, like me, alive), and – I cannot remember his name, the Principal Private Secretary to Eden, who later became Ambassador in Paris and a peer, and was by way of being a friend of Dr. Weizmann. Goldmann wanted me to convey to the relevant officials of the British Embassy that they, the Zionists, were not in favour of the violent demonstrations against the British Embassy, the White House, Congress, etc., which were then going on in Washington under the leadership of Bergson (who I think became a member of the Irgun). I duly reported this, and it no doubt gave some satisfaction to the British Embassy.

You speak as if these demonstrations did something which the silence of Stephen Wise and Co. failed to do. But what was that? I repeat again that it was shameful that there was no great cry of horror by the Jews – it might have done no good, but at least it would have been testimony to what was felt – but the practical consequences I do believe would have been zero. Hayter told me that he fully understood what the feelings of Jews must be about the horrors then going on in the Germany-occupied lands, and that he deeply sympathized; but that he did not know what either the British officials in America, or indeed Congress or the Government, could in practice do. Roosevelt, I think, was rather hard-hearted about the whole thing, and not the warm ally of Jews and Zionism which the American Jews fondly believed him to be. His last policies before he died were not favourable to the Zionist cause – as those of Truman were. The most interesting thing that Goldmann ever told me was that there was a secret Cabinet Committee which by 1944 had decided on the partition of Palestine between Jews and Arabs, and that this was to be kept secret until the end of the war. But that is another story, which I shall be glad to tell you if and when we meet.

IB

PS. If you do not agree with me about what Jews could have done during the war, and failed to do, do let me know – I should like to know your opinion. If you agree, then there is no need to answer this letter.

■ ■ ■

11 January 1995

Thank you so much for your illuminating letter concerning the guilt complex which the Allies, American and English Jewry should or should not have about their non-intervention during the Shoah.

You ask for my views. I need a little more time to think about this doom laden subject.

May I show your letter to David Morrison, the researcher I referred to in my letter?

FSW

■ ■ ■

1 February 1995

Dear Sir Isaiah,

In your letter of the 10th January you asked what my views were on the controversy whether or not the Allies should have bombed the railway lines leading to Auschwitz. You may recall that this arose from my reading of the manuscript of my friend, David Morrison's book on this subject where he recalled Nahum Goldmann's visit to you at the British Embassy.

I am not a professional historian; I am emotionally involved and probably the last person who is qualified to come up with an opinion based on facts. I have, however, passed on your comments to David Morrison who has written as follows:

"The most detailed treatment of the issue of bombing Auschwitz is in Wyman's "Abandonment of the Jews." He devotes an entire chapter to it. At the process level, the approach to this question is the same as the approach to the entire issue of the Nazi period – what were the choices and what choices were made by different groups and different individuals?

The bombing of Auschwitz, however, presents more difficulties than most for a number of reasons:

1. When the issue arose in 1944, the documentation of the magnitude of the extermination was massive and unchallenged.
2. The documentation of the callousness of the State Department and War Department vis-à-vis rescue efforts was clear and acknowledged. It was the threat of the exposure of this callousness in public debate in the Congress that in great part influenced Roosevelt to establish the War Refugees Board.
3. The Air Forces of the US and Great Britain had detailed maps of the area and were carrying out extensive bombing of industrial targets in the area; this is in direct contradiction to John McCloy's contention that bombing Auschwitz would be possible only by diversion of planes from important war operations.
4. The German war machine was a shadow of what it had been earlier in the war. In particular the German air force was

essentially out of the war – the Allies had unchallenged control of the skies.

5. The argument that bombing railway lines and bridges was of limited value was indeed an active argument during the war, but the weight of the evidence kept allied planes active in carrying out just such assignments again and again. By the summer of 1944, the Germans had little capacity to rebuild destroyed targets and certainly could not have kept Auschwitz at a killing capacity of 20,000 Jews a day, had it been hit from the air. Over 100,000 Hungarian Jews were killed at Auschwitz after the massive bombing of the immediate area in August of 1944.

6. In September 1944 the United States diverted a large number of heavy bombers to an airdrop of supplies over Warsaw to help partisans there, despite the fact that it was known they were doomed. An Air Force memorandum acknowledged that planes needed for the war would be lost for several days. Wyman cites the final paragraph of the Air Force report justifying the mission "despite the tangible cost which far outweighed the tangible results… America kept faith with its Ally." Why was the moral imperative to give support to a small group of Polish partisans greater than the imperative to save Jewish lives, especially given that the bombing of Auschwitz would have required no diversion of planes already in action in the area, whereas the Warsaw operation completely diverted a large number of planes from the war effort for over a week?

Whilst writing to you I take the opportunity of enclosing the European Jewish Publication Society's press release.

ISW

6 November 1955

Della and I were delighted to see you looking so hale and hearty at last Thursday's reception of the European Jewish Publication Society. Thank you for your encouragement without which Peter Halban and I would never have engaged in this enterprise.

Thank you also for having agreed in principle that I may quote extracts from our correspondence in my book which has been provisionally entitled "Frankfurt, London and Jerusalem." I am enclosing copies of the relevant letters herewith for your approval. It would mean a tremendous amount to me to be allowed to quote some of your obiter dicta.

FSW

■ ■ ■

9 November 1995

Dear Mr. Worms,

Thank you for your letter. I have made a very few trivial corrections to the tss of my letters, and marked two passages for omission – these are too obviously offensive (and have little relevance to the rest) and could cause pain to survivors.

Otherwise it all seems perfectly OK if you wish to use any excerpts that could be useful.

I was very glad to be present at that very nice meeting, which I thought went very well.

IB

■ ■ ■

15 November 1995

Thanks you so much for your letter of the 9th November. I am deeply grateful for your permission to allow me, in due course, to quote from some of your letters.

I spent the last weekend in Frankfurt, not by choice, but because I was asked to speak on the occasion of the 30th anniversary of the re-establishment of Maccabi in Germany.

In your letter of the 30th December 1987 you asked "whether the German Jewish community was vanishing?" At that time I was ambivalent. We were all rather hoping that they would be a passing phenomenon. The 30,000 in 1987 are now over 60,000, mainly due to the influx of Russian Jews. They are an interesting lot. By choice they would probably prefer to assimilate and disappear but in reality the inherent German intolerance of anybody who speaks their language with a foreign accent leads to a cohesion of the many minorities that are now *Gästarbeiter*. It is for this reason only that the Jewish Community is swelling and is now sufficiently established to build its own infrastructure such as schools and new synagogues.

It may be difficult to understand for some of us but it is in fact history repeating itself for the fourth time in the last eight hundred years.

FSW

12 August 1996

Dear Mr. Worms,

Sir Isaiah Berlin is still abroad, but I read him your letter, and he asked me to say that he was very touched by it, looks forward greatly to reading your book, and has longed to call you "Fred" but hasn't dared!

Pat Utechin, Secretary to Sir Isaiah Berlin

25 August 1996 *(in handwriting)*

Dear Fred

Thank you so much for your book. Don't sit on spilkes (Yiddish for in Russian SHPILVI = pins)

- I'll take your book to Italy tomorrow for my fortnight there – I am sure I shall love reading it – I'll take no other book.

Yours,
Isaiah

■ ■ ■

23 October 1996

Dear Isaiah

I should like to associate myself strongly with the sentiments which you, Immanuel Jakobovits, Martin Gilbert and Peter Levy have expressed in your letter to Mr. Netanyahu.

Having just spent a month in Israel, one is deeply troubled by the prevailing atmosphere of depression on the one hand and triumphalism on the other. Della and I returned to Jerusalem after a visit to friends in one of the moshavim in the Judean mountains more or less at the same time as the Prime Minister's cavalcade of cars swept in from the airport after his visit to Washington. The highway was lined by tens of thousands of his supporters holding up posters "Kol Hakavod, Bibi" and similar encouraging slogans. Needless to say that many of the men wore either knitted or black kipot.

To my sorrow I have found that engaging in a rational debate with otherwise high intelligent and sensible Likud friends is a wasted effort. The sense of self-righteousness is palpable. Arguments that this Government has undone in one hundred days what Rabin and Peres built up carefully over four years cut no ice. The growing isolationalism of Israel and the already manifest slow-down in investment by large international concerns does not bother them. God and Bibi are on their side!

There is a school of thought, probably optimistic, which believes that Mr. Netanyahu is playing a devilishly clever game which will bring about the following scenario: When, after the American elections, the Prime Minister will be compelled to make the concessions which he categorically at this stage says he will not make, the right wing coalition will collapse and he will then be able to form a National Unity Government with Peres as the Foreign Minister.

My own gut feeling is that Mr. Netanyahu is not devilishly clever but naïve and inexperienced, and if he carries on in his way he will do irreparable damage to the State of Israel. Only time will tell.

Speaking personally, with three daughters and ten grandchildren, all in Jerusalem, I have more than an academic interest in the peace process.

I trust you had an enjoyable holiday in Italy. We have just come back from a few days in Florence and Fiesole.

Fred

■ ■ ■

12 December 1996

I was delighted to learn at a meeting I had yesterday with the emissary of Rabbi Steinsaltz that you have established a close personal relationship with our friend, Adin. He is truly a remarkable man, ecumenical in the sense of the late Rav Avraham Isaac Kook, tolerant with those who disagree with him and contemptuous of the haredim who have tried to put him into a straight-jacket without success. He has done more for the study of Talmud with his enormous effort of translating it into modern Hebrew, English, Russian, Spanish and French than anybody since Rashi.

He also has a mischievous sense of humour, and like you and me, loves a little rechilut. [Ed. gossip] The fact that he attracts self-proclaimed agnostics like Felix Posen, who went with him to China, speaks for itself!

I have supported the Rabbi's publications for a number of years and have now agreed to host a dinner which is due to take place in London on Monday the 10th March. I understand that you have also been made aware of this date and that you have tentatively agreed to come along. I would be delighted if you could confirm this since your presence would be an additional attraction for our potential clientele.

Fred

■ ■ ■

10 February 1997

Dear Isaiah,

The Hebrew University, in partnership with Mort Mandel (one of the principal funders), Professor Seymour Fox and Alan Hoffmann (who happens to be my son-in-law) have run an educational project for a number of years under the title of "Jerusalem Fellows." The number is limited to 20 at any one time. They undergo intensive training in Jerusalem for a period of two years and they are expected to return to their country of origin for a minimum of five years to occupy senior positions in Jewish Education.

The current crop of 20 arrived in London last week to look at the educational infrastructure that we have in this country. They came to my office to be briefed and I found them to be quite outstanding. The majority already had their Ph.D.s but all of them were passionately involved in their vocation. Conspicuous by their absence were participants from the UK. There aren't any! It is a reflection of the arid landscape that applies to Jewish education in this country.

When Ahad Ha'am came to London in 1911 he arrived at a similar conclusion:

> The Anglo-Jewish establishment startled him with its stolid, serenely unbookish conservatism: he claimed that it was simply too painful to speak about Anglo-Jewry. Repeatedly once he settled there, he likened the community to a cemetery – serene, comfortable, dotted with grand artefacts and yet devoid of the requisite inner substance or human tension that makes life bearable

(I am quoting from Zipperstein's book). The scene is not quite so bad today but with the abysmal failure and demise of Jewish Continuity Mark I we have to build from scratch. Mark II with its cross-community instead of ultra-Orthodox leadership stands a much better chance and those of us, like Felix Posen and myself, who would disassociate ourselves from Mark I are willing to support its successor.

The Jerusalem Fellows also visited North London Collegiate School, one of the best girls' public schools in the country with quite a large contingent of Jewish girls. My three daughters went there before they made aliya.

I very much look forward to seeing you at the Steinsaltz Dinner on the 9th March

Fred

Berlin was unable to attend the Steinsaltz dinner. This last letter concludes the correspondence between Berlin and Fred Worms. Sir Isaiah Berlin died at his home in Oxford on 5 November, 1997.

All letters from Isaiah Berlin courtesy of The Isaiah Berlin Literary Trust.

Sport – and the Jewish Question

"Muscular Judaism"

Organized Jewish sport began only at the end of the 19th century. For 3,000 years – notwithstanding the young David hurling a stone at Goliath, and King Saul throwing a javelin at his son Jonathan – games for the sake of health and recreation were not part of the Jewish way of life.

There was a time when, under Greek and Seleucid influence, sports nearly caught on. Alexander the Great had the good sense not to interfere with the religions of his subjects. His rule on the whole was benign. The upper classes, including the High Priests, rather enjoyed the civilized way of life of the Greeks.

Greek sport competitions, performed by nude males, introduced a startling novelty to the local populations. Young Jewish men adopted many Hellenistic customs, participating enthusiastically in sports, and some went so far as to have a reverse foreskin operation in order to look the same as their Greek counterparts.

When Antiochus began to slaughter Jews and desecrated the Temple in 167 BC Mattathias the Hasmonean, his son Judah the Maccabee and brothers, led the successful rebellion, which is today commemorated in the festival of Hanuka. The rabbis pointed out, as had the prophets before them, that aping one's masters would quickly lead to idolatry and assimilation. This deep prejudice was strengthened by the subsequent conduct of the Roman conquerors. Their penchant for setting lions against gladiators and slaves against wild animals in their stadia and amphitheatres represented a spectator-sport, which was dramatically repugnant to the ethos of both Judaism and newly-emerging Christianity. Sport became synonymous with the hated customs of non-Jews and acquired a highly negative image which prevailed for 2,000 years.

In subsequent centuries, sport became the privilege of the leisured classes, particularly landowners. There was hardly an opportunity for the Jewish merchant to joust, nor were there Jewish knights. Once ghettos were established in Europe and the rabbis ruled supreme, the most one could hope for was to follow Maimonides injunction to teach one's child to swim – not in order to engage in competitions but to preserve life.

There were some exceptions to the rule. There are references in Jewish sources to ball games, fencing and horse-riding in Spain and Provence during the Middle Ages. The *Shulhan Arukh* (Rabbi Joseph Caro's guide to the Jewish way of life), published in the mid 16th century, discussed whether ball games were permitted on the Sabbath and festivals. It must have had some contemporary relevance since in the same century, Rudolph II forbade fencing competitions between Gentiles and Jews in Germany.

At the end of the 18th century, a young Jewish prizefighter, Daniel Mendoza, became boxing champion of England and was accorded royal patronage. It was the beginning of a phenomenon whereby ambitious young men from an underprivileged minority could fight their way to a better life.

The Zionist leader Max Nordau, put it well when he coined the phrase *Muskel Judentum* ("Muscular Judaism'") at the Fifth Zionist Congress in 1901: "Our history tells us that Jews used to be strong and muscular, but for a long time we have been concerned only with physical self-denial. In the narrow streets of the ghetto we forgot to exercise and stand straight. The weight has now been lifted; our will is free. No-one will now prevent us from attending to our physical recovery; the more Jews achieve in various branches of sport, the greater will be their self-confidence and self-respect."

Nordau himself was a contradiction in terms. Hungarian-born, he was a classic example of the Jews of the Enlightenment. His father was an Orthodox rabbi called Sudfeld ("Southfield"). When Nordau was 18, he rebelled against religion, called it a big lie, and devoted the rest of his life to pamphleteering against it. He became a doctor and journalist and never engaged in sport himself. He changed his name, in clear rebellion against his father, to Nordau ("Northmeadow"). He was a devoted follower of Theodor Herzl and was a co-founder of the World Zionist Organization.

When he made his famous clarion call, he was not really such a revolutionary as was generally thought. As a result of the Enlightenment in 19th century Europe, Jewish students at German, Austrian and Czech universities already wished to emulate the sporting prowess of their fellow students. They were barred from the fraternities which engaged in duelling. It was illegal to duel against a Jew or to accept a challenge from a Jew. It was not surprising, therefore, that the 1880s and the 1890s saw a proliferation of Jewish student societies at such universities as Berlin, Heidelberg, Munich, Prague and Vienna. They were the precursors of the Jewish golf and yachting clubs which were formed in English-speaking countries decades later.

In 1885, 400 out of 1,100 members of the Wiener Turnverein (Vienna Gymnastic Club) were Jewish, and in 1896, six Jewish athletes won 13 medals at the first Olympic games of the modern era in Athens.

The first all-Jewish sports club was founded in Budapest in 1888. It was followed by one in Constantinople in 1895, set up mainly by German and Viennese Jews living there at the time, and the first one to adopt the name "Maccabi," adopted from the Maccabees of old. Bar Kochba Berlin (commemorating in its name, the Second Jewish Revolt led by Simon Bar Kochba against the Romans in 132-5 AD), was formed in 1898 and thereafter the flood-gates opened. At the onset of the First World War in 1914, there were scores of Jewish sports clubs in Germany, Hungary, Switzerland, Yugoslavia, Russia and Poland. In Palestine, the first club was formed in Jaffa in 1906. By 1903, a roof organization called Die Judische Turnerschaft had been created.

Jewish sport began in Russia in Odessa in 1913, when the Hebrew Sports Club was formed, but in 1923, Jewish sports clubs were banned in Russia. In spite of this proscription by the Bolsheviks, many underground clubs sprang up in defiance. In the Baltic countries, Jewish athletic clubs were formed in Kovno, Vilna and Riga. A Remembrance Book can be found in the archives of the Pierre Gildesgame Museum in

Kfar Hamaccabiah, Ramat Gan, which lists, with painful details, many of these organizations which thrived and subsequently perished under Nazi rule.

In 1921, the Maccabi World Union (MWU) was founded in Carlsbad, Czechoslovakia, with its headquarters in Berlin. Many of these clubs prospered and produced world-class competitors. An outstanding example was Hakoah ("Strength") Vienna. Founded in 1909, it dominated Austrian sports until the Nazis closed it down. When their football team went to New York in the 1920s, it attracted the largest spectator crowd that had ever been seen there. Its weightlifting, swimming, water polo and football achievements were only equalled by those of Bar Kochba Berlin on the running track.

The headquarters of the MWU were transferred to London in 1937. At that time, the Union consisted of more than 40 national organizations, with a membership approaching 200,000. The clubs in the very countries from which the movement originated were doomed to extinction as the Nazi jackboot trampled first on German Maccabi; then in rapid succession, the Austrian, Czech and Polish clubs were forced to close. In 1947, there was a traumatic meeting of the MWU in Basel with the survivors of the camps, the emaciated remnant of the millions who had perished.

Under the indefatigable chairmanship of Pierre Gildesgame (an Anglo-Jewish industrialist of enormous charisma who was born in Poland, educated in Belgium and who died in London in 1982,) national organizations were re-established in Austria, Belgium, Denmark, Finland, France and Italy, to join forces with the United Kingdom, Switzerland and Sweden, whose Maccabiah clubs had survived the war intact.

The year 1948 witnessed further growth as clubs in Paris, Lyon and Metz were re-established, and the first Maccabi World Congress in Israel was held after the headquarters were transferred from London to Tel Aviv. Attending were representatives of Great Britain, Switzerland, France, Czechoslovakia, Argentina, Bolivia and the British and American zones of Germany.

In 1949, the Maccabi clubs in Argentina, Uruguay, Brazil and Chile formed the CLAM (Latin American Maccabi Confederation) that later included the rest of the Maccabi organizations of South and Central America and Mexico. These are, in effect, large Jewish sporting and social clubs, which serve as a focal point for the local Jewish communities.

The *yishuv* (pre-state Jewish community of Palestine) had enjoyed an unbroken tradition of sports since the establishment of the Rishon LeZion Club in 1906. It was founded in Jaffa by Dr. Leo Cohen, a Russian physician who worked at the local Jewish hospital. By 1912, they had a wide range of activities and renamed themselves the Maccabi Sports Society.

In 1941, a Maccabi company was formed in the Buffs regiment of the British Army, with the soldiers and many of the officers being drawn from the Maccabi clubs in Palestine.

Maccabi has played a leading part in placing Israel firmly on the international sporting scene. Football is the most popular national sport, followed closely by basketball in which Maccabi Tel Aviv has won the European Championship five times. Judo, swimming, sailing and tennis have produced world-class athletes.

Maccabi also sponsors a youth movement known as *Maccabi Tsa'ir* ("Young Maccabi") (from age nine to 18), which was founded in 1929 in Bratislava. It organizes sporting events, nature hikes, local history seminars, and is active in the field of social welfare. It has thousands of young members throughout the world, and holds regular national gatherings and competitions.

Maccabi sports clubs have been re-established in Russia and in other countries of the former Soviet Union and the former Communist bloc. Regional games take place in Europe, Australia, South Africa, Canada, the USA and Latin America at regular intervals.

The structure that has evolved over the years provides for local Maccabi clubs to be affiliated to a national organization, which, in turn, forms part of six regional confederations; Israel, Europe, Latin America, Australia, South Africa, North America.

The influential US Sports Committee for Israel, with representatives in virtually every sizable Jewish community, officially changed its name to Maccabi USA in 1996, thus joining their Canadian neighbours who have played a leading part with the MWU for several decades.

South African Maccabi dates to 1934. Shortly after its formation it was visited by Professor Selig Brodetsky, president of the MWU (and president of the Hebrew University of Jerusalem from 1949–1952). Their outstanding organizational capabilities manifested themselves immediately by sending a team to the Second Maccabiah in 1935, which, prior to its departure, was presented to the prime minister of South Africa, General James Hertzog who stated: "I cannot but rejoice at the great national movement amongst the Jewish people which would ensure to them their ancient heritage and inspire them with their national pride to which they are so justly entitled."

After the Second World War, Maccabi became a leading component of the South African Zionist Organization. Great technical difficulties had to be overcome during subsequent Maccabiah Games, since apartheid South Africa was banned by the International Olympic Committee from all international sports events. Nevertheless, the remarkable sporting prowess of South Africa Jewry was manifest at every Maccabiah, albeit sometimes in unofficial colours.

It is easy to forget that the astonishing growth of Australian Jewry is largely a post-World War II phenomenon, when Jews from Europe, and later from South Africa, settled there. Sports – Australia's overwhelming national pastime – began among the Jewish community in an organized fashion in 1920, although local activities commenced as early as 1912. The Australian *Jewish Herald* wrote in January, 1921: "Great events often have modest beginnings." The reference was to three young Jewish sports clubs in New South Wales, Victoria and Western Australia. A cricket match between Melbourne and Sydney in December, 1924, became the forerunner of the Annual Sports Carnival, in which many hundreds of competitors participate to this day. With a prosperous and well-organised Jewish population in excess of 100,000, and with outstanding Jewish schools, the Australian Maccabi confederation is one of the main bulwarks of World Maccabi. The rift caused by the bridge disaster (see page 181) is, hopefully, well behind us.

Germany deserves a special mention – both from the negative and positive point of view. My personal recollections as a member of Bar Kochba, Frankfurt, are roseate in retrospect, probably because I left for Britain at the beginning of 1937, aged 16, thus escaping the worst excesses of the Nazis and the closing of the Jewish clubs. 1936 was the year of the Berlin Olympics. Hitler was determined to make this a vast propaganda exercise for the Third Reich and to demonstrate the physical superiority of the Aryan race. Blatant anti-Semitism, including organized riots, were toned down in 1936, a condition demanded by the Olympic Committee.

In 1972, the Games were awarded again to the new post-war Germany. Eleven Israeli athletes and coaches were killed by Arab terrorists in the Olympic village in Munich. At these games, the Jewish swimmer, Mark Spitz, won seven gold medals for the USA (at the age of 15, in 1965, he had won three gold medals at the Seventh Maccabiah). Disaster met triumph in one week.

In 1965, the MWU reconstituted the Maccabi organization in Germany. The ceremony was held in Düsseldorf after much soul-searching. At that time there were less than 30,000 Jews in Germany, ostensibly with their suitcases packed. It was felt that we had a duty to the younger generation to keep them in a Jewish environment. In October, 1998, I travelled to Berlin to share in the 100th anniversary celebrations of the thriving Bar Kochba Berlin. Fate had gone full circle.

The Maccabiah Games is the unifying motivator for Jewish sportsmen and women throughout the world. Held every four years in Israel, it is open to all Jewish sports organizations including Hapoel, Betar, Elizur, the university sports associations, etc.

The First Maccabiah was held in Palestine in 1932 in North Tel Aviv at the then Levant Fair grounds. Three hundred and ninety athletes from 14 countries, including Syria and Egypt, participated. The Second Maccabiah, in 1935, became known at the "Aliya Maccabiah" with 1,350 athletes from 28 countries, including Germany. At a time when the British mandatory powers imposed severe difficulties on many of the athletes – particularly those from Germany – several "forgot" to return home. Lord Melchett, then president of the MWU led the opening parade with Tel Aviv Mayor Meir Dizengoff, on white horses.

The Third Maccabiah (the first in the new state of Israel) was held in 1950 with the participation of 19 countries. Competitors slept in tents on the Tel Aviv beachfront (where the Hilton Hotel now stands), offering rather different accommodation.

The new Ramat Gan National Sports Stadium was the venue of the Fourth Maccabiah in 1953, with 50,000 spectators attending the opening ceremony. At the Fifth Maccabiah in 1957, Kfar Hamaccabiah, the newly-established athlete's village was opened on a 20-acre site. Today this is a hotel and convention centre, with the largest function hall in Israel, a country club with 14 tennis courts, four swimming pools, squash and gym halls, a seminar centre, and the Pierre Gildesgame Sports Museum, in which the movement's archives are kept.

Recognition of the Maccabiah Games as a sports event of international standing was given by the Olympic Committee in time for the Sixth Maccabiah in 1961. At the Bar Mitzvah Maccabiah (the 13th) in 1989, athletes from the former Soviet Union took part for the first time, a truly remarkable turn of the sporting wheel.

All augured well for the biggest-ever Maccabiah, the 15th, which took place in 1997. Over 5,000 athletes were lined up on the far side of the Yarkon River running alongside the Ramat Gan Stadium, which was packed to its 55,000 capacity. We were standing in front of the VIP box to receive the president of Israel, Ezer Weizman, who was to enter in the traditional motorcade. There was an inexplicable delay. Then rumours filtered through of the collapsing of the footbridge across the Yarkon River over which the athletes were to enter the stadium, and which was to result in the deaths of four Australian athletes and 70 injured, some very seriously, among members of the Austrian and Australian teams, the first two teams to cross the bridge. In the subsequent trial, four defendants received prison sentences. The fact that the Yarkon was a lethal cesspool of toxic chemicals was the major cause of the deaths and injuries. This was an overwhelming disaster, unprecedented in the annals of the Maccabi movement, which has suffered from the consequences ever since. The wound is healing slowly but will leave a permanent scar.

The 16th Maccabiah, due to take place in July 2001 during the height of the Palestinian Intifada, was again going to become the largest ever with record participation and the first where both the opening and closing ceremonies were due to take place in Jerusalem. Years of preparation threatened to be frustrated when the USA, Canada and Great Britain, followed by other countries, pulled out. As terrorist atrocities mounted and insurance companies withdrew cover, it was felt by many athletes and Maccabi leaders that they could not send athletes whose safe return they could not guarantee.

The Israeli press was unanimous in condemning what at best was seen as a lack of solidarity. Actually, cancellation was fiercely opposed by the MWU leadership in Ramat Gan. An emergency meeting of the international leaders met five weeks before the scheduled opening. The meeting was addressed by the Israeli Minister of Sports and Culture, who pleaded in the name of the prime minister that, in spite of the situation, the games should proceed.

In the event, the Maccabiah took place; the countries that had pulled out, returned, and the opening and closing ceremonies were held as scheduled at the Teddy Stadium and at the Sultan's Pool in Jerusalem. Some 2,200 athletes came from overseas, about half of the original number and no sports records were broken, but the continuity of the Maccabiah and the loyalty of Maccabi to Israel was assured, as is the place of sporting activities both in Israel and in Jewish communities worldwide.

The next Maccabiah is due to take place in 2013 and the opening ceremony will be at the enlarged Teddy Stadium in Jerusalem. The Kfar Hamaccabiah has been vastly improved. The large new building has suites only, a large reception area, the biggest hotel lobby in Israel and the Kevahazi Synagogue and the Worms Business Centre. The latter is available for people who need secretarial assistance, meeting and eating facilities if they join this elegant club.

This article was originally published in Ariel: The Israel Review of Arts and Letters, *in Spring, 2002, and is reproduced here by permission.*

Address to the 26th Congress of the Maccabi World Union, May 2010

Maccabim and Maccabiot from the four corners of the earth, this is my last address as your honorary president. After serving for quite a number of years as chairman of the European Maccabi Federation, I became president of the MWU 1982-86, chairman of the board of Kfar Maccabiah, 1987-94 and honorary president, 1995-2010.

I look back with nostalgia to 1956 when Mayor Abraham Krinitzi of Ramat Gan, Pierre Gildesgame, Aron Netanel, myself and one or two others founded the Kfar Hamaccabiah without any money whatsoever. What we had was *hitlahavut* ("enthusiasm") and *bitahon* ("confidence"). The paradise in which we find ourselves today, after many difficult years is a tribute to the dedicated leadership of the movement over the last 54 years.

It has been my past practice to take a global view of Maccabi within world Jewry and I shall do the same today. Alas, world Jewry today is very unpopular; it says in the Torah, *ve'haaretz tishkot arbaim shana* ("and there will be peace in the Land for 40 years"). In biblical times when there was no strife for 40 years, it was worth recording. Now, after the Holocaust, we have had more or less 40 years of relative peace. The European nations were embarrassed, but those days are over, and good old fashioned anti-Semitism is back in vogue. Israel has become the scapegoat for everything that has gone wrong in the Middle East. In the meantime, I think we can look upon ourselves as tremendous achievers.

First of all, Jews, form less than two percent of the world's population. However, we have 54 percent of the world chess champions, 27 percent of the Nobel Prize winners and 31 percent of the Nobel medical laureates. In the United States, Jews are two percent of the population but they have 37 percent of the academy awards, they give 36 percent of national philanthropy, and are 51 percent of Pulitzer Prize winners. However of the 5.2 million Jews in the United States, only 3.4 million are affiliated to a Jewish organization. The rest have no formal attachment to Judaism; this is one of our biggest challenges to day – to pull them back.

Israel has more high-tech start-ups than any other country in the world except the United States. It is the only country which finished 2009 with more trees than it started with. The plan to have a tree for every Jew on the planet, 13 million, is on the way. Israel has more companies on NASDAQ which is a smaller Wall Street stock exchange than all the Europeans and Asians combined.

Why is this not appreciated in the rest of the world? First of all, as you can see, there is a big constituent of jealousy and envy to the fact that Jews are high achievers. We have always laid the biggest emphasis on education. Not just Jewish education, but secular education as well.

Some members of the prejudiced United Nations claim that Israel is an "apartheid state." This is the biggest Goebbels lie imaginable. I live in Jerusalem. From our balcony we have a wonderful view of the old city. What do I see first thing in the morning? Two towers, one a church the other a mosque. In the evening we see 17 mosques, and their flashing green lights. Is there one synagogue in Jordan or Iraq or Saudi Arabia? You go to an Israeli hospital, and you see wards filled with Arab men and women. Sometimes, they share a ward with Israelis, which is very embarrassing because when the Arabs visit, 15 come at the same time. You go on a Friday night to Gan Hapa'amon, the Liberty Bell Gardens in Jerusalem and the basketball players on Friday night are Arabs. During the week it's mixed.

When Ariel Sharon unilaterally, without asking for any compensating gesture, vacated Gaza, one would have expected the world community to applaud for giving up voluntarily land which we conquered, but what happened? The Palestinians took over the beautiful glass houses which were the biggest source of income for Gaza, for out of season fruits and flowers exported all over the world. Israel offered to export them for the Palestinians without making a charge. The first thing they did was smash it all up. The next thing they did was ignore the offer by American Jews to give money to erect buildings, so that the refugees could be taken out of the camps. It was their determination to keep their people in misery and bring them up as haters of Jews. One of the biggest dangers which we see today is that 42 percent of the Palestinians in Gaza and the West Bank are under 15 and all of these kids are brought up with the image of Jews equivalent to the devil.

Now what is so special about today? Not that I am retiring, but it is the 2nd of May. And today is the 150th anniversary of Herzl's birth date. Exactly today, the 2nd of May. The man who had the vision of *im tirzu ein zo agada* – "If you wish it, it is no dream." Herzl chose London for the Fourth Zionist Congress because he said, Britain was free of anti-Semitism. One wonders what he would think of the situation today. Jews are not safe to wear a *kipa* in public, our university students are physically threatened and at the famous Oxford and Cambridge Union debates, Israeli speakers are shouted down. The rest of Europe has jumped on the academic boycott bandwagon.

Today, Israel is 76 percent Jewish, 16 percent Muslim, and two percent Christians, who suffer under the Muslims, and six percent others. Israel today is an example of freedom of speech. It is the outpost of European and American culture, without which the Middle East would be a total disaster.

My friends, Maccabi has an enormous responsibility because we have the youngsters. They are the ones who can influence the universities. Hillel in England has prepared a booklet "How our students can stand up against anti-Semitism on campus."

Having made aliya and living in Jerusalem, with its golden glow, its culture and unique atmosphere, I thank the Almighty for having given Della and me the *zechut* ("privilege") of dwelling in the midst of our children, grandchildren and great-grandchildren. As we complete each of the readings of the books of the Torah, we stand up and call in unison *hazak, hazak ve'nithazek* – "Be strong , be strong and we will strengthen each other."

Book Reviews

Fred Worms has been a prolific writer of book review over the years and a selection of these follow.

Thelma Ruby and Peter Frye:
"Double or Nothing." Janus Publishing Company, 1997

When, in January 1995, with the encouragement of Sir Isaiah Berlin, I formed the European Jewish Publication Society together with six generous friends, one could not have foreseen how much it was really needed. The Society's aim has been to promote through grants and subsidies the publication of manuscripts on Jewish subjects of literary, educational or historical interest that would not have been commercially viable. Holocaust literature is no longer fashionable. Publishers who have to earn their keep shy away from it. Amongst the ten books that have seen so far the light of day are three from camp survivors. The Holocaust denial industry must be fought all the way whilst eyewitnesses are still with us.

Fortunately, there is also a more felicitous side to our endeavours. "Double or Nothing," the joint autobiography of Thelma Ruby and Peter Frye, is an encomium to marital bliss, albeit beginning in middle age only, with Israel as the catalyst.

Thelma comes from a sheltered, Orthodox Leeds family. Her father was Louis Wigoder, a prosperous dentist. Her mother was an actress on the music hall stage. Thelma followed in her footsteps. With enormous gusto and joie-de-vivre she threw herself into this notoriously unstable profession. She worked with Orson Welles, Tyrone Power, Judy Dench, Paul Eddington, Chaim Topol and many others shedding, alas, her traditional Judaism on the way.

Peter came from a deprived agnostic background in Canada. His family was closer to Stalin than the Almighty. He had a desperately poor early life, queuing at soup kitchens and sleeping in doss houses in New York. He persevered and succeeded and lived for the stage as an actor, designer, producer and director. Amongst his pupils were Lee Marvin, Walter Matthau, Rod Steiger, Harry Belafonte and Elaine Stritch. He had a powerful personality, great sense of humour and love of his fellow men. Sadly, he became the typical McCarthy victim. Having fought in the Spanish Civil War, he stuck his neck out on innumerable occasions. In 1952 he narrowly escaped indictment.

He married Thelma in 1970; they rediscovered their Judaism, worked wonders for the Tel Aviv stage and lived a blissfully contented life until Peter died in 1991. These bare bones are fleshed out with marvellous anecdotes and tall tales. This book is a record of the taped conversations between the two. It was edited by Thelma after Peter's death. It does not claim to be a literary masterpiece. What went informally into the tape recorder came equally informally out of it, yet it makes for absorbing reading.

What a pleasure it is for a change to participate in this joyous saga of two happy Jewish adventurers. Let me finish by quoting from the epilogue: "Three weeks before [Peter] died, during a sleepless night he had scribbled a note to me, now I have it framed and hanging beside my bed. It says, 'For Thelma. I just want you to know that every night before I go to sleep I say to myself: I hope she knows how much I love her and cherish her, my beautiful, talented, generous bubaleh, vaibeleh, my angel... dein mann, Pinye.'"

Amos Oz:
"A Tale of Love and Darkness"

Chatto and Windus, London, 2005

Amos Oz (born Amos Klausner) lives in Arad. He prefers the desert to Tel Aviv and Jerusalem. He is 65 years old and happily married, having achieved the status of a literary and political icon. He lectures at Ben Gurion University and enjoys the accolades that are flowing in. *The Guardian* calls him "a writer of revelatory genius."

This autobiography covers three generations over a period of one hundred years, drawing on the memories of grandparents, parents, uncles and especially loquacious aunts with total recall. These survivor generations reached Palestine under the turbulent British Mandate and lived through the War of Independence and the creation of the State.

Nicholas de Lange, the Cambridge don who translated the book from the original Hebrew, did a first-class job but some of the transliteration is irritating: Tsvi instead of Zvi; Shimon Hazadik becomes Simon the Righteous; Good Sabbath for Shabbat Shalom, etc. The absence of an index of names is a serious drawback.

Amos' highly educated parents – his father worked in 16 languages, his mother in five – had an uneasy relationship. The fastidious, elegant Mrs. Klausner suffered under her garrulous husband and his unceasing, didactic chatter. He did not have an academic degree until the end of his life and had to be content to work as a librarian at the National Library, then housed at Terra Sancta, whilst Mount Scopus was under Arab control. Amos born in 1939, was their adored wunderkind. The lonely only child had remarkable powers of observation, rivalling Proust's gift of describing minutiae.

Whilst there are many moments of sheer delight, poetically described, the darkness of the title flows from the suicide of Mrs. Klausner at the age of 38, when Amos was 12 years old. It is this heavy shadow that predominates. The book is an effort to clear his "guilty" conscience, a mental catharsis to lay the ghost, which alas stays right to the end.

To write about this superb book and to paraphrase its contents would be presumptuous. This is why I have allowed the author to speak mainly for himself. On Shabbat afternoons, Amos and his parents would leave their one and a half room basement flat beyond Geula to visit Professor and Mrs. Klausner in Talpiot. This ritual walk is described in the great detail, progressing through Mea Shearim, past the Bikur Holim Hospital on Strauss Street, into Jaffa Street, to Yemin Moshe, beyond which was no-man's land. To the reader familiar with Jerusalem, this is a joyous recall of beloved routes. His father, with his encyclopaedic knowledge, explained the history of every public building, the origin of street names and why one day they would like to live in leafy Rehavia.

It reminds me of Bernard Levin's book, "A Walk up Fifth Avenue," or Graham Greene's "Travels with my Aunt," where the peregrination was merely the framework for airing any subject which came into their head. Having crossed no-man's land, they finally reached Talpiot, where Joseph Klausner and his wife held their salon with leading intellectual and artists.

Professor Klausner was one of the most respected personalities of the Jewish community of Jerusalem at that time, a brilliant lecturer and a winner of the Israel Prize; he was also the uncle of Amos' father.

Uncle Joseph had a penchant for putting emotional inscriptions in books: each year, from the time I was nine or ten, he gave me a volume of the Children's Encyclopaedia, in one of which he wrote, in letters that slanted slightly backward, as though recoiling:

To my clever and hardworking
Little Amos
With heartfelt hopes
That he will grow up to be a credit
to his people
from
Uncle Joseph
Jerusalem-Talpiot, Lag Ba-Omer, 5710

The ancestral history on both sides, going back to Poland and Ukraine, shows prosperous families imbued with *haskala* and adherents of Jabotinsky and Trumpeldor. The immigrant generation revered Menachem Begin and looked upon the kibbutzim as Communist imposters.

Amos had relatively uneventful school years at the Tachkemoni school and the Rehavia Gymnasium, spending most of his time reading any book he could get hold of, giving himself a quasi-pre-university education. His mother's clinical depression hung heavily over the teenager who had lived through the siege of Jerusalem and the War of Independence – he was yearning for a new life amongst the muscular *halutzim* ("pioneers") who he thought never picked up a book. He rebelled against his background, changed his name from Klausner to Oz ("Courage") and became a socialist.

> I was about fifteen when I went to Hulda, two and a half years after my mother's death: a paleface among the suntanned, a skinny youth among well-built giants, a tireless chatterbox among the taciturn, a versifier among agricultural labourers. All my new classmates had a healthy mind in a healthy body, only I had a dreamy mind in an almost transparent body. Worse still, I was caught a couple of times sitting in out-of-the-way corners of the Kibbutz trying to paint water-colours. Or hiding in the study room behind the newspaper room on the ground floor of Herzl House, scribbling away. A McCarthyite rumour soon went round that I was somehow connected to the Herut Party, that I had grown up in a Revisionist family, and I was suspected of having obscure links with the hated demagogue Menachem Begin, the arch-enemy of the Labour Movement. In short, a twisted upbringing and irreparably screwed-up genes. The fact that I had come to Hulda because I had rebelled against my father and his family did not help me. I was not given credit for being a renegade from Herut.

His rampant inferiority complex soured his early years on Kibbutz Hulda:

> In vain did I endeavour to excel in farm work and fail at school. In vain did I grill myself like steak in my efforts to be as brown as the rest of them. In vain did I show myself in the Current Affairs Discussion Group to be the most socialist socialist in Hulda, if not in the entire working class. Nothing helped me: for them I was some kind of alien, and so my classmates harassed me pitilessly to

make me give up my strange ways and become a normal person like them.

As for me, I took it all with humility, because I knew that the process of getting Jerusalem out of my system and my pangs of re-birth rightly entailed suffering. I considered the practical jokes and the humiliation justified not because I was suffering from some inferiority complex but because I really was inferior. They, those solidly-built boys scorched by dust and sun and those proud-walking girls, were the salt of the earth, the lords of creation. As handsome as demigods, as beautiful as the nights in Canaan.

All except for me. No one was taken in by my suntan: they all knew perfectly well – I knew it myself – that even when my skin was finally tanned a deep brown I would still be pale on the inside. Though I forced myself to learn how to lay irrigation hoses in the hayfields, driver a tractor, hit the target in the rifle range with the old Czech rifle, I had still not managed to change my spots: through all the camouflage nets I covered myself with you could still see that weak, soft-hearted, loquacious town boy, who fantasised and made up all sorts of strange stories that could never have happened and didn't interest anyone here.

And then the miracle happened. Nili, one of the golden girls of the Kibbutz, of whom Amos dreamed at night – during the day he was much too shy to approach them – condescended to read his poetry:

To this day Nili is my first reader. When she finds something in a draft that is wrong she says: That just doesn't work. Cross it out. Sit down and write it again. or: We've heard that before. You've already written it somewhere. No need to repeat yourself. But when she likes something, she looks up from the page and gives me a certain look, and the room gets bigger. And when something sad comes off she says I've got tears from that passage. Or if it's something funny she bursts into peals of laughter. After her, my daughters and my son read it: they all have sharp eyes and a good ear. After a while a few friends will read what I have written, and then the readers, and after them come the literary experts, the scholars, the critics and the firing-squads. But by then I'm not there anymore.

This is Amos' subtle way of introducing Nili, his future wife, with his own version of Hallel:

> It emerged one day that sunlight had suddenly lit up the dark side of the moon. That day, in Hulda, the cows laid eggs, wine came out of the ewe's udder, and the eucalyptus trees flowed with milk and honey. Polar bears appeared from behind the sheep shed, the emperor of Japan was seen wandering beside the laundry reciting from the works of A.D. Gordon, the mountains dripped wine and all the hills melted. The sun stood still for seventy-seven hours above the cypress trees and refused to set. And I went to the empty boys' showers, locked myself in, stood in front of the mirror on the wall, tell me, how did this happen? What have I done to deserve it?

When they married, the traditional kibbutz wedding canopy was not held up by two rifles and two pitchforks but by four pitchforks. Yet his happiness was still marred by his mother's tragic end. How could his adored mother have done this to him?

> I was angry with her for leaving without saying goodbye, without a hug, without a word of explanation: after all, my mother had been incapable of parting even from a total stranger, a deliveryman or a peddler at the door, without offering them a glass of water, without a smile, without a little apology, and two or three pleasant words. All through my childhood, she had never left me alone at the grocer's, or in a strange courtyard or in a public garden. How could she have done it? I was angry with her on Father's behalf too, whose wife had shamed him thus, had shown him up, had suddenly vanished like a woman running away with a stranger in a comic film. Throughout my childhood, if I ever disappeared even for an hour or two I was shouted at and punished: it was a fixed rule that anyone who went out always had to say where they were going and how long for and what time they would be back. At least they had to leave a note in the usual place, under the vase.
> All of us.

> Is that the way to leave, rudely in the middle of a sentence? Yet she herself had always insisted on tact, politeness, considerate

behaviour, a constant effort not to hurt others, attentiveness, sensitivity! How could she? I hated her.

The book closes in mea culpa fashion. Amos recalls the post mortem atmosphere:

> Despite the silence and the shame, Dad and I were close at that time, as we had been the previous winter, a year and a month before, when Mother's condition took a turn for the worse and he and I were like a pair of stretcher-bearers carrying an injured person up a steep slope.
> This time we were carrying each other.
>
> We never talked about my mother. Not a single word. Or about ourselves. Or about anything that had the least thing to do with emotions. We talked about the Cold War. We talked about the assassination of King Abdullah and the threat of a second round of fighting. My father explained to me the difference between a symbol, a parable and an allegory, and the difference between a saga and a legend.
>
> I have hardly ever spoken about my mother till now, till I came to write these pages. Not with my father, or my wife, or my children or with anybody else. After my father died I hardly spoke about him either. As if I were a foundling.

When Amos finished his military service at the age of 22, the committee of the Kibbutz sent him to the Hebrew University in Jerusalem to study literature because the Kibbutz itself urgently needed a teacher of that subject; but Amos insisted on adding philosophy to the curriculum and this is where his personal story virtually finishes. We do not know what happened to him in his thirties, forties and fifties and, hopefully, these decades will form the subject of another masterpiece.

A deeply depressing yet deeply exhilarating memoir – a truly great book.

Ed. Following an attack on Amos Oz in The Jewish Chronicle *by Rabbi Jeffrey Cohen, Fred wrote the following letter to the editor of the paper:*

"My tolerant old friend Rabbi Jeffrey Cohen should not adopt the role of a fundamentalist haredi rabbi who wants nothing less than a 'Greater Israel.' His attack on Amos Oz, calling him a 'Jew-hating Jew' is wholly unjustified. Amos Oz's prize-winning novels show his deep love of his country in general and Jerusalem in particular. The majority of Israelis, including the modern Orthodox, resent the interference of some rabbis in strategic/military matters and their appeal to young soldiers to disobey their commanders' disengagement orders. I know Amos and cherish his warm personality. At a recent lecture in Jerusalem before a mixed audience he had a standing ovation. His iconic status is fully justified. He is good for the Jews."

Amos Oz received a copy of this letter and replied to Fred, "I had not heard about Rabbi Cohen's attack but your own words warm my heart."

Michael Bar-Zohar:
"Yaacov Herzog: a Biography" Peter Halban, London, 2005

Yaacov Herzog was sui generis. His elder brother, Chaim (Vivian), who became president of Israel, considered him to be the cleverest in the family. He was one of the aristocrats of the yishuv. His mother, Aura, of Jewish-Egyptian origin, was a sister of Abba Eban's wife, Suzy. Yaacov was born in Dublin in 1921 at a time when his father Yitzhak Halevy Herzog was the chief rabbi of Ireland. The family settled in Israel in 1936, where Herzog Senior became chief rabbi of mandatory Palestine.

Yaacov was an *ilui*, a Talmudic genius, and at his Barmitzvah in Dublin he delivered his dissertation in Hebrew. He studied at London University and at the Etz Chaim Yeshiva and other yeshivot in

Jerusalem. His father travelled throughout Europe to save Jewish lives and Yaacov became his chef de bureau, accompanying him, writing his speeches and learning the art of politics. At the same time, Yaacov began to translate the Mishna into English. The mandatory powers regarded him as a quasi upper-class Englishman and appointed him as a liaison officer to the Chief Rabbinate and the British-Jewish chaplains in the Middle East.

Yaacov had inherited the deep faith of his parents, whose hopes were that he would enter the rabbinate. On the other hand, his elder brother, Chaim, distanced himself from his Orthodox background. Some friction developed when Chaim chided Yaacov that the hiring of chauffeured cars and planes overseas was making a bad impression. Here Yaacov made it clear in no uncertain terms that the saving of lives could not be measured in monetary terms.

He became the principal advisor to prime ministers Ben Gurion and Levi Eshkol and the Irgun took him into their confidence whilst he was active in the Hagana. He received his rabbinical ordination with honours at the age of 27. After the Declaration of Independence he worked at the Ministry of Religious Affairs and showed, according to Teddy Kollek, that the wise young scholar was an efficient and thorough administrator. With his charm and acumen he understood the importance of land ownership. It is estimated that Yaacov Herzog purchased about one-sixth of the area of Jerusalem on behalf of the state.

At the age of 31, he married Pnina Shachor, whose father Zalman was the Chairman of Mizrachi in Tel Aviv. She was fascinated by Yaacov's activities and quietly sat in the corner while he was negotiating land deals with the Greek Orthodox Church. She survived him by 33 years, became president of Emunah and one of the world's leading activists on behalf of women's causes.

In 1957, Yaacov was appointed minister at the Israel Embassy in Washington at a time when his cousin, Abba Eban, was ambassador to the United Nations. Eban wrote then:

> His life is a unique drama in the story of our Foreign Service. His quick mind moved restlessly from scholarship to politics. He is Orthodox without being pious. He has always worked in somebody

else's shadow, first Ben Gurion, then Golda Meir, then Eshkol and then Golda Meir again. When he came to me in Washington, I had the feeling that I was advancing his release from his parents' custody which though doubtless warm, was restrictive. He had not time or thought for anything that was not directly connected with the interest of the Jewish people.

I have quoted this tribute because at a later stage, tension developed between Eban and Herzog when, as far as the territories were concerned, Eban was too conciliatory for Herzog, who adopted the traditional biblical attitude to a "Greater Israel."

The climax of his career came when, as ambassador to Canada, he held the famous debate with Professor Arnold Toynbee. On a cold morning in January 1961, Hillel House at McGill University in Montreal was overflowing. Loudspeakers were placed throughout the building when Yaacov Herzog, in a masterly fashion as a Jew intimately acquainted with the Bible and the Talmud, and as an experienced diplomat, secured a notable victory over the noted professor who had written off the Jewish people as a "fossil." A compact disc of the debate is included in the book.

Yaacov's tact and discretion enabled him to meet secretly with leading opponents of the State of Israel and he developed a close personal relationship with King Hussein of Jordan, whom he met regularly over a period of nine years at the clinic of a Jewish doctor in London. By this time his claim to fame was recognized and Isaiah Berlin described him as: "… one of the best and wisest, most attractive and morally the most impressive human being I have ever known."

However, the mutual admiration was not unqualified. Herzog wrote:

> I found him [Berlin] generally out of touch with the real political facts, a very complex man, a genius who has achieved universal standing. He plays down his Jewishness, probably to avoid damaging his standing in Western culture, yet his Jewish roots keep showing.

When Chief Rabbi Israel Brodie retired in 1964, Sir Isaac Wolfson thought there was only one man with all the qualities for his post and he invited Yaacov Herzog to become chief rabbi of the United Kingdom. This caused a dilemma and much soul-searching. Yaacov's parents and his wife were in favour of his acceptance, if only to reduce his 18-hour working day for the benefit of the family. Reluctantly, Herzog accepted:

> After much thought and inner struggle I have decided to accept. Providence has led me from the path I have been following for many years back to this sphere of religious thought, this sphere which has always been the deepest core in my life.

Alas, his sense of duty clashed with his conscience and he collapsed. Professor Zondek described this as psychosomatic. He concluded that Yaacov had to be isolated from all pressure and sent him to Geneva to recover. Yaacov later acknowledged that Zondek had saved his life.

Sometime later Prime Minister Eshkol invited him to become director of the Prime Minister's Office, a post which he accepted. When Golda Meir became prime minister, she felt that she did not need an advisor on communication in the English language since this was her mother tongue. She appointed Simcha Dinitz (later Chairman of the Jewish Agency) as her principal aide and gradually Herzog felt isolated and removed from the centre of power.

Once again he was afflicted by terrible backaches and sometimes he could not rise from his bed. His good friend, Nahum Goldmann, recalled: "He was the victim of his own career; he had a number of disappointments... he suffered and locked everything in his soul. To succeed in political life you need to be quite pitiless... he could not do it."

Yet the need to be in the corridors of power had become an addiction. In 1971 he had an opportunity to go to Harvard for a year. He refused: "I have to help Golda." Soon after he was delivered unconscious to hospital.

He had one more secret meeting with King Hussein in Aqaba; he met Pnina in Tel Aviv and three hours later flew to London. He then sent off to Canada, gave an excellent speech, went back to Tel Aviv and died. He was 51 years old. A brilliant, hypersensitive man had literally sacrificed his life for his country.

This biography was commissioned by Pnina and her children. After the book launch in London, there was another one in Jerusalem at Yakar, where Yaacov's daughter, Shira presided. Unfortunately, Pnina passed away after handing over family letters and documents to Prof. Bar-Zohar.

Friends who knew Yaacov well thought that the tenor of the book was too adulatory and few of his shortcomings were mentioned. Be that as it may, this publication offers a rare insight into Israel's formative years in which Yaacov Herzog played a prominent part.

Martin Gilbert:
"In Search of Churchill" Harper-Collins, London, 1995

This is an immensely readable book, the nearest thing to a historical thriller. For all those who are daunted by the vast quantity of Churchilliana extant, including 16 volumes by Gilbert himself, this is an easy entrée into the great man's long life.

Rabbi Adin Steinsaltz once said: "The Talmud is a vast sea; there is no end to its study." This could equally have been said about Winston Churchill. While still a young graduate, Gilbert worked for Randolph Churchill (Winston's son) who, right up to his death, employed a staff of researchers to assist him in writing the authorized Churchill biography. Alas, he got no further than 1916 when his tumultuous lifestyle led to his premature demise. He was a bully, a charmer and an exacting taskmaster. If any name, however, unimportant, was mentioned in Winston's correspondence, young Martin had to play detective, dig deep and write a concise profile of the hitherto unknown person.

When it came to major characters with regular contact with Winston, the temptation had to be resisted to be side-tracked into their lives, which could have been the equivalent of an additional commentary on Rashi.

For the period 1917 up to Winston Churchill's death, Martin Gilbert has been the official biographer. In pursuit of his quest during the last 30 years, he interviewed virtually all those survivors who worked with Churchill, met him socially or crossed swords with him. The family, politicians, the aristocracy, shorthand typists, secretaries, drivers – all came under the meticulous scrutiny of the author.

This book deals with the methodology of implementation and is better than a detective story. We learn about Churchill's private life, his idiosyncrasies, his moods, his compassion and his stubbornness.

Among the several researchers employed by Martin Gilbert was one Susie Sacher, the most gifted and persistent of them all. She is the daughter of the late Michael Sacher of Marks and Spencer fame who did such dedicated and lasting work for the Jewish community in general and our students in particular. What a pleasure it must have been for him to see his daughter thus employed.

Martin married Susie and between them they have enjoyed this remarkable journey of discovery and recording for posterity. They could easily have assimilated and disappeared into the upper middle class in which they move freely. This Oxford don, however, embarked upon a parallel career as a leading historian of the Holocaust and its geo-political connotations. His 12 atlases are essential tools for the future generation and an anathema to Holocaust deniers.

When not in their home in Jerusalem the Gilberts are active participants in the London Jewish community. Martin Gilbert received a knighthood in the last honours list, a most popular recognition of his talents and dedication.

Wim Van Leer:
"Time of my Life" Carta and The Jerusalem Post, Jerusalem, 1984

"Van Leer – Van Leer" you reflect, where have I heard that name before? "Well, there's the Van Leer Institute in its impressive grounds, next to the President's Residence in Jerusalem. There's that amusing writer who contributes regularly to *The Jerusalem Post* on a variety of esoteric subjects; and are there not these large trucks one sees on European motorways marked "Van Leer Industries"?

Your memory is correct. We are talking about the same family in all three instances. Wim's father, Bernard, was one of Europe's leading industrialists. With Dutch elementary school education and endowed with a complete lack of scholastic abilities, he went on to build a multi-national business in barrels, transportation and related industries, employing tens of thousands in scores of countries. His hero was Napoleon Bonaparte. His rapid rise to industrial eminence made him a lonely man. Having outgrown the social circle of the family, as a nouveau riche industrialist, he had no business friends in a field that was traditionally the preserve of old aristocratic families. Bernard took up solitary horsemanship, formed a circus and became his own ringmaster and star performer.

When the Nazis invaded Holland he signed over his factories in exchange for the family's and the circus' safe departure to the USA. After the war he returned to find that his enterprises had prospered mightily under the Nazis and that he was richer than ever. When I met him at a hotel in Wassenaar near The Hague, where we held a Maccabi Conference, he had the aura of the powerful multi-millionaire who merely had to lift an eyebrow to have his every wish instantly attended to.

It was the strong personality clash with his father that was to influence Wim's career and character. He was born in 1913 and was a troublesome boy. At the age of 15 he was sent away from home to live with a local teacher. "At 18 I left Holland for good, my father formulating the family sentiment by extending a standing invitation to drop by for coffee and a chat whenever I happened to pass through

Amsterdam, subtly insinuating that unnecessary loitering on my part would not be appreciated."

He became the black sheep of the family, an appointment which he much enjoyed and to which he devotes a whole chapter. He had two more major clashes with his father. On returning to Holland to discharge his flying duties as a Dutch Air Force officer, he visited his parents in the stately Amstel Hotel which naturally his father owned. The night before Wim had made some derogatory observations about one of Van Leer senior's grandiose scheme to a company executive. Father asked him to apologise. Wim refused. They almost came to blows and Wim walked out leaving his father who had tripped over, lying prostrate on the floor.

When Bernard asked Wim to "voluntarily" renounce all claims to the Van Leer fortune, factories and indeed anything that his father controlled, Wim complied. In his will Bernard left everything to the Van Leer Charitable Foundation, with many hundreds of millions, to be managed by his other son, Oscar. Yet in spite of their antagonism the old man could not help but to see in Wim a chip off the old block. Before he died, he invited Wim to rehearse a funeral oration in front of him. Wim, after considerable reluctance, complied and said:

> This is indeed a sad day for me, as for all of us. For today one of life's failures goes home to his Maker. If there has ever been a man who missed his vocation it was Bernard Van Leer, my father. I would like to remember the deceased not as I knew him, but as I should have liked to have known him. Others will today catalogue the numerous outposts of his industrial empire, whose founding absorbed all of his great energy. I cannot reconcile the foolish expenditure of so much devotion with so insignificant a task. I want to pay homage to the man who had the audacity to offer to finance the Concertgebouw Orchestra's strike for a period of 25 years, rather than have it submit to a Nazi-tainted baton. We are saying farewell to a man so gauche, so shy, so isolated, that he felt it necessary to keep an empty seat next to him on airplanes so as not to be close to one of his fellow-creatures, created, like him in God's image....
>
> We stand at the grave of a failure. A man with so many human possibilities, so much originality, so much sweetness. A man who

preferred to fill the canvas of his living days with industrial power, with the world of combative competition, of anger and telegrams, to the exclusion of all else. As a representative of the "all else," I stand here and pay my last respects.

This was the last time they met. Wim, like his father, had a minimum of formal education; he called himself a "student of the University of Life which has no graduates and only mid-term drop-outs." He learned the metal trade in Switzerland, played in a jazz band, worked in Italy, Trinidad and Germany, married and engaged in innumerable affairs; he became a pilot in the Dutch Air Force; he single-handedly snatched a group of young German Jews from a concentration camp and brought them to England, and smuggled a Czechoslovakian on his motor bike to freedom. He was 26 when the war broke out.

And that was only the beginning. In due course he would become a factory owner, industrial inventor, international adventurer seeking sunken treasure in Outer Mongolia, a builder of Israel's air force, a pioneer in aerial crop spraying, an originator of beef cattle raising and steel barrel and plastic sheet manufacture. He, together with his wife Lia, was the founder of the cinemathèques in Haifa and Jerusalem, and turned his hand to film producing (he received the Golden Bear Award in Berlin in 1961) and journalism.

If all this sounds like a Walter Mitty or a *luftmensch* career, let me make it clear that Wim is a formidable no-nonsense capitalist who occupies one of the most beautiful houses in Jerusalem's Yemin Moshe with his wife and innumerable cats.

His attitude to life appears to be that of the detached, amused aristocrat who cannot resist a challenge, whether it is in the guise of a beautiful woman or risking his life to save others. Commercial shrewdness is combined with an ability to assess other people's character and a ruthlessness in disposing of them when their usefulness has come to an end.

One of my successor presidents of B'nai B'rith in Britain, was Werner Lash who was one of the many who owed his life to Wim. Just before *Kristallnacht*, Wim, with his non-Jewish appearance and Dutch passport, was invited by the Quakers to Germany to see if he could do anything to help. This is a marvellous chapter of the committed, fearless man whose Jewish instincts, dormant for so long, came to the fore. With patience, perseverance and cunning and with the help of the legendary American, Captain Foley, and a sympathetic SS lawyer, he prised 22 Jews out of a concentration camp and brought them safely to England. But he was still ambivalent if not downright antagonistic to traditional Judaism.

If Wim did not care much for Judaism he also had little rapport with the Zionists, yet once again when the embryonic State of Israel fought for survival he could not resist the challenge. After the war, his mother could not settle down in Holland and took up permanent abode at the King David Hotel in Jerusalem. She involved herself in the building of the state and endowed the Van Leer Institute. Wim was with one of his more sensational girlfriends in Paris when mother dropped by. She introduced him to an *Aliya Bet* (illegal immigration) operative. Wim joined up and flew a Beechcraft Bonanza on a complicated route to Haifa to join the nascent Israeli Air Force. Instead of flying on missions he found himself sitting in the Yarkon Hotel in Tel Aviv trying to build up the scant equipment of the Air Force. That was the beginning of his "non-Zionist stay" in Israel where he has lived ever since. There he met Lia, the only woman who could hold him and with whom he has shared his life for over 30 years.

The last chapter of his book was cut out by the publishers. It has since been published in *The Jerusalem Post*. It deals with Wim's appearance in the hereafter, when he meets the Recording Angel at the "Golden Gates sparkling in the pure Ozone." In vain he looks for Heaven or Hell. He learns to his amazement that the only punishment is the penalty for missed opportunities, for unused talent, for waste during one's life on earth. On this basis he has written himself a one-way ticket to Heaven in which, alas, he does not believe.

This is an entertaining book written by a larger-than-life man, the like of whom they do not make any more.

David Sorkin:
"Moses Mendelssohn and the Religious Enlightenment"

Peter Halban, London, 1996.

Let us deal first of all with the basic facts of this remarkable man's life. He was born in Dessau, Germany, in 1729, the son of a *sofer stam* (religious scribe), suffered various childhood illnesses which left him a hunchback, received a Jewish and secular education and in due course mastered Latin, Greek and the principal European languages, mathematics and the works of the leading philosophers.

He became an outstanding leader of German Jewry and was recognized as such by the monarch. He was referred to as the Socrates of Berlin. As a progenitor of Jewish emancipation, his seminal writings and speeches hastened the *haskala* (Enlightenment) and he was actively engaged throughout his life in what nowadays is encapsulated in the work of the Council of Christians and Jews.

He wrote, alas somewhat optimistically: "It is a fortunate coincidence that the betterment of the situation of the Jews marches hand in hand with the progress of mankind." Unlike poor old Ahad Ha'am, who never progressed in business beyond being a clerk in Wissotzky's tea firm in London, Mendelssohn worked his way up from being an ordinary apprentice to a partnership in a Jewish-owned silk factory.

He married well – Fromet Guggenheim of Hamburg, who was a descendant of the wealthy Court Jew Samuel Oppenheimer of Vienna. Of their six children, four married out and only one of his nine grandchildren remained Jewish. One grandson was Felix Mendelssohn, the composer. Others became bankers and the respected firm of Mendelssohn, and Co. was finally absorbed into the Deutsche Bank in 1939.

One may well wonder why such a committed Jew should have such an appalling track record as far as his immediate family is concerned and there is, indeed, no simple explanation to this voluntary opting out of what could have become one of the great German-Jewish families – "Rothschilds of the intellect."

Moses Mendelssohn's proverbial tolerance, his friendship with G.E. Lessing and many other German writers and philosophers, coupled with the obvious advantages of conforming with the dominant faith to be absorbed into the upper strata of society were obviously contributory factors.

Having briefly dealt with his background, let us look at his philosophy which merited him the epitaph..... "From Moses to Moses, there was none like Moses..." I quote from Sorkin's book which examines the dichotomy between Mendelssohn and Moses Maimonides.

> The corollary to Mendelssohn's emphasis on practical knowledge is the limitation to theoretical knowledge – an idea that already played a role in his early philosophical works. This idea now took the form of a discernible opposition to Aristotelian naturalism. The introduction of Aristotelianism into Judaism in the Middle Ages had exacerbated the tension between philosophy and revelation; its naturalism cast doubt on divine omnipotence (pre-existent matter vs. creation ex nihilo), and its belief in the contemplative ideal (the pre-eminence of theoretical knowledge through a comprehensive science of the divine) challenged the status of ritual and commandment. Mendelssohn's consistent opposition to the Aristotelian elements often put him at odds with Maimonides. This opposition is evident in respect to two issues: the nature of Creation and the relation of reason to good and evil.

Nowadays we would probably define Mendelssohn as modern Orthodox. He kept the *mitzvot*. He acknowledged the limitation of human reason, believed in divine revelation but he was also a pluralist. He had no time for agnostics. In his book "Phaedon," Mendelssohn writes: "The transition in matter of religion from doubt to thoughtlessness or from neglect of public worship to deprecation of all worship, tends to be extremely easy, especially for those spirits who are not under the authority of reason but are ruled by greed, ambition or lust."

Mendelssohn is probably most famous for his translation of the Old Testament into German, which he did initially by using Hebrew letters for phonetically pure high-German words. Like most previous translations of the five books of Moses, the Mendelssohn version created controversy bordering on furore. The rabbinic establishment has never liked to have the mystique of its calling lifted so that the common man can draw his own conclusions or, heaven forefend, study the text without authorized supervision. For a time Moses Mendelssohn's translation was placed under a ban.

From the septuagint at the beginning of the common era to the Latin version of the fourth century, to Yiddish in the 13th century, to the English translation by Tyndale who paid for it with his life in 1536, there was opposition followed by a steady erosion of the arcane, priestly monopoly.

There is nothing new under the sun. In our time Rabbi Adin Steinsaltz's reputation with the ultra-Orthodox haredi community declined when he began the ambitious task of translating the Talmud into modern Hebrew, English, Russian and French.

"What next!" thundered the heads of some yeshivot. Such easy access with punctuated text, Rashi and other exegetes instantly at hand in the vernacular, undercut the need to spend years at yeshiva just to be able to master the text. History demonstrated that people quickly got used to the new facilities through which the Bible became the world's most translated book and the yeshivot's pupils did not diminish. The ultra-Orthodox answer to Steinsaltz, incidentally, was to produce their own translations through their ArtScroll publications.

Sorkin's book naturally draws fully on the large Mendelssohn literature extant but he follows his own system of dealing with the challenging task of grouping Mendelssohn's manifold activities under three principal headings: Philosophy, Exegesis and Politics.

Sorkin differs in his interpretation from some of his predecessors. For example, he writes on the conflict inherent in "Mendelssohn's belief in revealed religion and his full-scale participation in Enlightenment thinking." I wonder whether the late Alexander Altmann, one of the leading writers on Mendelssohn, would have agreed with him that there was such an enormous gulf. He referred to Mendelssohn as the "prototype for better or for worse of German Jewry."

Other experts, like Smolenskin and Franz Rosenzweig thought that Mendelssohn had left a harmful legacy in the shape of his own family.

Immanuel Kant pointed out unequivocally that the rationalism of the Enlightenment was in direct contradistinction to Sinaitic revelation.

Let us conclude with two quotations from Sorkin's book:

The religious Enlightenment represented a kind of Golden Mean. Mendelssohn's version was a middle way between the casuistry and Kabbala of baroque Judaism and the speculative rationalism of Maimonides."... "Since Mendelssohn thought the Bible offered practical knowledge in a form accessible and relevant to all Jews, his commentary contains no hint of the common distinction made by mediaeval rationalist exegetes between exoteric exegesis for the masses and esoteric exegesis for the initiates. ...For us this Torah is a possession... to know the commandments which God had enjoined us to learn and to teach, to observe, and to fulfil; it is our life and the length of our days.

David Sorkin has produced a valuable addition to the small library devoted to one of the greatest thinkers in European Jewish history. This volume demands time and concentration from the dedicated layman and is essential reading for the specialist.

Moshe Kaveh:
"Divinely Given Torah in our Day and Age (Studies on the Weekly Torah Readings)"

Bar-Ilan University Press, Ramat Gan, 1998

I do not know how many versions there are of explanations of the parashat hashavua (the weekly sedra) that have been written over the centuries by hundreds of rabbis and others, ranging from Rashi to Nechama Leibowitz, but even at the present time new and rehashed comments are offered weekly in newspapers from the pulpit and on the Internet.

For many years *The Jerusalem Post's* Friday edition featured contributions from the late lamented Rabbi Pinchas Peli whose incisive insight ensured him a large following. His place has now been taken by Rabbi Shlomo Riskin from Efrat, who is a great story-teller, whether they are relevant or not.

Our leading traditional commentators follow the Rashi pattern. They perform a didactic role. The Torah is infallible. Where the facts (*pshat*) are inconvenient, the Midrash or Aggada can turn black into white. Everything our forefathers did was good. Every act of Esau was evil even when he generously fell round Jacob's neck after his 22 years absence. The text states: *vayishakehu vayivchu* – "they kissed and cried," a most moving moment in their relationship. Rashi says that Esau wanted to kill Jacob by biting his neck, which fortunately turned to marble.

I am a *pshat* man. The Midrashic stories are rabbinic inventions, often of great charm but usually devoid of any factual basis. My heroes are Ibn Ezra, the Ramban (Nachmanides) and the Ralbag – Rabbi Levi Ben Gershon, also known as Gershonides. Under present day Talmudic political correctness, they would be looked upon askance by most yeshiva heads. It was therefore with some curiosity and trepidation that I opened the recently-published volume of the weekly portion written by faculty members of Bar-Ilan University.

A university is not a yeshiva. It can never adopt the inward-looking attitude of leading yeshivot, which eschew scientific study of the Torah as leading inevitably to questioning and disbelief. On the other hand, a rigorous academic approach is a sine qua non at a university.

For six years Bar-Ilan has published this weekly commentary which now has thousands of Internet subscribers. Maimonides' insistence that a knowledge of science was essential for the proper understanding of the Torah, has been largely ignored by the yeshiva world, which was surprised when Samson Raphael Hirsch came out with his dictum *Torah im derech eretz* – "Torah with respect." Rabbi Kook was criticized in his lifetime because he believed that the march of science was to be welcomed even if on the surface it seemed to clash with religious preconceptions. Aviezer Ravitzky, an Orthodox professor at the Hebrew University summed it up in a lecture given in London in March, 1997, which has since been published.

> A religious person may prefer the value of Good to the value of Truth in his/her personal life. But in one's academic studies, Truth will supersede Good. One may choose one's domain of study, and even refrain from a "harmful" study, but what one actually writes must reflect one's cognitive, not axiological World.

The Bar-Ilan publication is all the more intriguing, since the contributors are not the rabbis in the faculty of Jewish studies, but professors from other departments, including philosophy, physics, Land of Israel studies, sociology, anthropology, Hebrew and Semitic languages, physics, life sciences, Hebrew literature and Jewish history – a truly eclectic mix of multi-talented lecturers.

Their challenge is an enormous one. University students will not be satisfied with old wives' tales. They want explanations that make sense yet can be reconciled with the text. This causes frequent dilemmas. Let us take, for example, the creation of the world and how long ago it took place. I quote from Professor Moshe Kaveh (a physicist and current president of the university) introduction dealing with this particular point.

> It is interesting to note the approach taken by several great Jewish figures who, with characteristic Jewish insight, argue that God, being omnipotent, simply could have created the world in six days, even though this process, according to scientific research and human perception, would have to have lasted billions of years!

This clever comment, it turns out, has a scientific foundation! Fifteen billion years is a time span that assumes no change in the entire universe. We know, however, that close to the moment of creation (the "Big Bang") the universe was dramatically compressed into a small volume. According to Einstein's general theory of relativity, when mass is especially concentrated, reactions are dramatically accelerated, so that something which takes billions of years, could occur in a few minutes or hours. Prof. Gerald Schroeder, who wrote a book on the subject, recently made some precise computations, applying principles from Einstein's theory of relativity to the processes involved in creation of the universe, and concluded that 15 billion years could be compressed to six days of creation. Even if this explanation proves to be incomplete in the future (in the way that Einstein's theory can be said to be "classical" and was not aware of quantum theory) we nevertheless see that the basic concepts of time and place have changed in the 20th century, enabling ancient questions to be answered in the light of new scientific understanding.

This is intriguing. Does Prof. Kaveh believe that perhaps the world after all is only 5,759 years old? Prof. Aharon Arend, another faculty member, also uses the creation story to deal with Bible criticism, which he summarises:

> We have presented three intermediate views between the extremes of Bible criticism and the approach that does not permit direct original study of biblical verses: the first acknowledges the questions raised by research, but bases its faith on a divinely given Torah, not on the text's uniformity but on its eternity; the second maintain that the contradictions are the work of Heaven and do not detract from faith; the third ascribes importance only to halakha and the Oral Torah established by the sages, and does not subscribe to any particular theology. Approaches similar to these three have been formulated by various philosophers and commentators, each according to his views and understanding.

These are just two examples from this challenging publication, which faces contemporary problems courageously and with confidence, I recommend it highly to those whose concern is to reconcile the apparent dichotomy of text with modern science.

Philip M. Klutznick:
"Angles of Vision – A Memoir of My Lives"
Ivan R. Dee Inc., Chicago, 1991

In 1843, a number of worthy gentlemen of German Jewish descent met at the Sinsheimer Café in New York, in order to form B'nai B'rith, a fraternal organization which would bridge the confrontational disputes of the various sectors of the American Jewish community. They adopted the motto "Benevolence, Brotherly Love and Harmony." This admirable credo was not strictly adhered to during the first 100 years of its history, during which "Our Crowd" rigorously dominated the order.

It was not until 1938 when Alfred Cohen, then aged 78, gave up the presidency of B'nai B'rith as the last of the German Jewish potentates, that the 80 per cent majority of American Jews whose ancestry hailed from Poland and Russia flexed their muscles by the election of Henry Monsky.

Amongst the bright young men of the new regime was Philip Klutznick, born in Kansas City in 1907 into an immigrant family of Orthodox persuasion. He was short, overweight, brilliant at school and university, and wholly incapable of any physical exercise until a Dr. James Naismith, the inventor of basketball and director of physical education at the University of Kansas offered "to save his life."

Early on in the course of his legal practice, Klutznick specialized in the esoteric field of public housing. Roosevelt and Truman appointed him commissioner for public housing. Other presidents sent him as ambassador to the United Nations, whilst Jimmy Carter made him secretary of commerce. In six decades of public service, Klutznick mixed with the most powerful players in the world, many of whom became close personal friends, including those whose policies he opposed. His memoirs include pen portraits of the famous, ranging from Konrad Adenauer, Dean Acheson, David Ben Gurion, Menachem Begin, Jimmy Carter, John Foster Dulles, Dwight Eisenhower, Levy Eshkol, Nahum Goldmann, Mordecai Kaplan, John Kennedy, Golda Meir, the Roosevelts, Yitzhak Rabin, Anwar Sadat, Moshe Sharett, Adlai Stevenson, Harry Truman and Frank Lloyd Wright.

Whilst not in government service, Klutznick made himself a multi-millionaire through vast property developments which became models of ecological planning, human relations and architectural aesthetics. He also became the leader of the volunteer consortium which redeveloped Chicago slum neighbourhoods. His most sensational development was the Water Tower Plaza in Chicago where a shopping centre, hotel and luxury apartments are integrated into a skyscraper which became a worthy addition to the famous townscape of Chicago.

He also became a leading Jewish figure. He was co-founder of AZA (Junior B'nai B'rith) in 1922, and he became international president of B'nai B'rith, founder chairman of the B'nai B'rith International Council, acting chairman of the Presidents' Conference of Major Jewish Organizations, and president of the World Jewish Congress. Together with Oved Ben-Ami, the mayor of Netanya, he built Ashdod and, with another partner, the Hilton Hotel in Jerusalem. Levi Eshkol told him "make profits, but not too much." In the event, Klutznick gave his shares in both these enterprises to a number of educational establishments in Israel.

In 1956 – rather like Sir Moses Montefiore – he secured the release of 8,500 Moroccan Jews through his personal intervention. He held a famous debate with Ben Gurion in which he rejected the prime minister's dictum that you could only be a complete Jew if you lived in Israel. He agreed that America was in the Diaspora but not in the galut. Passionately committed to the Jewish people, he moved from Orthodoxy to Mordechai Kaplan's Reconstructionist Judaism. He followed a consistent course of what can best be described as right-wing economics and left-wing politics. His insistence that one must talk to the enemy (the PLO) and not to those who may be more convenient adversaries, made him unpopular in certain quarters in Israel. Honoured by many universities in the United States, he had to wait until his eighties to receive his first Honorary Doctorate in Israel – from Haifa University.

The book offers a remarkable insight into American Jewish history of the last half century. Autobiographies generally serve to illustrate that the author has been right and has worked to his entire satisfaction. Klutznick is not shy in pointing out his own shortcomings and occasional failures. To the student of modern Jewish history, this book makes compulsive reading. As an autobiography, it shows a man who succeeded in many fields whilst living up to the highest ethical standards.

The Jewish Quarterly, London, Spring, 1992

Hilllel Halkin:
"Letters to an American Jewish Friend – A Zionist's Polemic"

Jewish Publication Society of America, Philadelphia, 1977

Harold Fisch:
"The Zionist Revolution – A New Perspective"

Weidenfeld and Nicholson, London, 1978

Like Samson Raphael Hirsch ("19 Letters") and Victor Gollancz ("My Dear Timothy,") Hillel Halkin uses the device of writing letters to a friend, whom he guides relentlessly to his desired conclusions and whose counter-arguments he demolishes in a fashion strictly reserved to one who combines the roles of prosecutor and judge.

The early letters follow the old Koestler argument (albeit from a different angle) that there is no future for organised Jewry outside Israel. The dialectics are skilfully interwoven with lyrical descriptions of the Israeli countryside, around Zichron Yaakov where the author has been living for the last seven years.

Jewry in the Diaspora is doomed on demographic and religious grounds. This is how Halkin disposes of the 5.4 million Jews in the U.S.A (his figures). Falling Jewish birth-rates, intermarriage and rapid assimilation will reduce the number of those who identify with the community from four million to three million by the year 2000, of which "with luck one quarter might remain hardcore."

The reduced number will lose whatever influence Jews may have had on the American political scene. In a growing population, their percentage will shrink from three percent to perhaps one percent. Their resources will not be sufficient to maintain their own infrastructure let alone Israeli institutions. This will lead to a dichotomy, with internecine battles which will gradually reduce them to an ineffective, rudderless, drifting vessel, tossed about by storms which it cannot survive. The alternative is aliya and only aliya. Halkin wields a powerful pen and having read the first three letters, one can well understand why this book made such an impact on young Jewish intellectuals, particularly at American universities. In fact, with a little editing, this part of the book could form the basis of an aliya pamphlet published by the Jewish Agency.

"But what kind of an Israel do you want me to come to?" asks his bewildered friend. The answer is an astonishing one. The Israel of Halkin's dream is one which will have cut itself off from the "outdated religion" which served its purpose prior to the establishment of the state. Reform and Liberal Judaism are dismissed as artificial creations soon to be swallowed by assimilation. Of the Orthodox he writes:

> Even the greatest of religious myths that have served as the building block of civilizations have their longevity, their historical life-span beyond which, however inexhaustibly rich they may appear, they harden and die. Their demise may be gradual. For how many hundreds of years did the great nature cults of antiquity linger on in the West long after Christianity had won the decisive battles for men's minds and hearts? Still, it must come.

He goes on:

> One sometimes meets in our contemporary Jewish world a curious type of Jew whom I have fittingly heard referred to as "Orthoprax"

and who may be said to live the life of a Marrano in reverse, since instead of conscientiously believing in traditional Judaism though being unable to practice it, he conscientiously practices it though unable to believe in it.

My children, I know, will not have the opportunity to reject Orthopraxy as I did, since I have done that for them. Centuries of traditional Jewish life have come to an end with me, a responsibility that I do not take lightly. But they would have come to an end in the Diaspora too, and here, at least, I can still pass the torch in what seems to me the only honest way.

It is when we come to Hillel Halkin's "only honest way" that the mind begins to boggle. He would like to see a secular Jewish culture develop in Israel, symbolised by land and language.

It means having a state of our own to protect these two things. It means having our own educational institutions and media to transmit this past to us and to translate what we must take from the outside world into terms natural to ourselves. It means having our own economy that allows and compels us to participate in all aspects of productive life and to make them part of our national experience. It means having our own streets, shops, courts, criminals, factories, farms and football leagues. In a word, it means having the soil in which our own culture can grow. If we succeed, the long march that began nearly a century ago in Europe will be over. We will be home again. We will become like the Gentiles, an ordinary people with an ordinary culture of its own, which is like, in the words of our psalm, "A tree planted by streams of water that yields its fruit in its season and its leaf does not wither."

Hillel Halkin is not deflected by realities. His description of the "Ugly Israel," pushing, shouting, in tight-fitting jeans is, alas, most convincing. To me, his book is one of the most powerful polemics against aliya, unless of course it is to do battle with the new secularism which he propagates. Finally, and here we have a common denominator with Professor Fisch's book, Hillel Halkin is not prepared to give up any territory whatsoever. His answer to the demographic threat is mass aliya from the West.

And so we come from a leap into non-belief to a staunch defender of the faith. Harold (Harel) Fisch, the epitome of the didactic Anglo-Saxon professor, went on aliya in 1957 and has occupied the chair of English at Bar-Ilan University ever since. He writes brilliantly, his erudition is remarkable and his style is felicitous. Halkin's ideal that Israel should achieve normality in the world, and be like any other nation, is anathema to him. Fisch explains lucidly that Zionism is not a product of Western liberal tradition. It is primarily "the offspring of the Jewish myth." Israel will never be a state like any other state. He quotes David Ben Gurion addressing the Peel Commission. "The Bible is our mandate." Faith and the myth of the Covenant are the recurrent themes of his thesis. Herzl and Sartre are dismissed for their misconception of the Jewish problems. They did not understand the centrality of the Covenant, through which the people became partners of God.

Zion without Sinai is meaningless. Halkin's duality of land and language becomes a trinity of God, land and people. True Zionism is a spiritual return – "a going up to the mountain of the Lord." The survival of statehood is dependent on the resurgence of religious belief and practice.

Fisch analyses the Zionist concepts of four philosophers, Moses Hess, A.D. Gordon, Rabbi Yitzhak Hacohen Kook and Martin Buber. What have these four divergent characters, ranging from the Communist Hess to the "I-Thou" Buber and Chief Rabbi Kook in common? All are mystics. Their beliefs are dissected carefully and one gets a new insight into the minds of what one may have considered familiar landmarks in Zionist history. Fisch pleads for a state which is diametrically opposed to that dreamed of by Halkin. The abnormality he wants extends to a double calendar. In a veiled reference to Halkin he writes:

> There are some who deceive themselves that they can get along with one calendar only. Among them are the "Canaanites," so-called because they have decided to reject all that is Jewish in Israeli nationality and to return to some purer, non-Judaic identity based on land and language. They represent the Nietzschean revision of Jewish history and the Jewish value-system carried to its extreme. They believe they can live in the 20th century without coming to

terms with the 58th century anno mundi. For them there is neither Sabbath nor Sabbath-eve. Their complaint against the Jewish state is that as well as being founded on the 5th of the month of Iyar, it was also founded on the 14th May. This is for them a scandal and an absurdity. For the Canaanites there is neither history nor promise, but only the affirmation of contemporary existence."

On the other hand, Fisch allows some latitude to the ultra-Orthodox who oppose Zionism:

> Had they been convinced that Zionism was an authentic Jewish phenomenon and that its programme would have furthered the spiritual as well as the physical well-being of Jewry, they would not have hesitated to give it their support. But they sensed – correctly – that Zionism sprang from the Emancipation, and the Emancipation represented for them the intrusion of an alien life-style and an alien calendar into the life of Jewry.

Where does all this lead us? The political realities, as Professor Fisch sees them, are enshrined in the Begin policy. There are no doves among the Palestinian Arabs. Israeli moderates are out of touch with political realities. Concessions made by Israel will only hasten its disappearance. He says:

> The moderates are fundamentally unwilling to contemplate the existential uniqueness of Jewish history... To recognise the Arab hostility to Israel as diabolical, as a continuation of Hitler's war against the Jews, involves a recognition of the essential abnormality of the Jewish condition, and a recognition also, that this abnormality has not ended with the establishment of a Jewish state. There are still many who are not prepared for such recognition.

Here at last is the confluence of the two extremes. Between Hillel Halkin and Harold Fisch, the secularist, and the mystic, common ground has been reached not to give up an inch of land. The consequences of incorporating another million Arabs into Israel is conveniently ignored or answered with the messianic hope of aliya in the hundreds of thousands. It seems to me that the secularist is placing too much reliance on providential intervention, while the mystic, too, is taking too much for granted. God has not given us freedom of choice in order to save us in spite of ourselves.

If these two books reflect the extreme polarisation of the yishuv, peace still seems far away.

Alan M. Dershowitz:
"The Genesis of Justice.
Ten Stories of Biblical Injustice that led to the
Ten Commandments and Modern Law"

Warner Books, New York, 2001

Professor Dershowitz has made his name as a legal iconoclast. He is a professor of law at Harvard University where surprisingly he also teaches Bible classes. He has a yeshiva background and recalls with a modicum of pride that he made himself thoroughly unpopular with his teachers by asking awkward questions. This challenging book, written in a fluent style will appeal to all those – and this must be the vast majority of us – who have problems with the morality of some of the Bible stores relating to the conduct of our forefathers.

There is little doubt that if God was an American citizen, the professor would have taken him to court. Incitement to murder is only one of the accusations against the Deity which appears to meet out justice in a haphazard fashion. Dershowitz states categorically that he does not want to get involved in the question of the authorship of the Bible which he recognises as the greatest publishing masterpiece in the history of humanity.

He divides the classic biblical commentators into three categories. The first are the "defence lawyers." They are what we would now call fundamentalists of the ArtScroll school who will reinterpret the text whereby Abraham, Isaac and Jacob were faultless and Joseph was a zadik. Rashi is the outstanding example.

Next we have the Socratic commentators who acknowledge that they do not always have the answer. He quotes Maimonides who believed that scientific knowledge was essential for the understanding of the Torah and that reason and faith were not incompatible.

The third category consists of the subtle sceptics. These commentators employ veiled allusions and hint that theological purity is not as important as the observance of the commandments. Ibn Ezra is an exponent of this school. Dershowitz, like Chief Rabbi Hertz, is ecumenical in consulting outside sources. He cites Pope John Paul the Second:

> Fundamentalism likewise tends to adopt very narrow points of view. It accepts the literary reality of an ancient, out-of-date cosmology simply because it is found expressed in the Bible; this blocks any dialogue with the broader way of seeing the relationship between culture and faith. Its reliance on a non-critical reading of certain texts of the Bible serves to reinforce political ideas and social attitudes that are marked by prejudices – racism for example – is quite contrary to the Christian gospel.

We now come to the alleged specific injustices. God warns Adam and Eve that if they eat from the tree of knowledge they will surely die. Yet both of them lead long lives. Cain murders Abel and lives for seven more generations. God heard Abel's cry for help but did not intervene. God regrets that He created mankind and decides to destroy it with the exception of one family. Later He realises that the flood was a mistake and promises that He will not do it again. Abraham is incited to murder and receives a blessing. He is willing to intercede on behalf of Sdom but not on behalf of his son Isaac.

Dershowitz quotes Elie Wiesel who argues that not only did Abraham fail the test, but so did God. No God should ask a father to kill his child and no father should ever agree to do so. God may have saved Isaac physically but He crippled him emotionally whilst killing his mother in the process. Abraham also sent his son Ishmael into the desert where he would have died but for the intervention of God.

Lot's daughters sleep with their drunken father and produce the line of the Messiah through Ruth the Moabite woman. Jacob deceives his father and is deceived by his sons.

Dinah is raped. Her brothers Simon and Levi commit genocide but their tribes prosper and Levi receives the coveted priesthood. Joseph retaliates against his brothers. It may be said that he is merely paying them back in the same coin, but Dershowitz considers this story to be particularly didactic as the basis of quite a number of laws which appear later in the Torah. Only in a world without a legal system can such injustices prevail. False accusations unsubstantiated by at least two independent witnesses run counter to Jewish law and planted evidence becomes a criminal offence.

We now come to the climax and the conclusion of the book. It is brilliantly summarised in the slogan: "The Genesis of Justice in the Injustice of Genesis." In other words, we have a book of laws based on remembered experience, which was an essential preliminary to make the subsequent law palatable.

The Christian Bible and the Muslim Quran deal less with the development of law than does Genesis. The law already existed at the time of Jesus and the Talmudic period was at its height at the time of Mohammed. It is the genius of Genesis that it is involved so closely in the history of civilization in the days before the development of a formalised legal system. Genesis is the beginning of the common law of Justice. "Virtually all of the large jurisprudential underpinnings of modern law can be discovered in the book of Genesis."

This is where Dershowitz rests his case.

Arthur Miller:
"Timebend – a Life"

Grove Press, New York, 1987

Three wives – the first a Catholic whose family insisted on a church wedding, the second Marilyn Monroe, and the third, Inge, a German girl who made a name for herself as a photographer and who, for over 25 years, has given Miller the companionship that had previously eluded him, provide the background for the Brooklyn-born Jewish writer whose conscience compels him to take on an unsympathetic world.

His total recall of events, conversations, smells and other people's idiosyncrasies lead one to suspect that he must have kept a diary from the age of three! The son of a powerful, blonde entrepreneurial father who commanded instant respect in spite of his illiteracy, Miller writes with an evocative resonance and a compelling style that makes it hard to put down the book in spite of its 613 pages.

Moral indignation and outrage are his principal leitmotifs. He is continually appalled by the injustice and oppression of the last 50 years and finds his catharsis by writing highly charged plays that more often than not are ahead of their times and only achieve popular appreciation when they are revived.

The crash of 1929 and the unemployment of the 1930s with the loss of self-respect of millions, led to "Death of a Salesman" and "All my Sons." The corruption at the New York waterfront and the Union's domination of ethnic minorities produced the timeless "A View from the Bridge;" the McCarthy indignities, where Miller was arraigned and triumphed is depicted in "The Crucible" and "After the Fall" is his protest against the atomic bomb.

The Nazis' persecution of the Jews as experienced by his psychoanalyst, a Dr. Loewenstein, provided the theme for "Incident in Vichy." "The Archbishop's Ceiling" is not only about the fatigue of the synapses of the constrained writers behind the Iron Curtain, but also about the "bugged ceiling of the mind" in the West.

Arthur Miller became the conscience of his country. His identification with the underdog, his suspicion of the establishment, his contempt for the fast buck, made him somewhat reluctant to enjoy financial success with all it seductive accompaniments. His fastidiousness, his intolerance for the second-rate and his aversion to Hollywood corruption, made his affair and marriage to Marilyn Monroe all the more astonishing. The truth is that he was physically bowled over. It was the classic hitherto controlled middle-aged man's sexual explosion which, in spite of his intellectual rationalization, became the very opposite of "mind over matter." It could not last.

Monroe's continuous need for reassurance, her dependence on drugs, her chronic insecurity, her fecklessness engendered by her insecure childhood doomed her as a natural victim beyond rescue by any man. Amongst the many phobias that Miller battled with, none drew more acid contempt than Lee Strasberg's Method School of Acting. Marilyn Monroe was so totally enslaved by the dominant personalities of Lee and Paula Strasberg that she refused to act without Paula by her side, which inevitably led to continuous clashes with the producer.

This came to a climax in the film "The Misfits" which Miller especially wrote as therapy for Monroe. It proved an unmitigated disaster. Clarke Gable died of a heart attack within a week of completing the film. Lest it be thought that Miller's vindictiveness towards the Strasbergs was caused by personal prejudice, there is now abundant evidence that he was right. Simon Callow, in reviewing Lee Strasberg's book, refers to "his deadly practice, killing off the actor's mental response with baleful results." In a letter to me Callow adds: "It is my conviction that Lee Strasberg was a most deeply malign influence on the American theatre."

The story has a happy ending. Arthur Miller, loaded with honours, uses his presidency of PEN, to battle for freedom of expression wherever there may be a restrictive curtain. Accompanied by his wife and helpmate, Inge, he travels the world and talks to Gorbachev, presidents, prime ministers and to fellow artists dedicated to preserving a modicum of decency in a decaying world.

This is the autobiography of a supremely honest man who pours out his heart, which has shown a remarkable resilience to setback and suffering. It is, after all, a quintessential triumph of mind over matter.

"Theodor Herzl – Visionary of the Jewish State"

Edited by Gideon Shimoni and Robert S. Wistrich
Magnes Press, Jerusalem and Herzl Press, New York, 1999

Who needs another book about Theodor Herzl? Is there not a plethora of biographies, diary translations and eye-witness accounts from the many contemporaries such as Ahad Ha'am and Max Nordau?

The answer must be a categorical yes. This volume of some 350 pages with 20 contributions from leading professors in Israel, the United States and the United Kingdom is a most welcome addition with its new material, unlikely as it may seem 100 years after the main events.

The catalyst for its publication in the form of a *Festschrift* was the centenary of Herzl's "Der Judenstadt," the revolutionary vision of a future Jewish state evoked by a secular Jew with only tenuous affiliation to Jewish sources and practices.

The concept of a political solution to the Jewish problem was so extraordinary that when Herzl showed a draft of his book to his best friend, Friedrich Schiff, Herzl records in his diary: "In the midst of the reading he suddenly burst into tears. I found this natural enough, since he was a Jew; I too had wept at times during the writing of it. But I was staggered when he gave me an entirely different reason for his tears. He thought that I had gone off my head, and since he was my friend he was touched to tears by my misfortune. He ran off without saying another word. After a sleepless night he returned, and pressed me hard to leave the entire business alone, for everyone would take me for a lunatic ... I said: 'If this is the impression my ideas make on an educated and faithful friend, I shall give them up.' Schiff later changed his mind."

Herzl lived for only 44 years (1860-1904). He had a deeply unhappy marriage to Julia Naschauer. His daughter, Pauline, died in 1930 in a hospital in Bordeaux as a drug addict. His son, Hans, shot himself on the day of Pauline's funeral and his youngest daughter, Marguerithe died in 1943 in Theresienstadt. His only grandson, after serving in the British Army, also committed suicide.

Herzl considered himself a failed playwright and became a journalist only because he had to make a living. He was the correspondent of the *Neue Freie Presse* in Paris. Born in Budapest, the family moved to

Vienna because of their deep affinity to German culture. These are the well-known facts.

The attraction of this book, however, is that every one of the 20 contributors tackles a different aspect of Herzl's character and life. His ambivalence to the solution of the Jewish problem was clearly demonstrated so that at some stage he proposed a mass conversion of young Jews as a gesture to assimilation. Later he came to the conclusion that anti-Semitism which, throughout the 2,000 years of Christianity, had been based on religious hatred, was now becoming a racial problem which would not be solved by conversion.

A year after the publication of "Der Judenstadt" he convened the first Zionist Congress which took place in Basel, Switzerland in 1897. The 1890s were a truly seminal period for Herzl. In 1895 he witnessed the degradation of Captain Alfred Dreyfus and was there when his epaulettes were torn from his shoulders. His depression increased when, in the same year, the intensely anti-Semitic Karl Lűger was elected mayor of Vienna.

Herzl was a mixture of realism and naïve faith. In his utopian "Alt Neuland" published in 1902, he visualised a new Palestinian society of honour and dignity and friendship with the Arabs who would undoubtedly welcome the Jews who would elevate their living standards to unprecedented heights. He talked to the Kaiser and many other national leaders and suggested that Palestine could become a German protectorate, rather like Lord Strabolgi proposed 50 years later that the pending Jewish state should become part of the British Commonwealth.

The dignity of Herzl's bearing was matched by his majestic appearance and disenfranchised Eastern European Jews hailed him as *hamelech* ("The King"). Herzl, the neurotic dreamer, became a man of action. The Zionist Congresses matured into a political force, the World Zionist Organisation. He created the Jewish Colonial Trust which later became Bank Leumi. He published a newspaper *Die Welt* and prophesied that there would be a Jewish state within 50 years of his death.

Although he represented the epitome of secular Judaism, he recognised the importance of carrying the Orthodox with him. He wrote in his diary on 15 June 1895: "The rabbis will be pillars of my organisation and I shall honour them for it. They will arouse the people, instruct them on the boats and enlighten them on the other side. As a reward, they will be formed into a fine, proud, hierarchy which, to be sure, will always remain subordinated to the state." Alas, the Rabbis wanted nothing to do with him. They considered his plans a blatant interference with the Almighty's plans for his people.

Surprisingly, one of the contributors, Professor Mordechai Breuer, of Bar-Ilan University, recalls how his own father, Isaac Breuer (my own teacher in Frankfurt for ten years) admired Herzl's personality. He writes: "In the sense that Zionism was a call to Jewish people to work toward national emancipation and ascend to the historical stage of the nations of the world, my father was a Zionist. National redemption, however, was inconceivable without the return of the Torah to its rightful place and its recognition as the sovereign law of Israel ... Until his last days [Breuer writes] my father continued to be enchanted by Herzl's personality – as a man though, not as a Jew."

It is revelations of this kind which makes this book such a fascinating one.

Conrad Black:
"Franklin Delano Roosevelt – Champion of Freedom"

Weidenfeld and Nicolson, London, 2005

This is a book of considerable gravitas in both senses of the word. With its 1,280 pages it can either be used for weight-lifting exercises or, for a comfortable read, it has to sit on a lectern or lie on a table. One would have thought that two such experienced publishers as Lord Weidenfeld of Chelsea and Lord Black of Crossharbour would have given consideration to printing two volumes with a somewhat larger typeface. Nevertheless it has become an international bestseller and is a tribute to the intellectual capacity and literary brilliance of the author, rarely found amongst newspaper publishers. FDR, the hero of the New Deal who made the USA the most powerful country in the world, is considered by Black as one of the most important and influential figures of the 20th century.

Over the years, the books that I have chosen to review have usually had a personal angle where I was able to make a contribution, and this is no exception. In this vast magnum opus I have concentrated on FDR's relationship with the Jewish community and his personal attitude towards some of his "Court Jews." It is an astonishing coincidence that Conrad Black's literary triumph coincides with the collapse of his newspaper empire and reputation. *Eich naflu giborim* – "How have the mighty fallen!" A man who had literally everything, including a brilliant Jewish wife, Barbara Amiel (a North London Collegiate girl), is accused of stealing from his own companies to the detriment of the shareholders. These facts may seem irrelevant as far as the book is concerned, but Black's snobbery and arrogance are modelled on his hero, FDR. His publishing empire includes *The Jerusalem Post* and the change in ownership will not necessarily be beneficial for the State of Israel, which both he and his wife have supported over the years. They attended the opening of the Supreme Court in Jerusalem as guests of Lord Rothschild and they were most congenial company.

FDR was one of the world's greatest manipulators, a ruthless charmer who had his own clear vision of the relative importance of the American population. Number one: WASPs; number two: Catholics; number three: Jews; and number four: others. He was brutal with his political enemies. For example, the enormously wealthy Moses Annenberg, whose son Walter later became Ambassador to the Court of St. James, criticised the New Deal in his paper, The Philadelphia Inquirer, only to find himself in jail on some trumped-up charges.

The author sums up FDR as follows:

His record of four consecutive presidential election victories, his seven consecutive congressional election victories, the huge crowds that always came out to see and cheer him throughout his long reign, attest incontrovertibly to his genius of operating every lever of the vast and intricate political machinery of the United States. His insight into common men was the more remarkable because he was certainly not one of them, and never pretended for an instant that he was.

Thomas Mann was captivated by him – his combination of power, sensitivity, and physical vulnerability, his liberality in an age of dictators, and the immense popularity he had earned in his own country. He also had great style. His powerful, handsome, animated appearance, cigarette holder at a rakish upward angle, flamboyant gestures, hearty and contagious laugh, skill at repartee, and evident love of his work and his job, made him an irresistible personality. Even some of his sartorial flourishes, the fold in his hat, his naval cape, a walking stick, were widely emulated. His idea of how to be president was to be himself. He loved virtually every aspect of the job, and felt he held it by a unique combination of personal determination, popular adherence, and natural right, even predestination. He could not conceive that everyone would not like to be president.

He became and long remained the most publicized and visible person in the world, though rivalled in this by Hitler and Churchill. His confidence, flair, and sure judgment of occasion caused him never in over 12 years to embarrass himself publicly. His physical presence, eloquence, and command of his position and tasks were all, and at all times, impressive. This conferred upon him a unique status as a public personality. He was a natural leader. As Isaiah Berlin wrote, all through the terrible years of his presidency, he never once appeared to experience a moment of fear.

He was a phenomenon and, as in other fields, it was difficult to know when his unfailing intuition left off and cunning analysis began. He was a brilliant phrase-maker and epigrammatist, often finding expressions that would electrify the country: "A New Deal for the American people... Nothing to fear but fear itself... The good neighbour... rendezvous with destiny... one third of a nation... the dagger struck into the back of its neighbour... the great arsenal of democracy... the day of infamy." When pressed, as on D-Day, he could rise to heights of Lincoln-like eloquence.

And now to the Jews: Eleanor Roosevelt, his wife, described Justice Frankfurter as "an interesting little man but very Jew" and, after dinner with Bernard Baruch, said "the Jew party was appalling. I never wish to hear money, jewels or labels mentioned again."

During the 1930s, a time when German Jews were desperate to escape, Sir Isaiah Berlin was deputed to the British Embassy in Washington. In a personal letter which he sent me dated 10th January, 1995, he describes the scene in his inimitable style (see page 162 for the full text).

Yet at Yalta in 1945, FDR "declared himself unequivocally to be a Zionist" with which Churchill and Stalin agreed unenthusiastically.

On 1 March, 1948 a very frail president addressed a joint session of Congress. He underlined that Yalta would only become a success if his isolationist opponents would not prevail. American power would become irresistible. America had led the world to victory in a just war. It would do so again in pursuit of a just peace. This was his last public appearance. FDR died on 12 April, 1945.

The research carried out by Conrad Black is admirable in its detail and thoroughness. He has produced a masterpiece, which undoubtedly will become the authorised source book on the life of Franklin D. Roosevelt.

Miscellaneous

Ed. The following pieces do not fall naturally into one of this book's main categories, but I make no apology for including them – so "miscellaneous" will have to do.

Frederic Raphael: Correspondance

18 September, 1979

Dear Frederic Raphael,

Does your heart sink when you receive a fat envelope? Do you immediately suspect another painful offering from a budding author which you will be reluctantly compelled to return after a couple of jaundiced glances at it? Relax. The enclosed deals with your favourite subject. I don't suppose in a month of Sonntags* that the whole will be printed in the Jewish Quarterly – but we'll see.

You like the post in the morning. So do I. It is surely not just idle curiosity, but the zest for living and the unexpected. What news from the children? Have they left Taiwan for Korea? Has the baby – safely ensconced in an ex North London Collegiate womb – seen the dazzling daylight of Jerusalem? The time between 7 and 8.30 a.m. devoted to tea and papers in bed and reading the post, is the most cherished part of the day.

May I say on a personal note how much I disagree with your outright condemnation of dictated letters. If one has a deplorable handwriting and can't type, what does one do? Inflict the indecipherable squiggles on one's friends and children, who will look upon the solution of the jigsaw puzzle as a penance? "Oh dear, here's another letter from him.

---

* Ed. Jacob Sonntag, Editor of the *Jewish Quarterly,* London

See whether you can make head or tail of it?" Or do what I have practiced successfully for many years, and build up a fantastic communications network, by using Miss Bunsen. Only her name is Pamela – she does not feature "his and her Ref." on the letter and you have obviously never had a secretary who is ad idem with you.

My daughters, North London Collegiate, Hebrew University of Jerusalem, Harvard and Columbia and my two academic sons-in-law (both volunteer ex-parachutists in the Israel Army, both members of the "Peace Now" Movement, complain bitterly if more than two weeks elapse and they do not hear from me. We deal with politics, the arts, academic and personal matters – you name it, we knock it. My wife has kept them all, and has visions of the publication of the collected letters of the Worms family.

How good is your tennis? I would welcome it if our paths were to cross.

Yours sincerely,
Fred S. Worms

■ ■ ■

25 September, 1979

As from Lagardelle,
St. Laurent-la-Vallée,
24170 Belves, France.

Dear Mr. Worms,

Thank you so much for the damned fat envelope and its pleasures. I am not actually hostile, as you ask, to the arrival of envelopes from aspiring writers, though I receive less than you may think. Most people seem to imagine that writing, like making love, is a simple matter and that it can be learned as you go along. Making love probably can't be learned any other way, though the paperback industry would like to promise us otherwise, but writing certainly can, or at least it can certainly be helped along and should be. It is one of the pleasures of being a writer to remember how kind many people were to one (some were unkind, of course, but that's the way it is) and to be able to help others, when one can. It is easier, actually, when one is face to face with them than when one tries to correct their prep as it were. Having said that, please do not rush to send me your six volume masterpiece, in Yiddish, translated by your Israeli cousin-in-law, on life in the Kiev ghetto after the fall of the Kazar empire. I am a bit busy.

I appreciate greatly your generous words about Cracks in the Ice and I hope that old Sonntag splashes them big, though he seems never to find space to review any of my work, even the old standard, as they say in the record business, The Glit P.* You are not wholly wrong in alluding to my "favourite subject," by which I assume you mean me, but I should tell you that I actually do not grub after mentions of myself in the public prints, though I am capable of getting bored when I read the eight hundredth interview with some rival, if rivalry there is in the arts (and of course there is). If you have any inside knowledge of the secret life of Cavafy, or any poems of his which have escaped the printer, I should as soon see those as read even such nice things as you write about me.

Incidentally, if I may quibble nicely, my use of long words is nearly always either ironic or cribbed from the work in question. I am not a great one for the polysyllabic, though I can sometimes manage it when roused. I am easily reproached in German, since I have none, though I am not too penitent about the Ich bin ein Jud thing since if a European statesman of standing had actually called himself a Yid, as if to say, so what?, then it would have been ever better than all that dignified Jewish stuff. By the way, I don't dislike Arnold Wesker, I just get bored with him from time to time. We have recently made up and I should not like to take the stitches out of the wound prematurely. Arnold has made the easy and tempting and honourable mistake of diluting all talents by becoming a public figure, at least in his own eyes, with all the Private Office fantasies that go with naïve meliorism. This is no reason to dislike him, though it is something of an Awful Warning. I live in France not least because it obliges me to work, not talk.

---

* Ed. This is a reference to Raphael's 1976 best-selling novel "Glittering Prizes", subsequently made into a very successful BBC television series.

I accept that you have worked out an enviably symbiotic relationship with your Miss Bunsen (the light of your life, a punster might be tempted to crack) and I am not about to pass stern judgment, or any other kind, on your domestic arrangements. Obviously, as your letter proves, it is possible to be amusing, fluent and informative while in the process of dictation. Henry James even managed it (if he did) for creative work, this dictating business, but I, though I have a superb secretary (who lives in London), have always found that a sort of public-address falseness creeps into one's tone, a plumminess, a lack of that particular authenticity and shamelessness which is necessary if a letter is to disclose something to the reader as well as being the vehicle of the writer's conscious purpose. It is never a moral matter and I daresay that I should never have guessed that you had not written your enviably well typed letter yourself, but I can say, with hindsight, that it is a letter that lacks, at least, mistakes, which leaves the hunting analyst rather short of clues. You have sidestepped the Freudians, but that can always be a way of playing into their hands: why so careful?

Well, I must close by saying that I appreciate your close reading of my work and the generous remarks you make about it. I am happy, at present, to be retreating from personal declaration into the more modest clothing of fiction. However, one has, I think, a certain duty to allow oneself to be somewhat known and I hope you will keep this letter so that you may honour the call, in x years time, for anyone who has any correspondence etc. I can then be revealed as a self-conscious correspondent, of rather prosaic style, who obviously dictated his letters to a secretary, while the amiable and amusing Mr. Worms, despite his straight-faced "confessions," was evidently a natural and easy letter-writer of the kind who works directly, and without inhibiting intermediaries, onto the typewriter.

My tennis is sometimes powerful, usually erratic, unfailingly foul-mouthed, except for the first time of playing with strangers. Shall we dance?

Yours sincerely,
Frederic Raphael

Thinking Aloud

The demise of Sir Isaiah Berlin and Chaim Bermant has left an aching void, not only with their immediate families but also with their friends. There is no doubt in my mind that if they were still alive, I would have wished to share with them some of the experiences referred to below. Chaim, sooner or later, would have included some of these allusions in his *Jewish Chronicle* column, whilst Isaiah, after due consideration, would have written a letter which, with his lateral thinking, would have thrown an entirely new light on the issues.

Isaiah's name is now eternally commemorated, by the Isaiah Berlin Square in Keren Hayesod Street opposite the Dan Panorama Hotel (formerly the Moriah). Lady Berlin and 20 close friends participated in the simple naming ceremony. It is a felicitous location within a few hundred yards of the King David and Inbal Hotels on a route which Isaiah would take during his daily peregrinations when visiting Jerusalem.

Behind the Inbal Hotel is a well-tended garden with herbaceous borders, lawns and a playground for children. It slopes down gently from its main entrance in Pinsker Street. We, the grandparents, had been given 20 minutes notice that there would be an interesting ceremony in which our granddaughter, Second Lieutenant Ayelet Hoffmann, would be involved. Why only 20 minutes notice? Because Ayelet, in a mixture of modesty and pride, only advised her mother by cell phone half an hour before the event.

Some 40 young soldiers were sitting on the verdant lawn, a few enjoying the sun, other seeking the shade in a temperature of some 85 degrees. A smart woman officer in her late twenties, gave a pep talk stressing the importance of their service to the nation both from the educational and the security point of view. Promotions were announced and insignias denoting their new ranks were placed on their shoulders.

Why is it that people of my generation are so burdened with memories that we cannot participate in a joyous occasion without a painful incision from the past? As they pulled off Ayelet's shoulder straps in one quick movement to a standing ovation from her fellow officers, new straps with two bars were put on instead. I was reminded of Captain Alfred Dreyfus who, over a hundred years earlier, in 1894 went through a similar process but his was one of suffering the indignity of having his insignia torn off and being branded a traitor, innocent as he was, as a result of the rabid anti-Semitism then prevalent in the French high command. In a similar retrospective vision, I cannot see a goods train with its sealed trucks passing by without instant Holocaust connotations. I believe that the young generation is free from such hallucinations but, alas, genocide if rife in different parts of the world and the pressures on the young in Israel are not decreasing.

I resumed reading "The House of Rothschild" by Niall Ferguson, two enormous tomes which throw new light on what one had thought were familiar figures, yet I was astonished to read that Lord Victor Rothschild said in 1938 to a British audience, "…the slow murder of 600,000 people is an act which has rarely happened in history. In spite of humanitarian feelings, we probably all agree that there is something unsatisfactory in refugees encroaching on the privacy of our country." This extraordinary, ambivalent statement was totally unexpected from a scion of a family whose provenance derives from the very country whose refugees Victor Rothschild would rather have exposed to slow murder than to disturb the "privacy of our country" – whatever that means. A deplorable example of the Nimby* process.

One of the great dangers of the affluent meritocracy is that they are liable to lose touch with reality. A propos "the privacy of our country," I was reminded of an article by William Rees-Mogg in *The Times* – Lord Rees-Mogg, a brilliant man, former editor of *The Times*, political pundit, company director and adviser to the great and good, is satisfied with the "simple things of life."

He describes three days in his previous week. On Thursday he and his family went to the opera in Glyndebourne; on Friday he attended the House of Lords where he lunched at the long table where one sits informally next to whoever came earlier. (He says, incidentally, he is sorry that Lord Levy feels that he has met with snobbery and anti-Semitism in the Lords, a perception which Lord Rees-Mogg says is entirely incorrect.)

---

* Ed. "Not in my Back Yard."

On Friday afternoon he repaired to his country mansion in Somerset and on Saturday, helped his son canvass for a Parliamentary seat in Shropshire, the county with which his wife's ancestors have been associated since 1730. He concludes his report saying that within a matter of three days he has seen a superb performance of great opera, shared a heart-warming family weekend, followed a thrilling test match, enjoyed the House of Lords, his time in Shropshire and his country seat in Somerset. He concludes "what very sane people the British are!" (When did he last queue for a bus or travel on the tube during the rush hour?) Nevertheless one can only envy a man with such deeply-rooted traditions based on the same centuries-old location, secure in his identity. How many of us will be buried in the same country as our great-grandparents?

This brings me finally in this rather inconsequential wandering of the mind to "The President's Conference on Jewish Culture and Identity in the 21st Century," organized by the President of the Hebrew University partly at the instigation of Chief Rabbi Jonathan Sacks. During a memorable four days in May of this year we participated in symposia and listened to lectures from leading intellectuals of the Jewish world; professors from universities in Israel, United States and the United Kingdom, rabbis representing the different streams of Jewish pluralism, writers of the calibre of Eli Wiesel and politicians such as Yossi Beilin and Sallai Meridor. It was a thrilling, challenging, exhausting and possibly rewarding conference.

Why only possibly rewarding? Because to some extent we played Hamlet without the prince. The ultra-Orthodox were not there, either on the platform or in the audience. A consensus on Jewish Identity cannot be arrived at without the harcdim. Conspicuous by their boycott, in spite of the many invitations extended to their leaders, they made a statement by their very absence. This, alas, is symptomatic of our deep divide which ultimately represents a greater menace to our continuity as one people than our external enemies can inflict upon us.

Hot Under the Collar
or Canonical or not to Canonical

There was a time in the history of the United Synagogue when there was a high degree of formality and, indeed, uniformity about the dress of synagogue attendees. The minister-preacher and the minister-reader were dressed in canonicals: but this was as nothing compared to the sartorial splendour of the *shammas* (beadle), who combined canonicals with a top hat. The congregants came soberly dressed in dark suits (preferably black jackets and striped trousers), white shirts, ties and invariably hatted. Bowler hats were common (Barmitzva boys were expected to wear bowlers), but homburgs were acceptable. As for the all-powerful honorary officers – they attended in their dark suits and top hats and were the role models for all others, not least for the *Kol Nidrei* service on Yom Kippur when they appeared in dinner jackets.

So what has happened now? Gone are the canonicals and the top hats – indeed all hats have now been replaced by *kipot* of every hue and design. Gone are the dark suits and formal dress and in their place we have suits of all colours and materials, or just sports jackets and blazers. As for ties and shirts – the sober shirts of yesteryear have been replaced not only by all colours of the rainbow and as far as ties are concerned, by designs which sometimes border on the questionable. Of course, there are those who solve the dilemma of suitable neckwear, by wearing none at all, (even we are told in the hallowed box occupied by the honorary officers), whilst shirts may be worn apparently, either inside or outside the trousers.

It is an interesting halakhic question whether it is preferable to appear wearing an unsuitable tie in synagogue or to wear no tie at all. One can well imagine the heated arguments this would have aroused between the followers of Shammai and Hillel. One suspects that Shammai would have ruled in favour of strictly and only black ties, while Hillel would have accepted grey. But *no* ties?

The real question of course is – does it really matter? It certainly does not seem to be an issue which can simply be explained in terms of younger against older, nor in terms of more observant against less observant, for dress is an issue which divides people across these groupings. It really seems to be an issue between traditionalists and those who wish to be seen as independent of such constraints. It is interesting that in Israel, those who have abandoned jackets and ties seem to have changed them for a uniform dress of white shirts with short sleeves, and white kipot. This looks neat and that is probably the answer. We should dress for comfort but in such a way that we recognize *bifnei mi anu omdim* ("He before whom we stand").

Incidentally, nothing has been said about ladies' dress, partly because the writer naturally keeps his eyes down to avoid distraction, and partly because ladies are still expected to wear hats (heaven forbid that they should wear kipot, even white ones!) and decorous skirts and have their arms covered. One is told (hearsay, because one's eyes are downcast), that there are even signs of revolt in the upper galleries.

Perhaps this complex issue, which can distract congregants from their devotions, is worthy of sensible discussion to see if an agreed approach can be reached. After all, if the parliament of Bermuda can agree after a long and heated debate that members should be permitted to wear Bermuda shorts, and if a certain north west London synagogue can agree without debate that red is not an acceptable colour for worshipping ladies, then perhaps we can agree on one or more options. For example, an impressive development has been noted of late, when several gentlemen have appeared in elegant white straw hats, white linen jackets and grey trousers (after all, we are situated near a bowling green!). Whatever the outcome of such a debate, it should be possible to arrive at options which can combine comfort with the degree of decorum expected in a house of worship.

Modern Art

These two words cover a multitude of sins. The generic three-letter word "Art" is one of the most misused and abused words in the English language.

There are, in fact, insufficient definitions to categorise the different streams, which has led to solidity and an acceptability which usually sits easily within certain boundary lines. For example, Cubism and Abstract Expressionism are distinct and clearly understood labels. This is not so when we come to conceptualism, minimalism or installationalism, as I propose to demonstrate in this article.

It is a dangerous path to tread because all those who have dared to query the right of certain creations to be included under the heading of "Modern Art" have been dismissed as philistines, dinosaurs and reactionaries who will only recognise a work of art if it is within a frame. The truth is that even the modernists are deeply divided and not all of them are following the uncritical path of analysis for whom anything goes.

Our first difficulty is the lazy inclusion of most artists who have worked during the last 50 years under the generic term of contemporary art. One may well ask what Henry Moore, Epstein, Francis Bacon – an ad hoc collection of superb British artists – have in common with Damien Hirst, Gordon Matta-Clark, Ann Hamilton, Carl Andree, Tracey Emin, Bernard Jacobson and Jessica Stockholder. Since not everybody will be instantly familiar with these names, I shall describe some of their recent works.

Most of these "artists" would not survive for long were it not for the support of certain art critics or art historians who have made them famous through what can only be referred to as "arty-babble." Damien Hirst sold a shark floating in formaldehyde for £50,000 and subsequently sold his Stuffed Dead Sheep inside a glass case for £25,000. He failed to get into St. Martin's College of Art and Design. He himself says that he cannot draw and when asked what his stuffed animals are supposed to convey, his reply was that he had absolutely no idea.

Bernard Jacobson has shown a ton of lavatory paper casually heaped and asked £10,000 for it. Tracey Emin sold her Unmade Bed with surrounding, personal trivia for £120,000 to Charles Saatchi, the advertising guru and master sponsor of this type of modern installation. Jessica Stockholder punched a big hole through one of the Hayward Gallery's partitions as her artistic contribution and this became one of the official display items.

The Serpentine Gallery has acquired a reputation for giving houseroom to modern artists. An example of arty-babble is Richard Cork's description of a walking stick which was suspended on its own in the gallery. He described it as a walking stick robbed of its function by dangling far above our heads.

The standard reply to those challenged why these artefacts should have been included as examples of modern art is that most of the impressionists were misunderstood in their time. Look at Van Gogh or, better still, look at Cézanne. Alfred Munnings, when he was president of the Royal Academy, thought that both Picasso and Matisse were charlatans. The implication of this criticism is that any of the aforementioned artists is a potential Picasso or Matisse. This brings me to the greatest mystery in this intriguing scenario, i.e. the lemming-like, uncritical toeing of the party line of the modern young art historians who have totally abdicated individual judgement for the sake of the cause. Arturo Schwarz, a leading Italian art connoisseur and internationally-recognised expert in surrealism and dada and champion of Duchamp, said, in a personal conversation after he received an award from the Israel Museum in 1994, that most of the works of art based on products bought in a shop or factory, such as Carl Andree's bricks, have no merit because they are only a feeble imitation of Duchamp. He added that trouble is caused by writers who have a gift for words but little true knowledge of the history of art. In some countries, he stated, you call yourself an art historian after having received a BA degree. If somebody called himself a "Historian" with a similar degree, he would be laughed out of court. Furthermore, most historians specialise in certain centuries, whereas your art historians know it all from beginning to end. They regurgitate what they have read, and much of what they have read was written by their immediate predecessors.

Kenneth Snowman, the very sensitive art connoisseur – particularly in the field of precious metals and stones, writes:

One of the ugliest stains discolouring the fabric of our end of the 20th century has been contributed by an alarming number of stuntmen masquerading as painters and sculptors with the connivance of a further number of near-illiterate critics and gallery directors, cynical deals and ignorant patrons. The common factor which unites these pretentious individuals (the present tense is sadly mandatory since the situation largely persists) is a total lack of respect for, or knowledge of, their more cultivated forebears."

Why, indeed, should these people attempt to fulfil the demanding requirements of true artistic endeavour when they can so easily and profitably get away with fraudulent jumbles of brushstrokes and meaningless heaps of rubbish left on the gallery floor to be admired by the simple-minded?

How many times, one cannot help wondering, have normally responsible auction houses and galleries put on display non-figurative panels – painted by over-praised contemporary masters – the wrong way up? We know it happens but not exactly how often. On how many occasions has one found examples of these pointless trivialities portentously labelled "Untitled," as though profound creativity of the artist was quite beyond the understanding of a mere member of the public? Of course, the possibility that the perpetrator could not be bothered to think up a title for his or her masterpiece cannot be entirely dismissed.

It all goes back to Duchamp who, in 1913, sent – tongue-in-cheek – a mass-produced laboratory basin, coat hooks bought in a shop and a standard snow shovel for inclusion in an exhibition of modern art. As we all know, it caught on and there is hardly a modern curator who is prepared to blow the whistle on this nonsense, and this includes my good friend, the curator of the Israel Museum in Jerusalem.

"Et tu, Brute!" I exclaimed when I saw Duchamp's familiar household utensils on prominent display. "Why, oh, why?" I asked. "Because," he replied, "it is the epitome of modern art. These are seminal works."

"And the vacuum cleaner which stands there?" I enquired. "Oh no, that belongs to the cleaner, I think, and therefore is not a work of art!" Being somewhat dissatisfied with his answer, I asked him whether I could carry out an experiment. "Go right ahead" he said. I took a bunch of keys out of my pocket. One of them, a security key, was dome-shaped. I placed it on one of the little display platforms and started "lecturing" to the curator and Della.

"This is one of the most moving exhibits in the museum. It is clear that the artist was suffering from a deep personality split. The dichotomy clearly lies between sex and religion," I explained. "Does this domed shape of the key not represent the conflict between the male organ and a church steeple?..." and I waffled on in this learned fashion. Soon there was a crowd of some 20 to 30 people standing around, nodding earnestly, while some were avidly making notes. "Well," I turned to the curator, "have I not proved my point?" "You have proved nothing," he said, "You are not an artist."

One of the principal arguments of the protagonists is that the scoffers are in a time warp, hidebound by past experience and unable to get used to unorthodox ideas beyond the accepted painting and sculpting traditions. Art without creativity is an oxymoron. Leave off "oxy" and then you may be able to accept the party line.

I visited the Turner Prize Exhibition. The award went to one Rachel Whiteread who has learned to pour concrete, or at least has learned to supervise others pouring concrete. The wordsmiths – that is, the specialists in arty-babble, in which I can competently compete using the same weasel-words as they do – have compared her to Henry Moore. "Why should concrete be inferior to bronze?" they ask. Why indeed! The miracle is that it seems to have escaped the notice of the experts that Henry Moore created shapes with his own hands. A post factum explanation of her prize-winning concrete house is that it represents the poor man's cenotaph, as a memorial to a bygone era. A runner-up exhibited a few tons of rice spread over three long neon tubes glowing through the rice. Find your Indian supper – yes – but Art?

When Picasso picked up bicycle handles and converted them into a ram's head, he engaged in an act of creativity. You and I could not do this. What you and I can do is to ask workmen to pour concrete or liquid plastic over a mattress (another exhibit of Whiteread). If we did this, we would probably be considered vandals.

Why am I getting excited about this subject? The answer is perfectly simple. If the "expert art historians" give their seal of approval to this second-hand, non-creative art, they create an atmosphere of nihilism and undermine the morale of the serious students who subject themselves to the disciplines of learning to draw, to paint, to sculpt, to study anatomy and to go through all the challenges that this implies. Of course, there is the odd genius like Francis Bacon who never went to art school, but would he have qualified for the Turner Prize? Lest you think I exaggerate, let me tell you that there is a dramatic fall in the attendance of life classes in British art colleges since the students find that it is easier to make a fast buck through gimmicks for which you need no particular training.

A television crew was standing outside the Tate Gallery. Some visitors to the Turner Prize Exhibition were asked to express their views, a selection of which would be included in a television programme known as "The Right to Reply." I was fuming and accepted their invitation with alacrity. This is what I said:

"I want to congratulate Channel Four for giving the opportunity to non-professionals to express their opinion on the Turner Prize. The frontiers of art have always been extended but does that mean that there must be a complete abdication of judgement where the demarcation line lies? I have an artist friend. He lives in a cottage in the country. Next to the cottage is a beautiful meadow. On it are hundreds of cowpats – some cold, some steaming. With the sun setting on this random pattern symbolising both the creativity and the futility of human life, he is drained to the depths by this great emotional experience. His problem is how to transport the whole scenario into the Tate Gallery as his submission for next year's Turner Prize."

My broadcast words found an echo. Pamela, our friend and my secretary for over 25 years, found a poem on the Internet. I quote a part of it:

> I saw cows in a field dropping cowpats galore,
> I'm putting one in for the Turner.
> I'll first let it dry, then I'll daub it with gore –
> Should work out a treat for the Turner.

But what would work better, if the farmer allows,
Is to take his field with cowpats and cows
And present the whole lot – what a sight, what a wow! –
At the annual show call the Turner!"

On a recent visit to Italy, Della and I visited the Musei Civici di Verona, a magnificent building housing important collections covering the last 800 years. Outside in the piazza there was a fenced-in grassed area of 20 metres by ten metres. Inside were two masticating cows, surrounded by steaming cowpats. "Yes, this is a special installation for two weeks," the enthusiastic curator explained!

September, 2003

The Vwllss Lngg

I am continuously amazed how Israelis manage to read and write the equivalent of a vowelless language. Unaccustomed as I am, in German, French and English, to dispense with these vital five components of the alphabet, I am prepared to put up with consonants only in the Torah, but in books and newspapers?

You have to develop a sixth sense and look at the context and grammar of the paragraph to make sense of the sentence. Let us take a simple three-word example: "Uncle David's boiler" literally transcribed *hadud shel dod david* but spelled "hdd shl dd dd." How come my grandchildren under eight, the computer experts, can decipher this instantly?

Alas, it does not always work. The other day I climbed up the stairs leading from our house in Yemin Moshe to the car park. A stubble-chinned messenger with a large bunch of artistically wrapped flowers stopped me.

"*Ata gar po?*" – Do you live here?   I assured him that I did.

"*Ani mehapes Rehov Tura 39*" – I'm looking for 39 Tura Street. I said that this was actually my address.

He then told me that the flowers according to the Hebrew lettering of the address were for the Farad Vermes family. I asked him to hand the flowers to me, since I was indeed Fred Worms in person.

"*Hem lo bishvilcha, hem avur Farad Vermes,*" – They are not for you, they are for Farad Vermes.

I realised that I could not convince him of my double identity but I thought that seeing was believing and just like Abraham and Isaac, we walked together to the gate of our house.

There is a small inscription on the letter box in Hebrew and in English, "Della and Fred Worms" followed by the Hebrew letters – *fay, resh, daled, vav, vav, reish, mem, samach,*" undoubtedly Frd Wrms.

I unlocked the gate as a token of ownership identification. He gave me the flowers and pointed triumphantly to the vowel-less Hebrew name, "*Ani amarti lecha – Farad Vermes.*"

There it was in writing, black on gilt – my name was Farad Vermes.

I was reminded of the Frenchman who struggled with the illogical differences in the pronunciation of English words of similar spelling. door v. poor; slough v. enough; though v. rough, etc. When he arrived at Victoria station and saw a large poster advertising the musical "Chicago – pronounced Success" he shot himself.

In Israel you have to grn and pt p wth t.

Frd Vrms, Jrslm
פרד וורמס, ירושלים

Index of names

Abel 219
Abraham 25–27, 28–33, 151, 152, 153, 219, 220
Absalom 39
Abse, Danny 83
Adam 149, 219
Adonijah 39
Agnon, Shmuel Yosef 85
Ahad Ha'am 86, 108, 173
Ahasuerus 34, 35
Akhmatova, Anna 126, 133, 136
Alexander the Great 174
Allen, John 155
Allenby, Lord 108
Altmann, Alexander 206
Amiel, Barbara 226
Amnon 39
Andree, Carl 238, 239
Annan, Lord (Noel) 120, 125
Annenberg, Moses 226
Annenberg, Walter 226
Arend, Aharon 210
Aristotle 44, 52
Armstrong, Louis 145
Atlee, Clement 132
Auberon Herbert,
Auletta, Ken 159
Aumann, Robert 85
Austin, J.L. 126

Baal-Shem-Tov 81
Bacon, Francis (artist) 238, 242
Balfour, Lord 108
Bar Chaim, Rabbi 102
Bar-Zohar, Michael 194, 198
Barak, Aharon 109
Barkat, Nir 114, 117
Bartal, Israel 72
Baruch, Bernard 131, 228
Bathsheba 38, 39
Begin, Menachem 76, 85, 102, 189, 190, 211, 217
Beilin, Yossi 235
Beilis, Mendel 62
Belafonte, Harry 187
Bell, John 138
Belloc, Hilaire 142
Ben Gurion, David 70, 72, 78, 81, 103, 123, 132, 148, 150, 195, 196, 211, 212, 215
Ben Zvi, Yitzhak 151
Ben-Ami, Oved 212
Bergson, Peter 161, 162, 164
Berlin, Aline 124, 133, 233
Berlin, Sir Isaiah 59–60, 85, 108, 118–73, 196, 227, 228, 233
Berlin, Marie 123
Bermant, Chaim 233
Bernstein, Leonard 145, 146
Bettelheim, Bruno 83

Bevin, Ernest 132
Bialik, Haim 108
Bibi, Yigal 109
Black, Conrad 225, 226, 228
Bonham-Carter, Cressida 129
Bowen, Elizabeth 129
Bowra, Maurice 126, 129
Breuer, Isaac 225
Breuer, Mordechai 225
Brodetsky, Selig 127, 179
Brodie, Israel 96
Bronfman family 144
Bronfman, Edgar, Jr. 159, 160
Buber, Martin 72, 215
Bunsen, Pamela 230, 232, 242

Cain 219
Callow, Simon 221
Carter, Jimmy 211
Cecil, Lord 129
Cesarani, David 63
Cézanne, Paul 239
Chesterton, G. K. 142
Churchill, Randolph 126, 198, 227
Churchill, Winston 78, 83, 126, 148, 150, 198–99, 228
Ciechanover, Aaron 85
Cohen, Alfred 211
Cohen, Jeffrey 193–94
Cohen, Leo 178
Cohn, Haim 58–59
Cork, Richard 239
Cornwell, John 61
Cromwell, Oliver 86
Crossman, Richard 129

David (King) 27, 38–39, 174
de Lange, Nicholas 188
Dean Acheson,
Della Pergola, Massimo 67
Della Pergola, Sergio 67
Dench, Judy 186
Dershowitz, Alan 218–20
Dinah 155, 220
Dinitz, Simcha 197
Dizengoff, Meir 180
Dreyfus, Alfred 224, 234
Duchamp, Marcel 240
Duke of Norfolk 62

Eban, Abba 123, 195, 196
Eban, Suzy 194
Eddington, Paul 186
Eden, Anthony 163
Einstein, Albert 81, 209–10
Eisenhower, Dwight 211
Eliot, T. S. 121, 142
Elisha 122
Emin, Tracy 238–39
Epstein, Jacob 238
Esau 208
Eshkol, Levi 102, 195, 196, 197, 211, 212
Esther 34, 35, 36
Eve 219
Ezra 86

Federmann, Yekutiel 158
Ferguson, Niall 234
Fisch, Harold 213, 215, 216–217
Fisher, Mary 129
Flett, Martin 139

Foley, Captain 203
Foster, John 129
Fox, Seymour 172
Frank, Stephen 9
Frankfurter, Felilx 126, 131, 132, 228
Freud, Sigmund 81, 86
Frye, Peter 186, 187

Gable, Clark 221
Gellman, Jerome 31
Gershonides. See Ralbag
Gestetner, David 155
Gilbert, Martin 170, 198–99
Gildesgame, Pierre 177, 183
Ginsberg, Asher. See Ahad Ha'am
Goldhagen, David 62–63
Goldmann, Nahum 92, 132, 161, 162, 165, 166, 197, 211
Goldwyn, Sam 83
Goliath 38, 174
Gollancz, Victor 213
Gorbachev, Mikhail 221
Gordon, A.D. 215
Gore, Al 110
Goren, Shlomo 105
Grant Duff, Sheila 129
Greene, Graham 189
Gunzburg, Baron Horace de 124

Hacohen, Menachem 87–8
Hagar 31, 152
Halban, Peter 168
Halevy, Ephraim 134
Halkin, Hillel 213–18

Haman 33, 35, 36
Hamilton, Ann 238
Hardy, Henry 118, 130
Harrod, Roy 129
Hartman, David 32, 40–54, 73, 116, 147, 149
Hartman, Donniel 73
Hartman, Shalom 41
Hayter, William 161, 162, 164
Hazony, Yoram 72
Heine, Heinrich 147, 150
Henderson, Hubert 127
Hershko, Avram Hershko 85
Hertz, Joseph H. 31, 108, 219
Hertzog, James 179
Herzl, Hans 223
Herzl, Julia Naschauer 223
Herzl, Marguerithe 223
Herzl, Pauline 223
Herzl, Theodor 176, 185, 215, 223–25
Herzog, Aura 194
Herzog, Chaim (Vivian) 194
Herzog, Pnina Shachor 195, 197, 198
Herzog, Shira 198
Herzog, Yaacov 194–98
Herzog, Yitzhak Halevy 194
Hess, Moses 215
Hirsch, Samson Raphael 30, 46, 208, 213
Hirst, Damien 238
Hitler, Adolf 68, 72, 227
Hoffmann, Alan 172
Hoffmann, Ayelet 233
Hussein, King 196, 197
Hussein, Saddam 115

247

Index of names

Huxley, Aldous 127
Ibn Ezra, Abraham 86, 208, 219
Ignatieff, Michael 118, 124
Isaac 28–30, 154, 219, 220
Ishmael 31, 154, 220

Jabotinsky, Zev 189
Jackson, Michael 106
Jacob 31, 153, 155, 208, 219, 220
Jacobs, Louis 86
Jacobson, Bernard 238
Jakobovits, Lord 30, 88, 92, 122, 142, 170
James, Henry 232
Jay, Douglas 129
Jethro 86
John Foster Dulles 129
John Paul II 61, 219
Jonathan 38, 174
Joseph 220
Judah the Maccabee 174
Judah 27

Kahaneman, Daniel 85
Kant, Immanuel 150, 207
Kaplan, Mordecai 211, 212
Kaveh, Moshe 207, 209–10
Kelly, Aileen 155, 156
Kennedy, John 211
Kertzer, David 61–62
Kierkegaard, Søren 32–33, 152
Klausner, Amos. See Oz, Amos
Klausner, Fania 188, 189
Klausner, Joseph 189
Kléber, General 160
Klutznick, Philip 70, 211–13

Koestler, Arthur 141–42, 213
Kollek, Teddy 98–104, 116, 123, 195
Konrad Adenauer,
Kook, Abraham Isaac HaCohen 53, 108, 162, 171, 208, 215
Krinitzi, Abraham 183

Landber, Eugenia 123
Langham, Bo 138
Lash, Werner 202
Lehmann, Rosamond 129
Leibowitz, Nechama 207
Leibowitz, Yeshayahu 32, 54–60, 85, 153, 154, 155
Lessing, G.E. 205
Levi Ben Gershon. See Ralbag
Levin, Bernard 189
Levy, Lord 234
Levy, Peter 170
Lippman, Walter 124
Livnat, Limor 71, 73
Lloyd Wright, Frank 211
Loewenstein, Dr. 220
Lot 220
Lubetkin, Berthold 155, 156
Lűger, Karl 224
Lupoliansky, Uri 114
Lupu (pianist) 143

Madonna 106
Magidor, Menachem 112
Magnes, Yehuda s 72
Maimonides, Moses 43–44, 45–46, 47, 48, 49, 81, 148, 150, 175, 205, 207, 208, 219
Mandel, Morton 172

Mann, Thomas 83, 227
Maresky, Jonathan 9
Marks, Simon 148, 150
Martin, Rupert 138
Martin, Tom 138
Marvin, Lee 187
Marx, Karl 81, 86, 87, 147, 150
Matisse, Henri 239
Matta-Clark, Gordon 238
Mattathias the Hasmonean 174
Matthau, Walter 187
Matthews, Leslie 138
McCarthy, Joseph 187, 220
McCloy, John 166
Meir, Golda 196, 197, 211
Melchett, Lord 180
Menasseh Ben Israel 86
Mendelssohn, Felix 204
Mendelssohn, Fromet Guggenheim 204
Mendelssohn, Moses 204–7
Mendoza, Daniel 175
Menuhin, Yehudi 137, 143
Meridor, Sallai 235
Michal 38, 39
Michelangeli, Arturo Benedetti 145
Miller, Arthur 220–21
Miller, Inge 220, 221
Monroe, Marilyn 220, 221
Monsky, Henry 211
Montefiore, Sir Moses 212
Moore, Henry 238, 241
Mordechai 33–37
Morgenthau, Henry 131
Morrison, David 165, 166
Morrison, Richard 61

Moses 44, 58, 86
Munk, Elie 31
Munnings, Alfred 239

Nachmanides (Ramban) 26, 32, 208
Naismith, James 211
Namier, Lewis 126
Napoleon 62, 158, 160, 200
Nathan the Prophet 39
Netanel, Aron 183
Netanyahu, Binyamin 170–71
Neumann, Emanuel 132
Nicolson, Ben 129
Noah 149
Nordau, Max 175–76

Olmert, Ehud 104
Oppenheimer, Samuel 204
Oz, Amos 188–194
Oz, Nili 190–91

Pares, Richard Pares 127
Pascal, Blaise 147, 150
Pasternak, Boris 126
Peli, Pinchas 208
Pereia (pianist) 143
Peres, Shimon 81, 85, 105, 170, 171
Pharaoh 25, 151
Picasso, Pablo 239, 241
Pius XI, Pope 62
Pius XII, Pope 63
Plamenatz, J.P. 126
Pollini, Maurizio 145
Posen, Felix 172, 173
Power, Tyrone 186

Index of names

Prokofiev, Sergei 148
Proust, Marcel 188
Rabin, Yitzhak 54, 85, 108, 170, 211
Ralbag 208
Ramban. See Nachmanides
Raphael, Frederic 229–30
Rashi 171, 206, 207, 208, 219
Ravitzky, Aviezer 208–9
Rebecca 154
Rees, Goronwy 129
Rees-Mogg, William 234–35
Richler, Mordecai 144, 145
Richter, Sviatoslav 143
Riskin, Shlomo 208
Robespierre 150
Roosevelt, Eleanor 228
Roosevelt, Franklin Delano 126, 162, 163, 166, 211, 224–28
Rosenzweig, Franz 72, 206
Rothschild family 148, 157–58
Rothschild, Baron Mayer Carl von 161
Rothschild, Evelyn de 158
Rothschild, Jacob 158, 160
Rothschild, Lord Victor 130, 145, 233
Rothschild, Miriam 158, 160
Rubinstein, Amnon 71
Rubinstein, Elyakim 109
Ruby, Thelma 186
Rudolph II 175
Rumbold, Sir Anthony 164
Russell, Lord Bertrand 62, 152
Ruth the Moabite 220

Saatchi, Charles 239
Sacher Gilbert, Susie 199
Sacher, Michael 199
Sacks, Lord Jonathan 60, 61, 84, 142, 235
Sadat, Anwar 211
Sadat, Madame 156
Samuel, Sir Herbert 108, 152
Samuel the Prophet 38
Samunov, Ida 123
Sarah 25, 30, 32, 152
Sartre, Jean-Paul 215
Saul, King 38, 174
Schechtman, Daniel
Schiff, Friedrich 223
Schmool, Marlena 69
Schneerson family 128
Schneerson, Chayette 119
Scholem, Gershom 72
Schroeder, Gerald 209–10
Schwarz, Arturo 239
Scruton, Roger 139
Shabtai Zvi 86
Shachor, Zalman 195
Sharansky, Natan (Anatoly) 89–97
Sharett, Moshe 123, 148, 150, 211
Sharon, Ariel 102, 184
Shem 149
Shemer, Naomi 113
Shenhar, Aliza 71
Sieff, Israel 148, 150
Silver, Abba Hillel 131, 132
Simon Bar Kochba 176
Smolenskin, Peretz 206
Snow, C.P. 125

Snowman, Kenneth 239–40
Solomon 39
Soloveitchik, Joseph Ber 45, 153
Sorkin, David 204–7
Speiser, E. A. 31
Spender, Stephen 129
Spinoza, Baruch 81, 86, 148
Spitz, Mark 180
Stalin, Joseph 133, 228
Steiger, Rod 187
Steiner, George 84, 122
Steinsaltz, Adin 32, 116, 140, 148, 171–72, 198, 206
Sternberg, Sigmund 61
Stevenson, Adlai 211
Stockholder, Jessica 238, 239
Stokovsky, Leopold 145
Strabolgi, Lord 224
Straight, Lady Daphne 129
Strasberg, Lee 221
Strasberg, Paula 221
Stravinsky, Igor 148, 151
Stritch, Elaine 187
Sudfeld, Gabriel 175
Sulzberger, Arthur Hays 124

Tamar 39
Toaeff, Rabbi 137
Topol, Chaim 186
Toynbee, Arnold 196
Truman, Harry 211
Trumpeldor, Joseph 189
Tyndale, William 206
Tyson, H.A.M. 138

Van Gogh, Vincent 239

Van Leer, Bernard 200–201
Van Leer, Lia 202
Van Leer, Oscar 201
Van Leer, Wim 200–203
Vaughan, Cardinal 62
Vespasian 76
Vigdor, Moshe 112, 113

Walker, Rachel 129
Waller, Fats 145
Warburg family 137
Warburg, Edward 124
Warburg, Erich 136
Warburg, Sir Sigmund 79
Weidenfeld, Lord 225
Weill, Asher 10
Weizman, Ezer 109, 181
Weizmann, Chaim 108, 120–21, 123, 126, 127, 131, 132, 133, 148, 164
Welles, Orson 186
Wesker, Arnold 231
Whiteread, Rachel 241
Wiesel, Elie 219, 235
Wigoder, Louis 186
Wilson, Harold 120
Wise, Stephen 131, 161–62, 163, 164
Wolfson, Isaac 148, 150, 196
Woolf, Harry 156
Worms, Della 108, 116, 159, 160, 168, 170, 185, 241, 244
Wouk, Herman 77–78

Yochanan Ben Zakai, Rabbi 76
Yonath, Ada 85

Zadok the Priest 39
Zipperstein, Steven J. 173
Zondek, Professor 197
Zuckerman, Dov Behr 119, 120
Zuckerman [Berlin], Mendel 119, 120, 128
Zuckerman, Sir Solly 120, 144